The economy of later Renaissance Europe, 1460–1600

The economy of
later Renaissance Europe
1460–1600

HARRY A. MISKIMIN
Professor of History, Yale University

CAMBRIDGE UNIVERSITY PRESS
CAMBRIDGE

LONDON · NEW YORK · MELBOURNE

Published by the Syndics of the Cambridge University Press
The Pitt Building, Trumpington Street, Cambridge CB2 1RP
Bentley House, 200 Euston Road, London NW1 2DB
32 East 57th Street, New York, NY 10022, USA
296 Beaconsfield Parade, Middle Park, Melbourne 3206, Australia

First published 1977

Printed in the United States of America
Typeset by Jay's Publishers Services, Inc., North Scituate, Massachusetts

Library of Congress Cataloging in Publication Data

Miskimin, Harry A.

The economy of later Renaissance Europe, 1460–1600.

Bibliography: p.

Includes index.

1. Europe – Economics conditions. I. Title
HC240.M649   330.9'4'02   75–17120
ISBN 0 521 21608 7 hard covers
ISBN 0 521 29208 5 paperback

Contents

Tables, graphs, and maps

FOR ALICE S. MISKIMIN
A Fine Renaissance Scholar

Preface

The reader may find himself somewhat disconcerted to discover that a book devoted to the economic history of early modern Europe begins with a rather extended discussion of law and late medieval scholasticism, but I plead for his patience. The soubriquet "age of expansion" accurately describes the period, yet that expansion was more than geographical. Cultural, intellectual, legal, scientific, dynastic, artistic, philosophical, and economic matters were all in flux, and all shared in the "expansion" of the era. Each interacted with the others shattering accepted norms and destroying continuities. In a very real sense, flux and discontinuity were the common denominators, while the universal effort to confront, comprehend, and deal with the dissolution of received norms constituted the one cohesive and ordering element of the period. If I have been successful, the subsequent chapters will justify the first by building organically on that beginning.

The reader's patience and generosity are also solicited with regard to the endeavor as a whole. To compress and to attempt to structure so large and complex a period inevitably alters the tone, if not the facts, of history, and forces choices of both omission and inclusion. I am deeply aware that my priorities will often diverge from those of the reader and can do no more than ask his indulgence when he finds that my emphasis does not accord with his own. Equally, almost every sentence reflects a judgment among alternative interpretations of the past, but without trebling its bulk, the book could not do justice to the multifaceted and controversial secondary literature on which it often depends. Even if complete absolution proves impossible, I seek the reader's understanding in this sin. Though, if complete, it would dwarf the book, the bibliography offered at the end should guide the reader to the salient materials.

Finally, I should like to thank my wife, Alice S. Miskimin, for her remarkable strength and continuing support and for her invaluable suggestions and criticism. The errors, of course, are my own.

H. Miskimin

May, 1977

1
The abstractions of law and property

Witchcraft proliferates when fundamental premises are challenged and society itself appears unstable; it is thus no accident that the later Renaissance witnessed a profusion of witches. By definition, witches are supernatural creatures who exist beyond and in defiance of the laws of nature. They have the capacity to alter regular and expected patterns, to affect the cycles of fertility and regeneration, and to assume unnatural forms and powers. So long as witches are present, the homogeneity of experience is moot; the value of previous empirical observation is dubious; and the possibility of creating rational, scientific hypotheses on the basis of an orderly and immutable set of natural laws is questionable. Witchcraft, then, perhaps unfortunately, is antithetical to the more mundane craft of the modern economist. The latter conceives of the world as regular, bound by his version of natural laws – as, for example, those of supply and demand – and subject to innumerable constraints that enable him to predict, or at least rationally believe that he can predict, the reaction that will be caused by a given action.

Anomalous as it may appear to contrast modern economic thought with witchcraft, the contrast is illuminating. Those who concerned themselves with economic problems in the sixteenth century, particularly those cast as political figures or advisers, often seem to the modern critic to be naive or simply wrongheaded. One wonders, for example, how a thinker of Jean Bodin's genius could invent the quantity theory of money in 1568[1] and shortly thereafter, in 1576,[2] advocate the most sterile policies of bullionist mercantilism. The one position holds that the import of large quantities of bullion will cause domestic prices to rise; the other holds that domestic prices should be kept low so that large quantities of bullion may be imported. Clearly, the former insight should provide a limit to the effectiveness or success of the latter policy, but Bodin does not draw the obvious conclusion, and, indeed, it remained unexpressed for nearly a century and a half after his death. What prevented Bodin from making what appears to us so direct and simple a connection? Perhaps it is overly facile to point out that in 1580 Bodin published his *Démonomanie des Sorciers*,[3] a book that defends the existence of sorcerers and witchcraft against the attacks of skeptics, but it is suggestive of a cast of mind. If witches and sorcerers did exist, if there were supernatural forces, what were the constraints to action in the economic and political spheres? Could political power be substituted for, or alter, natural laws?

In his *Six Livres de la République*, Bodin carefully outlined his theory of the relationship between climate and the quality of government. Briefly, the cold of the north produces such torpor that the people of those regions are unfit to govern; in the south, the climate renders people so mercurial that they too are unfit. In regions such as his native France, however, Bodin found the climate ideally balanced to produce sound governors. Disregarding the historical or empirical credibility of the theory, the concepts do seem, at least to the author, to have something of the quality of a law of nature; the forces involved in molding political capacities appear too massive to be altered by the will of man. Bodin, on the contrary, draws the conclusion that one simply needs more forceful government in the extreme northern and southern regions to compensate for the natural defects of the residents. Through political intervention, it was possible to avert the normal consequences of natural forces.

Such an attitude, although it certainly does not resolve the internal contradictions in Bodin's writings, does perhaps make them more explicable. To the degree that political power and positive law (i.e., that of the state) wax, the constraints and limits imposed by divine or natural laws wane. At the extreme, political power becomes analogous to witchcraft, since both are viewed as capable of bringing about the unnatural and subverting the chain that leads from action to reaction. Perhaps one could indeed import vast sums of bullion without raising prices if enough political pressure were exerted within the domestic economy to control the cost of goods.

Bodin was, of course, but one figure, and it would be dangerous in the extreme to use him as symbol or even touchstone for the intellectual developments of the northern Renaissance, with its multitude of crosscurrents. Yet belief in demons, in witchcraft, and, even more generally, in the possibility of challenging the immutable character of law, political or natural, was a strong, and perhaps even dominant, aspect of the period. Louis XI of France (1461–83) was not above bargaining with the saints of those towns he sought to capture and in effect offering bribes to the patron saints in return for victory.[4] Even in the German mining industry, the center of the most advanced engineering and mechanical skills known to the sixteenth century, technologists included methods for propitiating bad demons and winning the favor of beneficent spirits when they were encountered beneath the surface of the earth.[5] In the political sphere, Machiavelli tolerated no external legal or moral constraints to the power of the prince save his own weakness.[6] Examples could be multiplied, but it will perhaps suffice to call attention to the prevalence of the idea that the limitations on political and economic action were far from certain in the sixteenth century, and that, in many instances, the abstraction, which law in one dimension is, seemed to have lost much of its force. What was true in the confrontation between witches and natural laws was also, depending on the region and to various degrees, true in regard to custom, written law, Roman law, divine law, and indeed the entire concept of law other than the will of the prince.

To sum together ethical, civil, and physical laws under one rubric may appear somewhat bizarre in our time; yet it is precisely this sum, this combined legal abstraction, against which sixteenth-century witchcraft mounted its assault. A single act of sorcery, after all, entailed transgression against all three dimensions of law. If the set of legal abstractions – ethical, civil, and physical – had been firm and sound in the sixteenth century, witchcraft would not have been possible or even conceivable and thus would presumably not have been attempted. The immutable homogeneity and constancy of church, state, and nature would have precluded the irregular and unnatural aberrations that sorcery sought to achieve. The very fact that witchcraft was deemed increasingly possible suggests that something had gone wrong with the system of legal abstractions. But before inquiring into the nature of the system's malaise, let us recall our main purpose and observe that those abstractions have real force in the sphere of economic behavior and organization as well as in the more arcane reaches of the supernatural.

In the first place and most obviously, the abstractions of law are basically conservative; they tend to preserve the status quo, to protect property and those who hold it, and to resist innovations of organization or method whether these originate from the private or governmental sector. The abstractions of law at once provide the constraints that limit the excessive assumption of power by any single agent within society and the framework within which to conceptualize and articulate the defense against any such endeavor to excess. It is through them that the disparate elements in the body politic find strength to counterbalance each other's power instead of degenerating into separate, anarchical, and warring entities.

Despite their importance for the preservation of social stability, the set of legal abstractions that had proved viable during the high middle ages was in pronounced disrepair by the beginning of the sixteenth century. As early as the beginning of the fourteenth century, William of Ockham (d. 1349) and Marsilius of Padua (d. 1342) had launched what amounted to an assault on the Thomist synthesis of faith, reason, philosophy, and law. Marsilius, in his *Defensor Pacis* (1324),[7] renounced the delicate Thomist balance between church and state, *regnum* and *sacerdotium*, and replaced it with the assertion of a single, indivisible sovereign power, the state, and a state for all earthly purposes superior to the church. More significantly for our present purposes, Marsilius separated and made independent the various levels of law that had formed a unity in Aquinas. Where Aquinas had postulated a congruent set of laws – eternal, divine, natural, and human – Marsilius limited law largely to that which could be enforced on this earth, that is, to that rendered by the state.[8] The Thomist conceptions of eternal and divine law are not so much abandoned as elevated to a sphere where they no longer impinge on matters of secular authority. To transgress against human or positive law is to transgress against divine law, since Christ commanded obedience to secular authority, but transgressions against divine law are not necessarily within the jurisdiction of secular law. Such sins neither concern nor violate human law, although "what is lawful and what unlawful in an absolute sense must be viewed according to divine law rather than human law . . ."[9] Marsilius also deviated from the Thomist view of natural law; he maintains that "natural right . . . is that statute of the legislator with respect to which all men agree that it is honorable and should be observed" and gives as examples "that God must be worshiped, parents must be honored, children must be reared by their parents, etc."[10] He further explicitly states that "although these depend on human enactment, they are metaphorically called natural rights."[11] Despite his claim to be following Aristotle, Marsilius's insistence on human enactment is a marked break from the ancient conception of natural law. Aristotle conceived of natural law as that law which was everywhere valid without regard to human action – a view that, not surprisingly, is far closer to that of Aquinas than that of Marsilius. For Thomas, natural law was at once above man, immutable with regard to his actions, and always in accord with the yet higher orders of divine and eternal law in the same fashion that valid human law must always be in accord with the natural law. In the Thomist system, man, through the use of right reason, could determine the prescripts of natural law, and thus it acted as a constraint and guide both for human actions and for human and positive law. It is this view of natural law that Marsilius specifically rejects "since there are many things in accordance with the dictates of right reason, but which are not agreed upon as honorable by all nations, namely, those things which are not self-evident to all, and consequently not acknowledged by all."[12]

Marsilius's rejection of the Thomist view of natural law as the model for human or positive law did not lead him to view political authority as independent of any constraints. The prince was expected to rule by law. Unfortunately, however, law was for him the creation of the *legislator humanus,* the whole body of the people or the weightier part thereof[13] and its interpretation depended largely on the ruler himself. Although the *legislator humanus* could, under certain rather ill-defined circumstances, correct or punish the ruler, the composition of this body is vague and the methods by which it might proceed so little considered by Marsilius that for all intents and purposes its restraining power is virtually nil.[14] In general, Marsilius appears to have hoped for a beneficent, but powerful, ruler and to have devoted only the barest attention to the potential necessity of constraining a malevolent one. Modern interpretations of the nature of Marsilius's state are in sharp disagreement. Some writers stress the strictures that the monarch must be elected, that he was to rule by law, and that he was subject to correction by the whole body of the people in order to find in Marsilius a prototype of later doctrines of popular sovereignty.[15]

Others concentrate on the primordial character of the election that introduces an hereditary monarchy, on the fact that the electorate was not the whole body of the people but only the weightier part in terms of rank and significance rather than number, and on Marsilius's definition of law as requiring an enforcing agent, inevitably the ruler, in order to find in him the precursor of Machiavelli or Hobbes.[16] Both views are perhaps correct; the apparent contradiction arises primarily from juxtaposing Marsilius's intent against the likely consequences of his doctrine. By removing the abstract constraints upon a weak empire in order to strengthen it against an overblown papacy, he sought to restore a benign balance; but in aiding the lamb, he released a lion.

Like Marsilius's, William of Ockham's work has generated a substantial and highly controversial secondary literature. Like Marsilius, he too was a polemicist on behalf of the emperor and against the abuses of papal power, and, perhaps for this reason, his thought resists simplification, and his influence is at once difficult to trace and probably greater than his intentions. More prolific and subtle than Marsilius, Ockham too attacked the Thomist hierarchy and balance, but he did so more effectively as a philosopher and theologian. In a formal assault on the then current philosophical systems, he denied the real existence of universals.[17] For him, concepts of a universal character were the result of "abstractive cognition" – "something abstracted from many singulars" – and hence had no reality of their own.[18] Such a doctrine would appear to cast considerable doubt on the viability of the Thomist structure of legal abstractions, depending as they do on the existence of natural law in a real and immutable sense and on the capacity of every human to recognize that law through the exercise of right reason. Ockham pursues the argument further and asserts that no universal could exist outside the mind, because that would mean that something of the individual would preexist his creation; as this would limit the power of God to create or destroy, it is rejected as impossible.[19]

Ockham does not draw the seemingly logical conclusion from the preceding; he does not renounce natural law nor the innate capacity of all men to recognize it. Instead, he maneuvers around the difficulties by doubling the number of systems of natural law. In his political writings, there are two distinct systems of natural law: the first is absolute, immutable, and largely irrelevant to the secular state; the second is subject to conditions and modifications.[20] The latter is that which is "licit, just, and expedient"; it is this version of natural law that governs secular political power.[21] The insertion of the word *expedient* in the traditional doctrine of natural law was fraught with overtones for the future of Western political thought, since almost any action can be legitimized under that broad rubric. To cite but one example, two centuries after Ockham's death, Jean Bodin, contrary to his property-conserving bias as a civil lawyer, uses a similar phrase to justify unlimited extraordinary taxation, observing that such "impositions are most just, for nothing is more just than that which is necessary."[22] Once natural law is seen as a variable, whose meaning is determined by what a secular ruler judges to be expedient, its value in constraining the unbridled will of the prince is very seriously diminished.

The influence of late medieval scholasticism on the subsequent development of political theory is acknowledge in general but disputed in particular. With rare exceptions, its influence on the development of economic analysis is left to a few specialists who are usually historians rather than economists.[23] The erosion of natural law, however, deeply affected the subsequent course of both political and economic theory. Theories of natural law, dependent as they are on the general prevalence of "right reason" among the populace, have a basically egalitarian bias. All men stand in the same relationship to a law that no man has the capacity to alter. This, of course, is not to deny the existence of distinctions of rank, status, wealth, and position. Medieval society was indeed hierarchical – dukes did not associate with peasants – but even within that rigidly structured world, each soul had value and the combined impact of Christianity and natural law acted to preserve and assert the importance of the individual. He had a soul, he could distinguish between right and wrong – a capacity that affirmed his significance and individual responsibility – and he was an integral part of the "public," benefiting from the sanctions of natural law which specified that political actions be for the public good.

When natural law came to require an enforcing agent and human enactment as in Marsilius, or an interpreter of that which was expedient as well as just as in Ockham, it was no longer true that each individual stood in an identical relationship to an immutable law. Marsilius's definition of the *legislator humanus* as the "weightier part" of the whole body of the people, by rank rather than number, is thus but an extension of a doctrine that denied the egalitarian component of the theory of natural law. The case of Ockham is, as always, somewhat more complex because, in his aversion to universals, he strongly emphasizes the particular and the individual by separating them from any universal.[24] The impact of such separation, however, is deceptive. On the one hand, the individual seems no longer embedded in the layers of medieval hierarchies, be they social or political realities or conceptual abstractions; in this sense, it is true that he seems more significant in himself. On the other hand, from a political point of view, the individual, by becoming separate, becomes more vulnerable, and, in this sense, less valuable. One effect of the disruption of the Thomist system of natural law was to set the individual adrift while at the same time removing the protective abstraction that had guaranteed his position in the hierarchy. It is not accidental, as LaGarde observes, that "neither the principle of submission to the common good, nor that of the autonomy of the human individual, nor that of collective sovereignty are effectively developed" in Ockham.[25]

Mutations in political values also affect their economic counterparts: Concepts of property are not independent from concepts of either law or the individual. Under the Thomist view of natural law, property was provided by God for the common benefit of mankind. In order to limit friction and disputes and to provide for better and more careful stewardship, however, the private division of property had been instituted through human law, but this division supplemented rather than displaced natural law. Property and its use were still designated for the common good, and, thus, its ownership implied obligation as well as rights; in cases of extreme necessity, all worldly goods reverted to common property.[26]

In a passage immediately following the one in which he defines natural laws as human enactments, Marsilius sets forth his theory of property. For him, one has the "right" to usufruct, acquisition, holding, saving, or exchanging "whenever these are in a conformity with right taken in its first sense," that is, humanly enacted natural law. "Right, then, taken in this sense, is none other than what is willed by the active command, prohibition, or permission of the legislator . . ."[27] Now although this doctrine appears at first sight to be but a small deviation from Thomist theory, the implications are considerable. Property remains, as it is in Aquinas, the creature of human law, but for Marsilius, whatever obligations might be entailed in the holding of property are equally the creation of human enactment. Property is essentially divorced from any higher moral sanction and title to it is entirely at the discretion of the will of the *legislator humanus*. Marsilius is quite explicit on this point and states that the legislator can "entrust to whomever it wants, and at any time, authority to distribute these goods."[28] Since the *legislator humanus* does not normally convene, this assertion would appear to mean that the secular ruler, acting in the name of the legislator, holds total and absolute power over property and its distribution among the citizens and institutions of the state.[29]

For his part, Ockham denies that property was ever held in common by all mankind. Instead, he maintains that at the moment of the fall, God gave each man the absolute power of dividing and appropriating the goods of this earth; this power, further, was not dependent on the consent of either the community or the state, but was in fact a true right, resident in each man.[30] Despite Ockham's retention of the almost universal proscription that in cases of extreme necessity the property of others may be appropriated, his doctrine would appear to be a considerable forward step toward unlimited private property. No perceptible moral or political obligations were normally attached to the rights of ownership. Unfortunately, however, in maintaining the individual property right, Ockham opens the way to its demise. In defending the property right, he asserts that no one may be deprived of his property "without cause or without blame."[31] But who decides the cause and by what criteria? Ockham would place this question under the civil law, but civil law is, as we shall subsequently observe, mutable. The Thomist correspondence between human law and the immutable natural law had disappeared in Ockham, and a natural law that was "licit, just, and expedient" was a pale substitute for maintaining the integrity of civil law. By becoming more individual and more private, property, as the person, had become more vulnerable.

There is a considerable difference between thought and action, and it is well to recall that the difficult and abstruse concerns of ecclesiastics do not always coincide with the temper of the times nor reflect historical reality. The works of Ockham and Marsilius, however, took their origin from and were formed by the historical context in which they were written. The fourteenth century had begun with the dramatic confrontation between Boniface VIII and the kings of France and

England over the issue of secular taxation of the church. In his final effort to defend the position of the church, Boniface issued the bull *Unam Sanctam* (1302), in which he claimed that "every human being to be saved must be subject to the Roman pontiff."[32] This seemingly excessive assertion of papal authority exacerbated the controversy over the relationship between secular and ecclesiastical jurisdiction and generated a substantial literature that included both Marsilius and Ockham. The clash was directly political, not simply an exchange of scholarly treatises. Edward I of England denied the protection of royal law to churchmen who refused to pay taxes, and Philip IV of France first prohibited the transfer of papal funds out of his country, and then, through his minister Nogaret, actually captured, and for a short time imprisoned, the hapless pope at his summer retreat at Anagni. The subsequent election of a French pope in 1305 and the transfer of the papacy to Avignon at once stimulated discussion of the political role of the pope and converted obscure scholastic arguments into political weapons. After his work had been condemned by the pope, Marsilius fled Paris, where he had written the *Defensor Pacis*, and sought the protection of the emperor, Ludwig of Bavaria, whose imperial election he defended against papal interference. In 1328, Ockham followed.[33] It was from this position that Ockham "defended the emperor with his pen" and even sought to justify Ludwig's matrimonial policy.[34]

Sometimes directly and sometimes indirectly, the events of the later middle ages continued to increase the relevance of the troubled writings of the later scholastics. The Franciscans, whose most brilliant intellectual leader was Ockham, had asserted as doctrine the absolute poverty of Christ and the apostles and preached that the ideal religious life was one that imitated Christ in this respect. Carried to its extreme, such a doctrine could not but prove embarrassing to a church that had grown rich over the centuries; Pope John XXII declared the Franciscan doctrine heretical in 1323.[35] Little could have pleased the revenue-hungry princes of the fourteenth century more than the opportunity to forward doctrines of ecclesiastical poverty, and, as a result, a natural alliance developed between the Franciscans and those princes who were out of favor with the pope. Indeed, during the period 1337–40, when Edward III, under threat of papal sanction, was briefly allied with the already excommunicated Ludwig, Ockham wrote his *An princeps*, defending the right of Edward to tax the wealth of the church in England and maintaining that the papal anathema would be invalid if employed in this instance.[36] Ockham's theory of property directly served the growth of the secular state in England at this juncture; at one remove, the legal theories of both Marsilius and Ockham converged in the same tendency. The strategy, devised by Edward I, of denying the protection of royal justice to clerics who were recalcitrant about paying taxes was pursued and elaborated as the century progressed. The Statute of Provisors (1351), the Statute of Praemunire (1353), and their subsequent manifestations in 1365, 1390, and 1393 formally asserted the right of the king, rather than the pope, to determine the nominees to ecclesiastical benefices and prohibited the appeal of any case to courts outside the royal jurisdiction; the 1365 statute specifically mentioned the papal court.[37] Although direct responsibility for these acts can in no way be ascribed to a philosopher such as Marsilius, his work was well known in Oxford and may have affected the intellectual climate in which they were passed.[38] In any event, he left no ambiguity concerning the right of the secular authority to redistribute the goods of this earth and it would be hard to imagine a more forceful attack than his on canon law and ecclesiastical claims to secular jurisdiction. In the first place, the existence of a separate legal system, counterpoised against that of the *legislator humanus*, transgressed against Marsilius's conception of unitary sovereign power and of law as dependent on an effective enforcing agent. His specific charges, however, are stronger still. He maintained that the Roman bishops and cardinals were afraid to call the decretals laws "for they feared resistance and correction by the human legislator, since by making such ordinances, they committed the crime of treason against rulers and legislators, and so from the beginning, they called these ordinances *jura canonica.*"[39] The political assault on ecclesiastical justice in England did not lack readily available theoretical justification.

The purpose of this discussion has not been to survey legal history in the later middle ages and early Renaissance, but rather to suggest in broad outline that the accepted certainties of earlier legal abstractions had been seriously shaken by the end of the fourteenth century. That real consequences could result is demonstrated by the English case, but even there an adequate treatment would have to include the reversals and setbacks wrought by Richard II on the forceful and shrewd policies of Edward III.[40] Restorative compromise, however, could not revive general acceptance of such legal abstractions as the Thomist version of natural law. Once they had been questioned, doubted, and subjected to conflicting definitions in a polemicized atmosphere, their value in providing an almost universally accepted vocabulary for political and legal discourse was severely reduced and they could not easily be replaced.

Two other bodies of law, less metaphysical than those considered earlier could assert some claim to immutability, to power to constrain secular princes, and to the capacity to establish the limits within which man must act. Custom, since it was safely embedded in time past, was to some extent immune from alteration in any given present, while Roman law was equally a received body of law, preserved in the *Corpus juris civilis*, codified at the instruction of Justinian in the sixth century. In fact, of course, neither custom nor Roman law was immune to change. Custom, particularly in the early middle ages, was largely a matter of remembered precedent, and because memory varied and precedents were simply the random acts of men, made legitimate through time or repetition, custom was at first a highly fluid form of law. Further, since it developed as a response to the general collapse of centralized government, it was always particular and local in application and provenance, and thus alien to the restoration of strong secular authority. Roman law, on the other hand, was the written remnant of an absolutist government with an obvious bias toward centralization. It could well serve the aspirations of princes interested in assertion or expansion of authority of an intensity unknown to the early middle ages; as a result, it provoked strong opposition from many quarters.[41] Perhaps for this reason as well, it gained the support of such emperors as Frederick I, who, by his encouragement of legal studies throughout the empire, aided the revival of Roman law in the university of Bologna.[42] In any event, from small beginnings at the end of the eleventh century, the study of Roman law proliferated throughout the twelfth. Although it had never been wholly forgotten, the *Corpus Juris* became increasingly important in the university curriculum and its study became competitive with even that of canon law. Roman law, at first glance, would appear to be the nemesis of customary law, but as Marc Bloch observed, the initial impact of the study of civil law was to improve and formalize the study of custom and to transmute custom into written law.[43] The potential conflict between the two systems was thus postponed rather than averted, as custom, increasingly codified, became a more worthy opponent to the centralizing tendencies of Roman law.

By the mid-thirteenth century, Roman law had found practical application as a device for subverting custom. After 1230, Frederick II successfully sought to recover control of Sicily by main force, and once this had been accomplished, he was in a position to impose new political and legal structures. In 1231, accordingly, he promulgated a comprehensive legal code, the *Lex Augustalis*, which was based on Roman law and which superseded all other conflicting laws and customs.[44] An efficient superstructure of government officials constituted a centralized bureaucracy, and though they did not replace the traditional feudal structure, they dominated it. Frederick was able to rule with a degree of absolutism unknown elsewhere during the thirteenth century, but the experiment proved premature, and on the emperor's death, Sicily quickly regressed into anarchy and petty factionalism.

Castile provides an example more appropriate to the thirteenth century of an attempted wholesale adoption of a legal code based on Roman law. In the 1260s, with the help of Italian-trained legists, Alfonso X endeavored to introduce a code similar to the *Lex Augustalis* and known as the *Siete Partidas*.[45] The new code would have replaced the customary law that preserved municipal liberties and aristocratic privilege and would, if implemented, have allowed Alfonso to rule as absolutely as Frederick had in Sicily. Castile was not yet ready to submit, however, and a relentless and persistent opposition first prevented the code from being formally adopted and subsequently led to the deposition of Alfonso in 1282 and the naming of his son, Sancho IV, as his successor.[46] Alfonso died unmourned in 1284.

Both the Sicilian and the Castilian attempts to substitute a Roman code for existing customs failed, but they serve to dramatize at once the tendency of Roman law to produce absolute rule and the awareness of this implication by those who ruled and those who were ruled. Although rapid and comprehensive adoption of such a code was dangerous and likely to generate intense resistance, more subtle and delicate measures found greater success. Everywhere in Europe, with the exception of England, Roman law had in some degree the force of common law and was consulted when specific custom failed to provide the solution to a legal problem. Despite contradictions – Roman law, for example, allowed absolute ownership whereas feudal and customary law was primarily concerned with the right to use rather than to possess – the two systems did coexist, but the détente became increasingly fragile as time passed and princes recognized the value of employing trained civilian lawyers to staff ever more efficient courts.

Reference to the emperor remained a serious obstacle to the wider application of Roman law in national states. Emperor Frederick II found no difficulty here, of course, but his very pretensions to universal dominance frightened the monarchs of Christendom and led in part to the frustration of his political ambitions. If kings were initially fearful of the imperial bias of Roman law, however, royal lawyers readily resolved the difficulties by inventing such phrases as *rex imperator in suo regno est* ("the king is emperor in his own kingdom"). After the reference point had been thus shifted, concepts drawn from Roman law could usefully serve national monarchies; the tendency was reinforced after 1250, when the death of Frederick II so weakened the empire that it could no longer pose a real threat to increasingly powerful kings. In France, for example, an ordinance of August 1374 incorporated the Roman formula *princeps legibus solutus est* ("the prince is the only law").[47] The formula was more hopeful than valid in the fourteenth century, but the precedent was established, and with continued repetition and the steady pressure of the royal lawyers, it grew in acceptance and force over the course of the next century. True enough, customary law did not die out – indeed, in 1454, a royal edict decreed the compilation and recording of all the customs of France, with the intent of rationalizing and confirming them.[48]

Several interpretations of the 1454 edict are possible. On the one hand, the codification of custom in the fifteenth century might appear to indicate a resurgence of its role as a normative legal system, but this view misses the import of the act of confirmation by the king. Once the formulae of Roman law had gained currency and the royal lawyers had developed into a formidable force, confirmation of custom became a means of coopting it. If the prince was the only law, custom existed solely by sufferance and royal confirmation was required to give it the force of law. Custom, in theory, then, drew its authority only from the will, direct or indirect, of the prince. As persistent confirmation imperceptibly converted the theory to practice, the ability that custom had drawn from its origin in time past – in an era unalterable by present action – to resist expedient mutation was largely vitiated. Roman law gave the prince a weapon against time itself.

The French ordinances of the later fifteenth century repeatedly confirm both the acts of earlier kings and the customary rights of such organizations as guilds, churches, and municipalities.[49] The effect, however, was not to expand the role of custom but to limit it; rather as if our own government, in reasserting the Bill of Rights, confirmed the identical document but changed the title to the "Bill of Privileges." This apparently minor alteration would undermine deeply the philosophical premises of the Constitution: If rights become privileges, they are no longer inalienable and rooted in natural law. In the French instance, Charles VII, and more persistently and shrewdly, Louis XI, used confirmation of preexisting custom as a means of converting rights into privileges and thereby extending royal authority and jurisdiction. Almost imperceptibly, the justification for the existence of guilds ceased to derive from the right of individuals to associate in their own interests, but came instead from the sanction of the king and at his pleasure. The same fate befell municipal liberties and ecclesiastical privilege. Custom was less and less a force of constraint on the will of the king, as it was converted, at first theoretically but increasingly in practice, into an aspect of that very will.

Roman law maintained that the will of the prince had the force of law, but, even so, certain constraints tempered the action of the ruler. First, the Roman system assumed that there was an abstract law, higher than that promulgated by the state; ideally, the purpose of positive law was to serve justice as measured by that higher law.[50] Thus, although the formula stated that the prince was the only law, his will was guided by its correspondence to the higher natural law. Second, because the emperor derived his authority from the "people," though obviously not in any democratic sense, there was at least a theoretical presumption that his actions would be on their behalf and in their interest. Finally, Roman law embodied considerable respect for contracts and private property and consequently provided a vocabulary for the protection of ownership and property rights against excessive incursions by other citizens and by implication by the government itself.

We have already noted some of the conceptual complexities that natural law had fallen into at the hands of such philosophers as Ockham and Marsilius of Padua. Once it had been adjusted to serve expediency or made dependent on enactment by the secular ruler, natural law could no longer serve as a normative standard for positive law. Arguments from it tended to become increasingly circular as the prince became the arbiter of the very law that was expected to modify and control his actions. At best, the limits imposed by natural law became obscure; at worst, they evaporated. Roman law had always incorporated a tension between the assertion of the absolute will of the prince and the presumption of a higher justice, but the intellectual developments of the later middle ages heightened the tendency to shatter that balance. Royal lawyers found it both intellectually satisfying and politically expedient to emphasize the voluntarist aspects of Roman law and to disregard notions of abstract justice.

More damaging still to the integrity of Roman law was the impact of Renaissance historical and philological scholarship. Ironically, the same intellectual ferment that had, through its respect for and emulation of classical antiquity, greatly expanded the provenance of the *Corpus juris* began in the late fifteenth century to undermine its authority. Lorenzo Valla, who is most noted for having proved that the "Donation of Constantine" was a crude forgery, applied the same techniques to the *Corpus juris* and revealed that it was "a product of time and circumstance, a historical artifact rather than a body of universally valid legal wisdom."[51] Once opened, this line of attack was pursued by a series of distinguished sixteenth-century jurists; the impact was devastating. Guillaume Budé, seeking to provide a verified and clear text of the *Corpus juris*, carefully studied the texts and discovered that the medieval version was based on faulty manuscripts and riddled with errors. Even more significantly, he found that the errors had led to substantive misinterpretations and even inversions of key points of law.[52] To question the basic validity of the text of the *Corpus juris* was tantamount to challenging the whole fabric of late medieval jurisprudence which had been constructed on that text, but the assault did not cease there. Budé recognized that the laws collected under the general fabric *Corpus juris* were not, in fact, a single body of consistent law, but rather the emanation of an extended period of historical time, and, therefore, that their meaning could only be comprehended through a program of study placing them firmly in their historical context.[53] Such a treatment of Roman law inevitably weakened its authority. Even though a more accurate and complete understanding of classical jurisprudence ultimately resulted, the initial effect was to reduce the salutary influence that a received body of "ideal law" had in providing a basis and a vocabulary of the defense of property and the concept of rule, limited, however slightly, by law.

The endeavor to place the received body of the *Corpus juris* in its proper historical context led, in the mid-sixteenth century, to a more generalized effort to reconstruct normative law through the study of history.[54] In 1566, in his *Methodus,* Jean Bodin wrote that the only way "to arrange the laws and govern the state . . . is to collect all the laws of all or the most famous commonwealths, to compare them and derive the best variety."[55] Although a task of such monumental difficulty could only have been justified by loss of confidence in any received body of law, so radical an approach could but further erode the normative quality of any extant legal system. The process of selecting the "best variety" was essentially limited to two possibilities. One might attempt to select those laws that most societies had held to be just, but the reductive nature of such a process is quickly apparent; very few laws, and those extremely basic, would emerge from this comparative approach. The alternative of selecting only those laws from each society that are "best" immediately poses the question of the standard of selection. Yet if the need for the comparative historical approach arose from the absence of a clear and accepted set of judicial abstractions, it was precisely that touchstone by which the quality of any given law was to be judged that was itself in doubt. On the one hand, the surviving laws would be so few and so basic as to provide little guidance or constraint for public action; and on the other, the ability to select such laws as seemed useful – one might say expedient – would again free rather than constrain the behavior of a government that had picked and chosen its operating rules from among the world's laws. By the middle of the sixteenth century in many areas on the Continent and to a lesser degree in England, the set of legal abstractions that had served in the middle ages was dismantled and there was yet no replacement. The assumptions to which one might appeal, and the vocabulary of that appeal, in defense of the individual, of property, of traditional liberties, had ceased to be the common heritage of European man.

Legal abstractions are of relatively minor concern when society is stable, when tradition and traditional modes of behavior seem strong, and when venerable institutions preserve their integrity and sustain the social balance. The sixteenth century was not such a time. The papacy had been damaged by schism, by the conciliar movement, and, increasingly, by the loss of prestige engendered by an unfortunate series of Renaissance popes. The church itself never recovered from the disintegration of the Reformation, on the one hand, and the establishment of national, though still Catholic, churches, on the other. Almost everywhere, religious conflict raised real concern over the legitimacy of secular authority. Institutions were no longer stable. Armies grew in size and destructive potential as traditional weapons retreated before firearms, and mercenaries became ever more important. With the geographical discoveries, the very boundaries of the world altered and the medieval cosmography, based on a Jerusalem-centered world, collapsed. New and more powerful navies fought over economic resources at vast distances from their home countries and the cannon became an instrument of commerce. Unique forms of economic organization were required for the exploitation of a wider world. Even in science, the received truths of Aristotle bowed before the onslaught of Copernicus and Kepler. Yet between the destruction of the older system of scientific natural law and the firmer creation of the seventeenth century lay a period of confusion filled with astrology, witchcraft, alchemy, and magic.[56]

Political, religious, intellectual, and economic ferment conjured a vast array of questions that demanded answers if society was to function. What were the rights of monarchy and the limits to power? Was there a limit to taxation as war became more international and expensive? To what extent could international trade be directed and controlled and in whose interest? What were the rights of peasants as population rose and food became scarce? Who owned the mineral rights in the new mines? If "money was the sinews of war," was there any limit to internal regulation of the commerce and manufacturing needed to earn foreign exchange? Under what law could Spain and Portugal regularize their claim to possessions in the New World? Could ecclesiastical and other land be redistributed by the monarchy and, if so, were there any limits to such redistribution? Were there natural limits to a monarch's ability to manipulate economic resources in his own interests? If larger companies were required by the expanding

European hegemony, did they exist by royal charter or by associative rights inherent in their individual members? Was there a substantive distinction between war and commerce? These are all economic questions, posed by the events of the later Renaissance; the answers are the major decisions of sixteenth-century economic policy and the basic fabric of the economic history of the period. Yet the nature of those answers cannot be understood without comprehension of the state of the system of legal abstractions to which they would normally have been referred.

2
Recovery: population and money supply

In the year 1453, Constantinople fell, and after an effort that had required more than a century, the Turkish drive to conquer the eastern shores of the Mediterranean was complete. In the same year, the Hundred Years' War between France and England came to an end and peace allowed France to seek solutions to long-standing problems and to recover from the accumulated disasters of the preceding century. England too found internal peace in 1485, when the coronation of Henry VII instituted the Tudor monarchy and ended the civil distress known as the Wars of the Roses.

Foremost among the catastrophes that Europe had suffered in the century prior to 1450 was massive depopulation. Perhaps a third of the total population had perished as a result of the Black Death, or bubonic plague, whose first appearance in 1347–50 was reinforced and intensified by persistent recurrences at the national and local levels for more than a century. Normal demographic recovery through enhanced birthrates was impossible until the virulence of the plague subsided and immunity increased. As a result there is little doubt that the overall population of Europe was considerably smaller in the middle of the fifteenth century than it had been at the beginning of the fourteenth. Available numerical estimates do not withstand close scrutiny (figures offered by leading authors vary by as much as 50 percent), yet despite disparities in the actual numbers, they all confirm the same overall pattern. The population of Europe grew, though at varying rates, from the eighth to the fourteenth century and then fell precipitously. M. K. Bennett provides the figures given in Table I.

Loss of close to one-third of the population of Europe during the latter half of the fourteenth century could not fail to cause severe

Table I. *Population of Europe (in millions)*

1300	73	1500	69
1350	51	1550	78
1400	45	1600	89
1450	60		

Source: M. K. Bennett, *The World's Food*, New York, Harper & Row, Publishers, 1954, Table I, p. 9.

economic problems and major dislocations. Population decline led naturally to a reduction in demand for basic foods, but because farmers could concentrate their efforts on the best and most productive land, the output of agricultural commodities did not decline in proportion to the reduction in demand. Prices for food grains fell as bread became relatively more plentiful and the earlier pressures on agricultural resources abated. Land grew cheap as labor to work it became scarce and as the bullion price of the product declined. Finding that they paid relatively less for necessities, consumers enlivened their diets with luxuries; meat, butter, fish, wine, and more exotic spices were consumed at ever lower levels of the social scale. Landholders everywhere attempted to adjust their production to the new market conditions. Land-extensive forms of agriculture such as sheep raising became more prevalent as labor prices rose, and specialized cash crops such as dyestuffs, barley for brewing, and livestock both for dairy production and for direct meat consumption were substituted for bread grains in an effort to meet the realities of the altered demands of a depopulated Europe.

Despite efforts at diversification, landholders were unable to protect themselves; rental income and land values fell precipitously throughout western Europe. In France, England, and Germany, surplus land, no longer worth farming, was abandoned and allowed to revert to forest or waste. In Scandinavia, cheap imported German grain virtually destroyed cereal culture on farms that had always been marginal because of the climate, and commercial fishing replaced agriculture. Only in some portions of the Netherlands and of northern Italy, where the presence of large cities provided markets, and in some regions of eastern Europe, where thirteenth-century conditions were even worse than those in the fourteenth century, could the traditional uses of agricultural land be sustained.

Declining population had a more severely adverse effect on the production of manufactured goods than it had on agricultural output. Skills, more difficult to acquire, were consequently more difficult to replace, and the nature of late medieval technology was such that labor, rather than machines or capital goods, was the crucial ingredient in the manufacturing process. As the prices of basic foods fell, the prices of manufactured goods rose, for a greater portion of income could be diverted toward the latter. Since life seemed short and death imminent, luxury was valued dearly. As a result, urban centers, benefiting simultaneously from falling grain prices and from rising prices for their own products, briefly tended to prosper and to draw the wealth of the countryside to themselves. In the period immediately following the great plague of 1348–50, money no longer flowed from the cities in search of food, but from the countryside in search of luxury and manufactured goods.

The new pattern was inherently unstable. Balance would have been restored in time as the funds of the agricultural sector were expended and the resultant lack of demand forced down the prices of manufactures. Such a balancing mechanism, however, is viable only in a closed economy in which the temporarily affluent townspeople would have had no other use for their wealth beyond internal trade. But fourteenth-century Europe was part of a world economy that included the Levant, India, and even Russia and the Far East. Momentarily favored by the commercial balance between town and country, townsmen sought to spend their gains on scarce luxuries and these came from the East. Spices, silks, fine brocades, damasks, ivory, coral, pearls, and diamonds were imported in increasing quantities, and silver and gold were exported to pay for them.

Between 1360 and 1460, but especially during the last four decades of that period, precious metal flowed away from northwestern Europe, through Italy and the Baltic, and ultimately found a resting place in the Near and Far East.[1] The countries of the northwest increasingly suffered from bullion shortages and the loss of the circulating medium necessary to sustain profitable and healthy economies. In England, where mint figures are more available and reliable than elsewhere, silver coinage output in the century after the Black Death averaged less than 4 percent of the levels attained in the early fourteenth century.[2] France and, somewhat later, the Burgundian Netherlands endured similar losses; in Spain, the period was remembered as the era of the *evacuación de oro* ("flight of gold").[3] Military expenditures, particularly for mercenary navies, combined with papal transfers to worsen the drain and soon adverse economic effects became manifest. Kings sought expert advice from merchants; laws were passed prohibiting or severely restricting the export of bullion, and sumptuary laws limiting the consumption of luxury goods became general. Everywhere currencies were debased as governments sought to preserve their revenues and perhaps to answer the demands of the governed for adequate means of payment. The attempted remedies, however, universally failed. Bullion flows were not reversed and medieval men were wisely too suspicious of royal motives to accept debased currency at face value. A monetarily induced recession followed the demographic dislocations, and trade, both domestic and international, appears to have contracted in the early fifteenth century.[4] Italian merchants found it increasingly difficult to receive acceptable payment from bullion-starved customers in the northern regions of Europe and such indices of the volume of international commerce as remain to us show an inexorable decline during the first six decades of the fifteenth century.[5]

Population growth

Throughout most of Europe, the interrelated demographic and monetary crises ebbed after 1460 and a period of recovery began, slowly at first, but gathering momentum with the coming of the sixteenth century. Some dislocation persisted and indeed some areas paid for the gains of others with intensified crises, but, in general, Europe's path after the mid-fifteenth century was ascendant. Bennett's figures, cited in Table I, indicate that between 1450 and 1600, the overall population of Europe increased by something on the order of 50 percent – a figure we may reasonably accept as an order of magnitude, even though considerable caution is advisable with regard to the actual numerical estimates.

Demographic history in the sixteenth century is a particularly frustrating enterprise because the period is one rich in tantalizing numbers and partial statistics, yet, at the same time, one for which hard knowledge is extremely difficult to obtain. Just enough real evidence is available to generate effective challenge of almost any generalization but not enough survives to support definitively any consensus. Population surely grew, and grew quite rapidly. Literary evidence, land use, rent rolls, urban statistics, and migration patterns all confirm and document the pressure of increasing numbers, but no overall figures seem reliable; the varying quality of regional statistics precludes simple addition. The most recent estimates for England suggest that population grew from 2.2 million in 1500 to 3.75 million in 1600 – a 70 percent increase.[6] The kingdom of Castile may have doubled, rising from 3 to 6 million between 1530 and 1594[7] and comparable growth seems likely for the kingdom of Naples, which, excluding the city itself, recorded 254,000 hearths in 1505 and 540,000 in 1595.[8] The figures are vague for France, but population appears to have recovered its preplague level in the first half of the sixteenth century and to have grown rapidly in some, if not all, regions.[9] Lyons may have grown from a village of twenty thousand in 1470 to a bustling city of between sixty and eighty thousand in 1530,[10] but it is difficult to generalize from such local evidence, because the civil and religious wars undoubtedly produced cotemporal regional declines and because even Lyons lost its prosperity late in the century. German population proliferated after the mid-fifteenth century, and in one area, the principality of Osnabrück, the increment amounted to 84 percent between 1500 and 1604.[11] Figures for Italy as a whole indicate growth from 11.6 million to 13.3 million between 1550 and 1600 – a somewhat slower rate than elsewhere as a result of the exclusion of the more vigorous increases that occurred earlier in the century.[12] Perhaps the most spectacular rise took place outside of Europe proper; estimates show the population of Constantinople soaring from one hundred thousand in 1453 to seven hundred thousand in 1580.[13]

That Europe's population increased sharply during the sixteenth century is beyond doubt, even though our estimates of magnitude are often tainted by a spurious precision. Beyond the simple increase in numbers, however, there was, perhaps more significantly, a change in location, concentration, and relative density of population. Economically, socially, and culturally, it makes a great deal of difference whether population merely expands proportionately or whether the expansion causes nodes of concentration in active cities that then serve as centers of economic growth, of financial stimulus, of the dispersion of technology, and of expanding networks of consumption and distribution. Where we are fortunate enough to have simultaneous estimates of demographic patterns for cities and for the country or region in which the city was located, it is possible to construct an urbanization index that allows us to make some comparisons across Europe. This is done by giving all late sixteenth-century population figures an arbitrary value of 100 and then calculating the percentage value of the earliest sixteenth-century estimate in each case. When the early value for a city is divided into the cotemporal value for the country or region, the result is an index of urbanization. If the city was small relative to the country at the beginning of the period and increased relatively, the urbanization index is proportionately large. The results of such manipulations are given in Table II.

Because of absence of data, our index unfortunately excludes certain cities that grew rapidly during the early sixteenth century. Antwerp, for example, by 1570 had expanded to nearly two and one half times its 1480 population;[14] the swift rise of Lyons has already been mentioned; Venice regained its medieval population level of perhaps 120,000 by 1500 and pressed upward to nearly 190,000 by 1575.[15] Antwerp and Lyons would almost certainly have merited quite high figures on the urbanization scale, although Venice and, even more clearly, most other Italian cities would have held lesser ranks because urbanization came early to Italy and the sixteenth century was for Italy a period in which efforts were made to regain or to hold ancient prosperity rather than a time of positive advancement. Even in the cases of Lyons and Antwerp, however, it is reasonable to argue that omission from the index is justified or at least compensated for by the very fragility and brevity of their demographic significance. Antwerp lost nearly half its population in the two decades following 1568 as a result of political and religious turbulence in the southern Netherlands; Lyons suffered heavily during the Wars of Religion; and Venice yielded a third of its population to virulent plagues in the years 1575-7.

The index effectively identifies two of the most durable and prosperous cities of the early modern period, Amsterdam and London, and it marks the lesser ones. The low index numbers of Neapolitan and Sicilian cities accurately reflect the backward and dismal economies of these regions in the sixteenth century, whereas those of Castile mirror the anomalies of Spain, the richest country in Europe yet one of the

Table II. *Urbanization in selected areas of Europe*

	Urbanization index
Holland, 1514–1622	
Amsterdam	3.19
Next six largest in	
the South Quarter	0.99
England, 1500–1603–5	
London	2.82
Castile, 1530–91	
Zamora	2.43
Leon	1.83
Toledo	1.43
Madrid	1.34
Seville	0.81
Salamanca	0.75
Burgos	0.60
Sicily, 1501–1607	
Messina	1.56
Palermo	1.13
Kingdom of Naples, 1505–95	
Naples (1500–95)	0.86

Sources: Holland: Jan de Vries, *The Dutch Rural Economy in the Golden Age, 1500–1700*, New Haven, Yale University Press, 1974, Table 3.1, p. 86. England: J. Cornwall, "English Population in the Early Sixteenth Century," *Economic History Review*, XXIII (1970) 32–44, and F. Mauro, *Le XVIe siècle Européen – aspects économiques*, Presses Universitaires de France, Paris, 1970, p. 160. Castile and the Kingdom of Naples: F. Braudel, *La Méditerranée et le monde Méditerranéen à l'époque de Philippe II*, I, Paris, Armand Colin, 1966, pp. 370–1. Sicily and the city of Naples: Mauro, *Le XVIe siècle*, p. 160.

least advanced economically. Even Madrid, the artificial capital of a vast colonial empire, shows little relative urbanization. The only real surprise is Zamora, now a sleepy Spanish town but then an important center for the wine trade of the Duero valley, a way station on the migratory sheep routes of the Mesta, or sheepmens' guild, and one of the four largest textile-producing areas of Castile.[16] Zamora and, to a lesser extent, Leon grew in relation to the surrounding countryside because each was poised upon a firm economic base and each was the focus of an extensive regional trade. To flourish, a city required more than local economic contacts. The early and spectacular rise of Antwerp was consequent on its selection by Portugal as the prime European port for the newly opened ocean trade in Eastern spices, its ties to the prosperous new mining regions of southern Germany, and its role as the continental entrepôt for the expanding English textile industry. Antwerp's decline had economic as well as political causes, since established trading patterns proved fluid and traditional sources of prosperity waned during the latter part of the sixteenth century. Lyons' demographic expansion, initially the inspiration of Louis XI, who granted extensive privileges to its international fairs in order to destroy the affluence of Geneva, was sustained by a firm, though temporary, economic base as the fairs prospered and the city became a center of international banking. London, during the sixteenth century, became increasingly important both in regional and world trade, and Amsterdam replaced Antwerp as the most significant port for European and international commerce.

The economic activities that sustained and supported each of these cities will subsequently be considered in more detail, but enough has been said to establish not only that the urbanization index identifies cities that experienced high relative population growth, but also that such population growth was very closely connected to the broader economic environment. Cities – by definition, concentrations of people within limited areas – do not merely depend on the surrounding economic structure; they greatly influence it. The greater the size of the city, the less feasible is it for the inhabitants to supply their own food, and they inevitably become more dependent on cash purchases of supplies over an ever wider area. With growth, individual occupations become more precisely defined and more specialized, and a host of tradesmen are required to handle the logistical problems of urbanization. Carters and shippers must travel greater distances to obtain supplies; wholesalers are needed to receive goods and divide them into units that can be retailed in smaller, more convenient shops. Credit must improve to sustain more complex markets, and more financial specialists are called for. As marketing structures and financial arrangements become increasingly sophisticated, ancillary professions and professionals multiply; lawyers, police, and regulatory officials proliferate, and, in their turn, they further increase the market impact of the city. As the urban population expands, the number of cash transactions, both within the city and between the city and the regions that supply food and raw materials, rise more than proportionally. The number of steps that it takes for a primary good to reach its final destination in the hands or mouth of a consumer multiplies. The need for ready money to negotiate the greater turnover and enhanced quantity of transactions is magnified.

In the sixteenth century, urbanization at once increased the demand for transactions cash and accented the potential inconveniences of an insufficient supply. Under certain circumstances, the latter element can contribute to the willingness of the general public to accept money substitutes, either in the form of more extensive credit arrangements or in the form of fiat money, whether printed on paper or stamped on metal. Happily for the economies of the late fifteenth and early sixteenth centuries, the supply of precious metal expanded along with the demand for increased quantities of specie, so fiat money was not an immediate necessity for the ongoing development of the cities. The money supply recovered at the same time as the population.

The mining boom

As we have noted, precious metal became scarce during the first half of the fifteenth century because of dislocations in the balance of payments between Europe and the Near and Far East. The situation was worsened by technological failures in the gold and silver mines of Europe. Around 1300, mines that had been successfully exploited during the affluent years of the commercial revolution began to lose their productive capacity. Old ore beds were exhausted and additional minerals could only be extracted at ever increasing depths. Such depths, however, were beyond the technical capacity of late medieval mining engineers and problems of mine drainage proved insurmountable. Depopulation, by bringing to an end the prolonged eastward migration of Europeans in search of fertile lands in central Europe, had a negative effect on gold and silver production as well. Fewer people settling new lands, clearing forests, and turning over the earth meant fewer opportunities for important strikes of new mineral resources. With rare exceptions, most notably in Bohemia and Hungary, the mines of Europe experienced a prolonged period of low productivity and poor results from the mid-fourteenth century to the mid-fifteenth.[17]

The requisite solutions to the problems that had arisen in mining were partly technical and partly economic. The most elaborately developed and deepest mines had always been those exploiting precious metals, although copper, both because of the innate utility of the metal and because it was often found in conjunction with silver, was also in some instances mined at considerable depths. Only when the value of the product could recover the cost was it worth investing the capital and labor required for timbering, supporting, and draining deep mines; in general, only the precious metals could repay the costs of capital-intensive mining. The extended, but persistent, drain of precious metals from western Europe increased the scarcity of bullion and, consequently, its value; the less there was the more a given unit could buy. Conversely, the commodity price of bullion rose, and as time passed in the fifteenth century, greater and greater expenditures of labor and goods could economically be devoted to the search for precious metals. It is hardly accidental that the century witnessed the shattering of the old geography as men strove literally to reach the ends of the earth, motivated at least in part by the quest for gold.

The high and rising commodity price of precious metal in all probability enhanced both the desire to experiment with new mining methods and the willingness of investors to bear the expense of more capital-intensive operations. Devices that previously had been known experimentally, and even sporadically used, were by the mid-fifteenth century widely adopted and refined. In the heavy clay soils of Germany and central Europe, seepage and water accumulation presented the greatest obstacle to deep mining and received the most ingenious attention, although the simplest solutions were perhaps the most effective. Where mines were located in hilly or mountainous regions, water could be drained off by constructing adits, or long drainage tunnels, from the bottom of the mine to the surface of the hill at a lower level. Such tunnels attained great lengths, extending in some cases for as much as a mile beneath the surface of the earth. Remarkable feats of engineering, the adits were not only expensive but dangerous to construct. Because the water trapped in the mine prevented further digging from within in the first place, the adit had to be excavated from without and dug upward toward the floor of the mine shaft. Successful completion of the excavation exposed the miner to a rush of accumulated water from the mine as the tunnel began to drain the flooded shaft. Similar difficulties impeded the maintenance of the adit once it had been built, and it is clear why considerable effort was devoted to developing less expensive and dangerous alternate means of mine drainage.

Literate and trained scholars joined pragmatic and inventive working miners in devising and diffusing advanced techniques; comprehensive tracts on mining and metallurgy appeared during the first half of the sixteenth century, bringing together old techniques and describing and spreading the newer methods.[18] Georgius Agricola, in his compendious treatise on mining and metallurgy, describes, in addition to adits, numerous devices for draining and ventilating mines.[19] Simple lift pumps, manually operated and fashioned from hollowed trees, provide the starting point for a survey of drainage techniques. Such pumps, of course, are limited by the physical capacity of air pressure to raise a column of water, and this limit is reached at just over 30 feet. Deeper mines required more complex engines, and with complexity came increased weight and greater friction; manpower proved insufficient. Although air pressure set the limits for simple lift pumps, friction and weight were the only barriers to pumping by means of a series of such pumps, arranged so that each emptied into a trough around the base of the next higher one. Waterwheels and treadmills, either man or horse powered, could then provide sufficient energy to set such engines in motion, especially when transmission ratios were governed by gigantic wooden gears. Further, the pumps could be combined with adits midway up the mine shaft in order to reduce the height to which the water had to be raised. More practical still, because it eliminated dependence on air pressure, was a variant of the Arab *norias*, or chain – bucket pump. In Agricola's version, a chain moved continuously around two wheels or pulleys, one at the surface and one at the bottom of the mine. The chain passed through a long pipe, which extended from beneath the water level in the shaft to the surface of the mine, and was equipped at regular intervals with balls of horsehair. As the balls rose into the pipe from below, they trapped a quantity of water, compressed against the wall of the pipe, and drew the water to the surface. The process was continuous and the depths at which the pump could be employed were limited only by the strength of the power source and the nature of the materials used to construct the device. With such engines, depths could be attained and mining effectively undertaken at levels not considered practical for more than a thousand years preceding the sixteenth century.

In smelting and refining as in drainage and excavation, the extensive application and systemization of known older methods was more important than any substantial technological breakthroughs.[20] Once capital costs could be justified by the high commodity price of precious metals, great ingenuity was applied to recombining and developing techniques at every stage of metal production. Water-driven trip-hammers, huge vertical beams lifted and released by protrusions on the axle shaft of a waterwheel, were used to crush ore. Similarly powered bellows were linked in tandem to provide a continuous blast of air to the smelting furnace. Attainable temperatures rose greatly, but intense heat was more important in the production of ferrous metals than in gold and silver smelting. More crucial for the latter metals was the intensified application of the amalgamation process employing mercury to separate gold and silver from base ores. The method was known in Roman times (it is described by Pliny) and was not lost during the middle ages; Chaucer's Canon's Yeoman impressed his fellow pilgrims with his knowledge of the arcana of alchemy and the vocabulary of refining by amalgamation. The technique requires crushing the ore – most notably silver, since that metal normally occurs in complex compounds, whereas gold is often found in its elemental state – and then sprinkling it with certain chemicals and mercury. Silver and gold adhere to mercury and form an amalgam so heavy that the base materials present in the ore may be washed away. Part of the mercury can be recovered simply by squeezing it out of the amalgam, and much of the remainder can be recaptured by heating the amalgam, vaporizing the mercury, and then condensing it, leaving behind the purified gold and silver. Vaporization is at once dangerous, because mercury is a deadly poison, and expensive, because not all the mercury can be recovered; indeed, as the sixteenth century progressed, mercury became an increasingly strategic and critical item in working the mines of the New World. For the early decades, however, alternate methods supplemented amalgamation and sufficient mercury was available from the ancient and rich mines of Almadén in Spain for the silver production of central Europe; later in the century, the mercury of Huancavélica in Peru supplemented this source.[21]

Although not, in general, new, the techniques employed in mining in the late fifteenth and early sixteenth centuries reinforced each other. Deeper mines provided more bullion, but improvements in bellows and furnaces yielded better tools for working deeper mines and more iron for cutting the timbers needed for deep shafts and for supporting the moving parts of elaborate drainage engines. Improved tools meant more efficient refining as well and perhaps helped to assure an adequate supply of mercury. The combined effect was dramatic. Production of silver in central Europe – in Saxony, Bohemia, Hungary, and the Tyrol – increased some fivefold between 1460 and 1530 to almost 3 million ounces, or roughly 90,000 kilograms, a year; in other regions such as Sweden production rose nearly as rapidly.[22] By the late fifteenth century, the mining boom in central Europe had done much to replace the precious metal that had been drained away during the preceding hundred years; almost everywhere, the last decades of that century witnessed heightened mint activity as bullion was once again available to be struck into coin, the life blood of economic activity.

The riches of America

Although Christopher Columbus died in 1506, disappointed in his dream of finding the riches of the East, his followers and successors saw to it that the Western economies would not need to depend only on the precious metals of central Europe. Haiti, then Cuba and Panama, served as bases for further exploration and conquest: Cortés moved against the rich Aztec empire in 1519 and Pizarro struck at the equally wealthy lands of the Incas after 1531.[23] Plunder was perhaps the initial objective of those few thousand truly remarkable, though cruel, men who conquered empires inhabited by millions, but as the Vikings had discovered six hundred years earlier, plunder has its own natural limits. Soon, more peaceful forms of economic exploitation replaced outright force. After accumulated treasures had been seized in Mexico and Peru, the predators turned to the source and to mining. Table III, which gives the American gold and silver imported by Spain, measures their level of success.

We will consider the economic impact of this massive influx of silver shortly, but first it is worth noting that the new mines and mining itself posed a number of problems closely interwoven with the legal abstractions discussed in Chapter 1. The vast additions to the geography of the world resulting from the discoveries of the late fifteenth century simultaneously distressed the comfortable security of the older, medieval, Jerusalem-centered world and forced consideration of the poten-

Table III. *Total decennial Spanish imports of fine gold and silver (in kilograms)*

Period	Silver	Gold
1503–10	—	4,965
1511–20	—	9,153
1521–30	148	4,889
1531–40	86,194	14,466
1541–50	177,573	24,957
1551–60	303,121	42,620
1561–70	942,859	11,531
1571–80	1,118,592	9,429
1581–90	2,103,028	12,102
1591–1600	2,707,627	19,451
1601–10	2,213,631	11,764
1611–20	2,192,256	8,886
1621–30	2,145,339	3,890
1631–40	1,396,760	1,240
1641–50	1,056,431	1,549
1651–60	443,257	469

Source: Earl J. Hamilton, *American Treasure and the Price Revolution in Spain*, Cambridge, Mass., Harvard University Press, 1934, Table 3, p. 44. Reprinted by permission of the publisher.

tial legal bases for establishing ownership of those additions. By what means could one formalize legal title to half the world? Some precedents existed as a result of the early fourteenth-century Atlantic explorations: In 1344, Spain had obtained papal sanction for her claim to the Canary Islands, and in 1434, Portugal, though not without protest, had been able to gain a similar title to islands not yet occupied by Spain.[24] The papal titles did not prevent discord, however, and military force was quickly substituted for judicial process; eventually, an uneasy truce was established by the Treaty of Alcaçovas in 1479, by means of which the Portuguese abandoned their claims to the Canaries, but won a monopoly of the African coast. Fifteenth-century experience, then, offered two essentially different methods of regularizing titles to newly discovered lands – conquest and papal sanction. The choice conjured deeper implications than mere legalisms, and the two methods became major poles in the debate concerning the Spanish crown's power over the colonies in the New World.

As we have noted, thirteenth-century doctrines of property customarily started with the assumption that the earth and its resources were given by God under natural law for the common use of all mankind and that they were subsequently divided into privately held units by human or positive law in order to avoid friction and to ensure proper custodianship. Under such assumptions, it was perfectly reasonable to seek title to newly discovered lands – presumably still part of the Lord's undivided endowment – from God's earthly agent, the pope. This was the course chosen by Spain after Columbus's unlucky landing in Portugal on his return voyage had provoked a competitive Portuguese claim to the new Atlantic territories. In May and September of 1493, Alexander VI, a Spanish pope, issued two bulls granting Spain all new lands west of a line drawn arbitrarily down the Atlantic Ocean. The second bull, *inter caetera*, was so generous to Spain that the Portuguese protested and war was averted only by means of the political Treaty of Tordesillas; signed in 1494, it pushed the papal line 275 leagues further to the west, and as a result gave Portugal the Brazilian coast. In 1506, a further papal bull, *ea quae*, reconfirmed the division, and in 1514, Leo X made the balanced nature of the division explicit by granting Portugal all new lands that could be reached by sailing eastward from the demarcation line.

Convenient though it was to obtain a recognized legal basis for the vast territorial claims, the nature of the title conflicted with the economic interests of the colonists. If Spain's ownership of most of the New World depended on the abstractions of natural law, the use and exploitation of the region should logically have been in accord with divine justice. On the other hand, colonists were few and labor needs were great. It was not long before Indian slave labor was employed and justified through arguments based on secular theories of conquest and supported by appeal to Aristotle's doctrine of the legitimate enslavement of naturally inferior peoples. The church labored for the conversion of the Indians and against slavery; the efforts of the Spanish monk Las Casas on behalf of the native populations were not only courageous, since opposition was great, but brought the luster of humanity to the generally sordid story of Spanish–Indian relations. Success in abolishing Indian slavery after 1560 was attained through a combination of ecclesiastical pressure and the political interests of the Spanish crown, which sought to prevent the growth of powerful feudatories in the New

World. One may also note that the increasing availability of Negro Slaves – paradoxically excluded from the sentiments reserved for Indians – may have alleviated the economic needs for native labor.[25] Cynicism should not, however, obscure the very real impact of the church, of doctrines of natural law in mobilizing ecclesiastical efforts, and of the earnest belief of devoted mendicants that each Indian had a human soul that belonged to God in mitigating the lot of native labor.

If labor conditions were to some degree softened through the influence of the church and natural law, the actual ownership of the mines was not referred to that jurisdiction. Medieval custom, perhaps derived from late Roman counterparts, gave the prince regalian rights to precious metals beneath the earth's surface as part of his sovereignty.[26] The reemphasis of Roman law in the jurisprudence of Europe during the later middle ages and the concomitant growth in the authority of the secular prince served to strengthen and extend such claims to regalian rights over the riches of the earth, and, in some cases, to expand those claims even to the base ores that had not been within the prince's authority before the sixteenth century.[27] Throughout Europe, territorial princes increased their control over mineral rights – in some cases over entire mines – and multiplied the number of royal officials engaged in the supervision and regulation of miners and mining operations. In the New World, perhaps as a result of distance and consequent uncertainty, the Spanish crown chose to lease its rights to the riches of the earth in return for a set share of one-fifth of the output, rather than to become a direct participant in the mines.[28] Once again we may note that Renaissance princes were not overly scrupulous in adhering to any one normative standard of justice and law, but rather benefited from the confusion that emerged as legal systems and controversies proliferated by referring selectively to whichever of the various legal standards favored the needs of the moment. If natural law was a useful rubric for claiming new territories, so be it, but it was more profitable to refer the issue of mineral rights to ancient custom and to doctrines of sovereignty derived from Roman law.

Monetary resurgence

The combined output of the central European and new American mines quickly ended the prolonged silver famine of the later middle ages, and when the depleted stocks were replaced, the phenomena associated with that depletion waned and long-established trends were reversed. The secular price deline of the late fourteenth and fifteenth centuries changed course and prices began to recover. In a sense, the mines of central Europe, by their very success, sowed the seeds of their own downfall. They had become economical in the late fifteenth century because extreme scarcity had raised the purchasing power of gold and silver to artificial heights; abundant output of precious metal drove commodity prices up fairly sharply and thus increased the capital costs of mining. After 1530, growing imports of precious metals from Central and Latin America further supplemented the European monetary stock, accelerated the fall in the purchasing power of gold and silver, and reduced even more the prosperity of the European mines. The political turbulence generated by Turkish attacks in central Europe and by the civil wars of Reformation Germany caused additional disruption in the mining regions. As a result, the mines of central Europe appear to have reached a peak in the 1530s that they were not to attain again until well into the nineteenth century.

The sixteenth-century inflation that played a major part in the decline of German prosperity was common to all of Europe, but its causes were not clearly comprehended by the men of the time. Some might add that the causes of inflation are not yet fully understood. Confronted by the inescapable evidence of rising prices, men everywhere sought to find an explanation; two Frenchmen engaged in a public exchange of views. One, Jehan de Malestroit, maintained that there had in effect been no increase if one but adjusted for the debasement of the currency. Reducing the money of account to constant silver content would, he argued, show that prices in France in 1566, the year in which he wrote, were no higher than they had been in the time of St. Louis, and thus, that the inflation was illusory.[29] The other, Jean Bodin, offered a series of explanations that included those drawn from the general wisdom – action of monopolies, war and the consequent reduction of supplies, the luxury of kings and princes, and debasement of the coinage – but focused his main attention on the great influx of gold and silver.[30] In so doing, Bodin appears at once to have invented the quantity theory of money, relating prices to the amount of specie in circulation, to have defeated his opponent decisively in the eyes of subsequent historians, and to have loosed an avalanche of commentary that sought to elaborate on this initial theme.

The spectacular and romantic dimensions of the conquest of the New

World have caused historians to concentrate their inquiries primarily upon the impact of American treasure and to understate, to the detriment of their work, I believe, the importance of central Europe. Even so, the ongoing discussion has been fruitful and provocative. Bodin's early version of the quantity theory remained primitive in that it simply noted the connection between bullion inflows and price increases, without closing the system so as to include variations in the output of goods and services or the effects of credit and other factors that affect the velocity of monetary circulation. Over time, however, the rudimentary theory was slowly developed and improved; Cantillon especially, writing in the eighteenth century, deserves credit for having been the first to comprehend clearly the importance of monetary velocity in closing the theory.[31] The quantity equation found its modern form – the one that has deeply influenced the historiography of our period – in the work of Irving Fisher, who rendered it in the following notation:[32]

$$MV = PT$$

This equation simply states that the money supply times its velocity of circulation (the number of times the money supply turns over) is equal to the price of goods and services times the number of transactions. Two dimes turning over five times will buy twenty plums at a nickel each. In this form, the equation is at once deceptively simple and tautologically true.

The quantity equation, perhaps because of its very simplicity, has provided the theoretical core for much of the discussion of the economic history of the sixteenth century, and that discussion has fallen into two broad categories. On the one hand, there is a very substantial literature that continues in the tradition of Bodin and Malestroit and seeks primarily to explicate the causes of the so-called price revolution. On the other, there is a continuing effort to weigh the influence of price increases on such factors as capital accumulation, industrial growth, relative rates of economic growth among countries, social structure (particularly that of the landed classes), and even the birth of capitalism. Let us consider first the question of the nature of the price revolution itself.

One of the difficulties that has plagued those seeking to elucidate the price history of the sixteenth century is a general failure to be precise with regard to what is to be explained and with the definition of the variables. The traditional periodization, which places the end of the middle ages and the beginning of the modern world around the year 1500, has had the unfortunate consequence of isolating early modern historians from medievalists. Those who work in the early modern period often appear reluctant to press further backward in time across the artificial barriers set by the traditional date. As a result, the price inflation of the sixteenth century is often measured only against price levels encountered in the late fifteenth century – a period marked by bullion scarcity, low population levels, surplus land, and reticent economic activity. Yet one may recall that Malestroit's challenge to Bodin was predicated upon comparison of prices in the time of St. Louis, king of France in the thirteenth century, when times were prosperous. Bodin, although he denied Malestroit's proposition that debasement accounted for all price changes since the thirteenth century, was more concerned with his present era and thus drew his explanations from the immediate past. These two opposing temporal perspectives continue to affect present-day perceptions of the connection between bullion inflows and price changes in the early modern world.

That there were massive importations of silver during the sixteenth century is beyond doubt, and the invaluable work of Hamilton has documented their size.[33] Yet *massive* is a relative word and even measurements precisely stated in kilograms are meaningless without some point of comparison. Some recent scholarship starting from the import levels of silver has questioned the validity of the quantity equation as a device for explaining the price inflation of the sixteenth century, since prices rose more rapidly in the first than in the second half of the period. If, it is argued, Spanish prices climbed at the rate of 2.8 percent annually during the first sixty years of the century and subsequently rose only at the rate of 1.3 percent during the remaining forty, with the most swift growth in the decade 1521–30, there must be something wrong with the quantity equation.[34] Because the greatest quantity of American bullion flowed to Europe after 1560, the influence on prices should have been greater at the end than at the beginning of the century, the critics assert, and because the price figures contradict this expected pattern, they renounce the quantity theory as a sufficient explanation of the inflation.

It is well to recall here our earlier statement that the quantity equation is tautologically true; it does not exist in, or depend on, historical time. It is a logical identity, immune from historical facts. Now without abandoning the historian's for the theorist's world, however, one may find a rather simple explanation for the reputedly peculiar behavior of Spanish prices in the face of ever-increasing imports of bullion. Because the European and Spanish monetary stocks appear to have been heavily depleted at the end of the fifteenth century,[35] a relatively small quantity of metal would have represented a substantial percentage increment; the impact on prices would have been proportionally great. As the stock of precious metal grew with each annual addition, however, each successive increment would have had to have been proportionally greater in order to have had the same impact on prices as the earlier, smaller imports. The price pattern of rapid initial increase followed by slower rates of inflation is thus precisely what the quantity equation would lead one to expect; it is not an awkward phenomenon that casts doubt on the validity of the quantity equation.

Although the most rapid rise in Spanish prices occurred in the decade 1521–30, before significant quantities of New World bullion had arrived, we must recall that that decade marked the maximum output from the mines of central Europe. During those years, European mines were producing roughly 90,000 kilograms of silver annually – a figure not surpassed by Spanish imports until the 1570s. Simultaneous consideration of European and American silver production leads to the following conclusions: that the influence of silver mining on prices should have been particularly sharp in the early part of the century; that European output would have greatly augmented the European monetary stock by the late 1530s; and that, as a result, when the American gold and silver arrived, its percentage impact on the monetary stock, and consequently on prices, would be less than that of the earlier additions derived from Europe's own mines. This is, of course, precisely what the price statistics show.

Careful distinction between the size of the monetary stock, which does affect the price level, and the size of the increments to that stock, which affect the price level only in proportion to their size when measured against the extant monetary stock, has enabled us to disarm arguments against the quantity theory that were based upon false expectations for the behavior of prices. What, however, of Malestroit's contention that debasement of the currency, rather than expanding metal supplies, produced the inflation? Here the issue depends to a great extent on the base period selected for anchoring the variables of the quantity equation. From the latter half of the fourteenth century forward, kings and princes everywhere indulged in extensive currency debasement as they found that there was less and less bullion available at the mints. Pressured by short supplies of bullion and growing needs for revenues and means of payment, they progressively reduced the metal content of the money of account. By the latter half of the fifteenth century, these actions had had considerable effect in weakening the intrinsic value of most currencies; yet it is precisely this period – largely because more price statistics are available than for any earlier time – that is most often chosen as the base period against which to measure the extent of the price revolution. The consequences of selecting the late fifteenth century as the base period are twofold. On the one hand, since debasement had been practiced in most countries for more than a century by that time, the money of account had already been greatly weakened; further debasement occurred in most cases during the sixteenth century, but it was probably not sufficient, as Bodin pointed out, to account for the great rise in prices during that century. On the other hand, the selection of a base period that incorporated an acute shortage of specie tends to exaggerate the impact of the incremental bullion from central Europe and from the mines of the New World. Moreover, since much of the long-term and continuous debasement of the various monies of account occurred because of, and in conjunction with, the bullion famine of the fourteenth and fifteenth centuries, the potential price-raising effects of debasement were to a large extent offset by the price-reducing effects of bullion scarcity. Nominal increases in the money supply that resulted from debasement were canceled by the reduction in the quantity of precious metal. There is, in addition, considerable evidence that the debased coinage was not publicly accepted at face value in any event, so that reductions in the intrinsic values of Europe's monies of account had only limited influence on the money supply as defined for the purposes of the quantity equation.[36]

The intent of this somewhat technical discussion of monetary matters and of historical periodization has, of course, been to place the conflict between Bodin and Malestroit in historical perspective. Once we have established the late fifteenth century as the point of comparison, Bodin was clearly correct that subsequent currency debasement was insufficient to account for all of the price inflation of the sixteenth century. Given these premises, historians have been judicious in aligning themselves with his views, although one might wish that they had been more explicit in stating those premises. Malestroit, taken on his own terms, however, is less easily dismissed than is generally conceded. French historical records have suffered too greatly to uphold meaningful comparisons between the thirteenth and the sixteenth centuries, but let us give Malestroit the belated benefit of our access to the richer archives of medieval England and test his hypothesis in the history of that more documented country.

Surviving records from the London mint are virtually complete, so we may compare coinage outputs over long periods of time; lacunae exist but they tend to balance each other. Thirteenth- and fourteenth-century outputs are somewhat understated in the aggregate because of the absence of records from the subsidiary mints of Canterbury and Durham; sixteenth-century levels are similarly understated as a result of the confused state of the documents during the troubled years from 1547 to 1551. In the course of the century from 1501 to 1600, the London mint struck 105,433 Tower pounds of fine gold; by comparison, the mint coined 106,699 Tower pounds of gold in the thirty-one-year period from 1344, the date of the first English gold coinage, to 1374. In three fourteenth-century decades, the London mint struck more gold than the amount coined during the entire century of the price revolution. For silver, the results are remarkably similar. Between 1273 and 1372, the London mint coined 1,960,058 Tower pounds of fine silver; this may be compared to the 2,276,356 Tower pounds struck in the sixteenth century. Malestroit, ironically, had he had access to these figures, might well have reversed Bodin's taunt and pointed out that the difference between the sixteenth century's 2.3 million pounds of silver and the medieval 1.9 million was not great enough to account for the considerable inflation in the later century. Further, even if one compares only the years of maximum importation of Spanish bullion with the earlier period, the results are not significantly changed. English silver coinage output from 1552 to 1594 was 1,432,436 Tower pounds; between 1279 and 1321, a similar forty-two-year period, the figure was 1,404,891 pounds of fine silver. Mint output levels, of course, are only an indirect reflection of the money supply; one may also compare years of recoinage, when the government attempted to call in all the old money in order to melt it down and reissue it in the form of fresh new pieces. These figures are perhaps a more direct indication of the size of the monetary stock at a given time. During the great recoinage of 1279–81, 367,000 Tower pounds of pure silver were minted – a quantity significantly larger than the 276,000 pounds struck during Elizabeth's revaluation and recoinage in the years 1560–2. If anything, these figures would lead us to conclude that the late medieval bullion supply was greater than that extant in England during the price revolution.[37]

If the period of comparison is extended over two hundred years, it appears that Malestroit was neither irrational nor obtuse in placing but slight emphasis on the quantity of money. Let us see how well his main contention – that debasement was primarily responsible for the inflation – withstands empirical testing. First, however, we must consider the scope of the inflation itself. Meaningful price indices or series are notoriously difficult to construct; over long spans of time, they mask changes in taste, variations in productivity, the introduction of new commodities and goods, and alterations in the overall economic structure. Granting these caveats, the best price series for England is an index of the prices of an adjusted composite unit of consumables that was developed by Phelps Brown and Hopkins.[38] Employing this index, we may compare the price level in 1323–72, when both gold and silver were minted in substantial quantities, with the price level in 1551–1600, the years of soaring imports of American treasure. In the five fourteenth-century decades, the average price index level was 121.3; the late-sixteenth-century average was 349.8. In nominal terms, sixteenth-century prices were approximately three times their fourteenth-century counterparts.

The Phelps Brown index measures prices in terms of money of account; as a result, it responds to the effects of debasement as well as to the influence of changes in the money supply and shifts in broader demographic and economic variables. If debasement were minor this would result in little distortion, but between 1323 and 1550 the silver content of the pound of account fell by nearly two-thirds in a series of irregular steps. Once the Phelps Brown index is adjusted to money of constant silver value, the average price index for the fifty-year period 1323–72 drops to 106.5, whereas that for the last half of the sixteenth century is reduced to 124.5. Expressed in pounds of constant intrinsic value, the price series indicates that the rate of inflation over a span of three centuries was minimal, or conversely, that debasement, in fact, does account for the greatest portion of the English inflation during those centuries. Given an extensive enough period – that, indeed, of his own choosing – Malestroit, at least on the basis of English evidence, appears to have been essentially correct; on the other hand, for a more limited period beginning in the fifteenth century, Bodin's position is sustained by the English figures. This is not surprising, of course, because by selecting the early fourteenth century for comparison with the late sixteenth, we have chosen two periods in which the stock of bullion appears to have been at roughly the same level; price changes, consequently, must have resulted from some other influence than variations in the quantity of precious metal. These observations do not deny the existence of the price revolution, nor the impact of inflation on the economies of sixteenth-century Europe, but they do make explicit the reasons for emphasizing the dimension of recovery in the discussion of both population levels and the money supply throughout this chapter.

Inflation and profits

Measured against conditions in the late fifteenth century, there is no doubt that prices, both nominal and real, rose steadily during the sixteenth century in most areas of Europe. The consequences of this persistent inflation have fascinated historians and economists alike. Scholars have indulged in a lively debate, extending through the pages of numerous books and journals, since 1929, when E. J. Hamilton first published an article with the provocative title "American Treasure and the Rise of Capitalism."[39] Hamilton, quite cautiously in this early article, drawing his evidence from then extant price indices, maintained that wages lagged behind prices in the inflationary price spiral of the sixteenth century and that the lag in wages tended to favor the accumulation of capital and consequently the rise of modern capitalism. In order to illustrate the mechanics of the process, he offered the following hypothetical example shown in Table IV.

Since the rise in the sales price of goods was far steeper than that for wages and rents, Hamilton asserted, profits automatically swelled to very high levels and contributed greatly to capital formation. J. M. Keynes, the economist, concurred in the analysis, writing that "in these

Table IV. *Profit inflation, after E. J. Hamilton*

	1500 (£)	1600 (£)
Sale price of a quantity of goods	100,000	250,000
Less wage costs of production	60,000	75,000
Less rent costs of production	20,000	50,000
Profit as a residual after costs	20,000	125,000

golden years modern capitalism was born," and indeed, going even further, drew "the attention of historians to the extraordinary correspondence between the periods of Profit Inflation and of Profit Deflation respectively with those of national rise and decline" in the cases of France, England, and Spain.[41] Needless to say, an idea of such rudimentary simplicity that purported to explain not only the birth of capitalism but the origins of national greatness itself, and one that had the explicit support of the greatest theoretical economist of the era, won many converts.

Ideas of such magnitude rarely go unchallenged and opponents quickly appeared. J. U. Nef, carefully considering the economic histories of the three countries together, observed that, whereas price inflation was greatest in Spain and profit inflation – the disparity between price levels and money wages – was perhaps greatest in France, economic growth was in fact greatest in England.[41] After an extended discussion of wage rates, prices, and industrial technology in both France and England, Nef concluded that although his study did not disprove the thesis that the price revolution stimulated capitalism, the influence of price movements was considerably more complex than the early proponents of the thesis had believed.

Some twenty years later, David Felix, in a brilliant little article, picked up some of the suggestions left by Nef and again focused attention on the problem of the price indices.[42] Hamilton, he observed, had based his example on an aggregate index that indeed demonstrated a two-and-one-half-fold increase in the price level over the course of the sixteenth century, but that did so only at the cost of concealing much valuable information. Looking at the separate components of the index, one discovered that for both France and England, the greatest rise in prices occurred in the agricultural sector, whereas the increase for manufactured goods was far more modest, when it was present at all.

Employing a base of 100 in the period 1451–1500, Felix pointed out that unprocessed agricultural products attained a price level of 402 by 1613, whereas assorted industrial products climbed only to 176 and textiles to 130 during the same period. Between 1521 and 1592, the price index for cloth actually fell from 85 to 80; during the same period the wage index rose from 93 to 134. Noting that such figures failed to support the existence of a profit inflation of the sort proposed by Hamilton and Keynes, Felix considered the possibility that swollen agricultural revenues might have been transferred to the industrial sector and thus have provided an alternative and indirect source of capital accumulation. The historical evidence for England did not reveal such transfers, so Felix concluded that the profit inflation thesis could not be "rejuvenated by grafting an agricultural artery on to it."

The disparity between the trends of agricultural and of manufactured goods' prices has led some to raise again the question of the validity of the quantity equation, because they assumed that an influx of precious metal would affect all prices in the same degree. That this would be so if the only variable to change was the money supply seems likely, but the actual divergence between the two sets of prices does not disprove the theory. Other factors – demographic change, shifts in taste, and divergent elasticities of supply and demand – all comprehended within the quantity equation, affected the equation at the same time as the output from European and American mines increased the monetary stock.[43] Grain and foodstuffs, produced on a limited amount of land, had relatively inelastic long-term supply curves, so that when population grew and the money supply expanded, the prices of agricultural produce rose sharply. On the other hand, the elasticities of supply for manufactured goods were greater, so that when demand increased, supply increased as well, damping the pressure on prices and accounting for the lesser degree of inflation that Felix observed in the manufacturing sector.

With these factors in mind, let us reconsider Hamilton's notion of profit inflation. Those readers with some knowledge of either economics or accounting will perhaps already have noted certain peculiarities in his hypothetical example of profit inflation. Profits are measured by the distance between labor and rent costs and sales price without any consideration of raw material costs and without regard to sales volume. Presented in such simplistic terms, the concept of profit inflation is extremely vulnerable to critical attack based on the relatively low rate of price increase ascertainable within the manufactured goods sector. The problem, however, is not so simple. Economists define profit as the difference between total revenue – unit sales price times quantity sold – and the total cost of producing the number of units sold. To measure profit effectively, in short, we require much more sophisticated information than is available from rather crude price indices, and indeed more perhaps than can be extracted from surviving sixteenth-century records.

Postponing for the moment examination of individual industries, we may note that in many areas of Europe, the sixteenth century was a period of economic growth and recovery marked by increased production of goods and services. In most instances, the prices of manufactured goods increased as well, although not so swiftly as did those of agricultural goods. Given these conditions, total revenues in each industry must inevitably have risen, because greater quantities were sold at either constant or rising prices. Calculation of total cost, either within an industry or within a single firm, is virtually impossible for any extended period of time, given the nature of surviving sixteenth-century records, so precision in estimating real profit – the difference between total cost and total revenue – is an illusory goal. One may still endeavor to identify in a qualitative fashion those factors that would have affected the cost functions of manufactured goods. If there were economies of scale, innovative technologies, new and more efficient marketing methods, or other cost-lowering influences at work in the economies of the sixteenth century, then it is, in fact, possible to rescue the notion of profit inflation – albeit a more sophisticated version than Hamilton's – and to connect it to the influx of bullion. Thus, if the consequences of the enhanced supply of precious metal were to increase the output of manufactured goods, to expand total revenues, and to permit economies of scale that lowered average cost, profit inflation would have resulted and would have contributed to more rapid accumulation of capital, given a political environment that permitted entrepreneurs to retain their earnings. In Chapter 4 we will pursue these lines of investigation in considering the technology and organization of industry; first, let us examine the impact of the price revolution in the agricultural sector. It was there that the most prominent price movements occurred.

3
Agriculture: the rising demand for food

The quickening pace of population recovery after about 1460, and particularly the concentration of substantial numbers of persons in a few burgeoning and prosperous cities, greatly increased the need for adequate food supplies. The availability of increasing quantities of precious metals, wrested from the mines of central Europe and Latin America, converted the clear biological need for food into effective market demand. There were more consumers and they had money. As a result, market conditions for agricultural products improved throughout the whole of Europe and sixteenth-century agrarian history appears as the almost perfect inverse image of its late medieval counterpart. Whereas the earlier period had witnessed a long secular decline in the price levels of the basic food grains, the sixteenth century experienced an extended upward movement, slow at first and then increasingly rapid, but always and inexorably upward. Fernand Braudel and F. C. Spooner have sought to provide a pan-European index of the rise in wheat prices across the century and to do so both for real prices in silver and for nominal prices in money of account on the basis of an arithmetic average of fifty-nine geographically distinct series.[1] Because averages tend to conceal diversity, these authors have attempted to preserve the range of variation by presenting their material graphically, with the average line set within a surface defined by the maximum and minimum values of the individual series. In considering Graph 1 it is well to remember that neither the maximum nor the minimum values are set by any single series from a particular region, but are instead the envelope curves of all maximum and minimum values. The segments of the graphs that are relevant to the fifteenth and sixteenth centuries follow.

From the graph it is apparent that prices in money of account rose

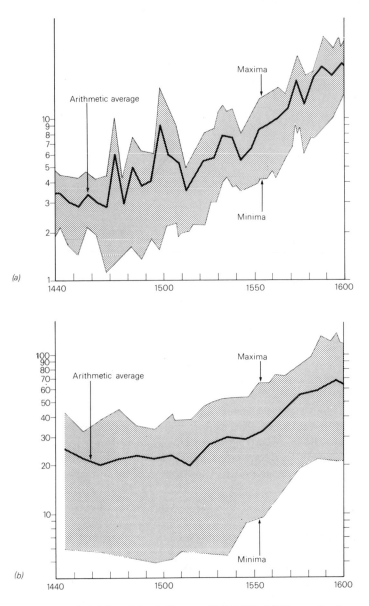

Graph 1. Wheat Prices in Europe; 1440–1600. (a) Wheat prices in money of account: five-yearly averages of fifty-nine series of wheat prices in Europe. (b) Wheat prices in grams of silver per hectoliter: ten-yearly averages of fifty-nine series of wheat prices in Europe. *Source:* F. P. Braudel and F. C. Spooner, "Prices in Europe from 1450–1750," in E. E. Rich and C. H. Wilson, eds., *The Cambridge Economic History of Europe,* IV, Cambridge, Cambridge University Press, 1967, pp. 470, 475.

much more sharply – note that the scale is semilogarithmic – than did prices expressed in silver. The many debasements of the sixteenth century are clearly reflected in the nominal price levels of wheat, so a substantial portion of that century's inflation must be attributed to monetary mutation. We are here concerned with investigating more basic economic forces, however, and for this purpose, the silver price of wheat is a more sensitive indicator of shifts in the nature and structure of agricultural markets. By the sixteenth century, grain was widely traded on international markets and fluctuations in the multitude of regional and national currency standards had only limited effects on price levels determined by international exchange.

The graph of wheat prices in silver may be divided into two quite distinct segments: First, there is a prolonged period of price stability, continuing through the latter half of the fifteenth century and into the second decade of the sixteenth; thereafter, the curve moves sharply and persistently upward. Together the two segments accurately reflect economic conditions as they shifted during the course of the entire period. Both population growth and monetary expansion were omnipresent influences on the European economy after about 1460, but their initial impact on the food supply and food prices was muted by the events of the preceding century. In the depressed era following the plagues of the later middle ages, landlords had found that falling grain prices and scarce and expensive labor meant declining rents; indeed, so drastic was the decline in many regions that vast areas of arable land were allowed to revert to pasture, to waste, and in some instances even to forest. In effect, the marginal revenue product of land had fallen to zero; such land consequently ceased to retain economic value. By the middle of the fifteenth century, there was a quantity of surplus land, either totally unused or devoted to such marginal activities as swineherding, where pigs were allowed to range widely through semi-forested land in search of acorns. Given such slack in the agrarian economy, the initial consequence of the recovery of the population and the money supply was to call forth some of the surplus land reserves that had accumulated in Europe during the preceding century. For a time it was literally true that each new mouth came with two productive hands and that the rising population essentially replaced the labor that had been lost to the epidemics of the fourteenth and early fifteenth centuries. In the first stages of recovery, population growth acted to restore the agricultural balance between men and land, to increase agricultural output, and to bring waste land back into cultivation rather than to place upward pressure on prices.

In the long run, however, land is a limited resource, and as demographic and monetary growth changed from recovery to positive expansion, surplus land no longer existed to act as a cushion against price increases in the basic food grains. This fact is, of course, evident in the sharp upward movement in the silver price of wheat that begins around 1520 and that is continuous throughout the remainder of the sixteenth century. Yet it was not simply population growth that placed upward pressure on prices; shifts in the very structure of the sixteenth-century economy exercised a strong influence as well. Deeper and more extensive urban concentration meant that increasing numbers of people were totally removed from the land and, consequently, that an ever larger portion of the population depended entirely on the market for its nutrition while contributing nothing to the production of food. Nor did they affect food supplies and prices only as consumers. Because urban life necessitates nonagrarian pursuits such as marketing and manufacturing, the urban population and the manufacturing segment of the rural population required raw materials to sustain their economic activities; these took a number of different forms. On the one hand, and perhaps most obviously, because cloth was the prototype product of the economically advanced centers of sixteenth-century Europe, the demand for raw wool encouraged the employment of scarce land as sheep pasture rather than as arable. Confronted by conflicting demands for the soil, landlords and governments tended to produce that which provided the most profit, and since if more land was used to pasture sheep, less was devoted to grain, price increases in one product generated parallel increases in the other. Land without labor, particularly land planted in relatively labor-intensive grain crops, is worthless, but with rising pressures on a limited supply of land, control of agricultural labor became even more crucial to landlords. In a sense, then, urban areas, by offering alternative occupations and thus drawing the labor supply away from the land, reduced the resources that could be focused on grain production at the same time that they heightened the demand for grain.

Expanding agricultural prosperity consequently created tensions over the distribution of resources both within individual economies and across the face of Europe. Once the wastes and the abandoned lands had again become major economic assets, the issue of their control was of vital importance; intense conflict over title to agricultural lands spread through the European economy from Spain to Russia. Landlords were pitted against peasants, cottagers against sheep farmers, and, in many instances, the state against the land-rich church. As property rights engendered conflict, so too did the question of access to labor and of individual liberties and rights to the fruits of each individual's productive powers. High grain prices tempted landlords to reassert long forgotten feudal dues and labor services in an effort to maximize their profits and to reconstitute the power they had lost in the difficult times following the great fourteenth-century plagues. Throughout Europe it was in the interest of the powerful to regain control of the land, to evict all who stood in their way, to repress individual liberties, and, if possible, to reconstitute the old labor services and rents in kind rather than in money.

The success of landlords in achieving these virtually universal ends varied greatly from region to region. Where the monarch was strong, he tended to resist the reassertion of feudal claims, since if made effective, they would have caused the reemergence of precisely those powerful feudatories that centralized governments had been struggling against for centuries. Where the monarch was weak or impotent, landlords were able to seize control of both land and labor and to reimpose the burdens of serfdom. Even where lords were frustrated by the presence of strong kings, the peasant was not necessarily the beneficiary. In some regions, the king's role was simply that of the most powerful lord, and he confiscated land and assimilated labor services on his own behalf. In others, the very strength of the king, dependent as it was on his ability to marshall the economic resources of the country, weakened the position of small farmers and peasants by forcing them into the clutches of moneylenders in order to raise sufficient cash for royal taxes. In such cases, neither the lord nor the peasant benefited, because the almost inevitable default turned the land over to sharp-dealing and market-conscious city dwellers.

Questions of land ownership and of individual rights are the stuff of jurisprudence. The soaring prices and booming market conditions of the period, by lending urgency and the intensity of greed to such issues, strained the already frail fabric of the sixteenth-century's inheritance of legal abstractions. Feudal law and custom were biased toward rights of seisin or use, but Roman law posed the question of absolute ownership. Given the pressures of the marketplace, it was inevitable that the two systems would be brought into opposition and that the vocabulary of property rights and of individual liberties would be tested. To a considerable degree the constitutional and legal histories of the various areas of Europe affected – and were in turn affected by – the outcome of the struggle for control of increasingly valuable agricultural assets. To perhaps an even greater extent, particularly in the eastern portions of Europe, the ultimate outcome was simply the result of main force. The general patterns and motivating influences in agricultural politics were common to Europe; to proceed further, we must consider individual histories on a regional basis.

The Low Countries

Since the grain market in the early modern period was truly international, we must begin somewhat arbitrarily and focus either on the centers of production or on the major consuming areas. Since the one could not exist without the other and since the internal developments in each were to a large extent externally determined, the approach is less than totally satisfactory, but let us start with the Netherlands, the prototypical consuming region of Europe. For centuries the southern Netherlands had been the most highly urbanized and industrial area in northern Europe; nowhere outside of Italy were urban centers so heavily populated, so close to each other, and so dependent on non-agrarian pursuits for their economic sustenance. Paris was perhaps larger than any city in the Low Countries, but the collective population of Ghent, Bruges, Ypres, and the other lesser towns represented a far larger proportionate burden than the French capital on the surrounding countryside and its capacity to provide sufficient food for the urban population. Indeed, by early fourteenth century, the Flemish towns were enough dependent on the importation of wheat that Philip Valois could confidently hope that by embargoing exports from northern France, he might force the Flemish to his side and break their English alliance, formed in the early stages of the Hundred Years' War.[2] Population recovery in the sixteenth century and particularly the spectacular growth of Antwerp following that city's selection as the central entrepôt for the Portuguese spice trade[3] made it inevitable that the southern

Netherlands would remain dependent on imported food supplies to supplement domestic food production. Though highly fertile, the countryside was simply too limited to support its densely populated cities.

Perhaps as a result of early and intensive urbanization, the agrarian history of the southern Netherlands differs from that of much of the rest of northern Europe. Depopulation in that food-short region did not reduce the urban demand for grain enough to ruin the prosperity of regional agriculture, nor did it force the abandonment of large areas of land, although some adjustments in the nature of the crops occurred in response to price differentials. As a result, the nobility seems to have been able to retain tight control over rural production and to have benefited from the later rise in grain prices without the prior need for reasserting their dominance in the agricultural sector. In Hainault, for example, nobles controlled 62.1 percent of the land revenues in 1474, 69.3 percent in 1502, and 57.1 percent in 1564;[4] their power obviously did not undergo major change either in the later middle ages or in the early modern period. Because the soil was rich and the market large and proximate, much land was kept in cereals during the sixteenth century; imported supplies supplemented but did not displace domestic production.

Grain is a crop that quickly exhausts the land unless fertility is maintained by means of complex crop rotation patterns or massive applications of manure. The Flemish pioneered in developing methods to assure an adequate supply of fertilizer, reinforcing the gains from convertible husbandry – the alternation of land between arable and pasture – by carefully stalling the cattle, by means of a variety of manure substitutes, and by employing the night soil from the towns.[5] To some extent, the very presence of those cities that provided markets raised the fertility of the surrounding fields and thus contributed to the region's ability to compete effectively against grain drawn from the international marketplace. During the sixteenth century, intensive methods enabled the farmers of the Netherlands to attain far higher yield-to-seed ratios than those reached elsewhere in Europe until recent times, although toward the end of the period English yields were rising impressively. Throughout most of Europe medieval yields of 4 or 5 to 1 prevailed; in the Netherlands, the average yield-to-seed ratio appears to have approached 10 or 11 to 1.[6] Despite high yields, imported grain was required for the populous towns, and until about 1500, traditional sources in northern France seem to have sufficed. From that date forward, however, the French role progressively contracted as cheaper and more abundant supplies were drawn from the Baltic region for redistribution through Amsterdam. After 1546, Antwerp and the other towns of the Low Countries rarely sought grain in France.[7]

The ascendancy of Amsterdam as the major grain market through which the produce of the Baltic was transshipped to almost all of Europe during the sixteenth century naturally affected Holland's own agricultural production. A few particularly well-endowed regions in the northern Netherlands continued to produce grain. Portions of Friesia expanded cereal production during the sixteenth century, and in Holland the island of Voorne marketed substantial amounts of grain in the various towns of that small country,[8] but cereal cultivation became increasingly the exception and was limited to geographically favored regions. The more usual course of action chosen by the farmers of the northern Netherlands was to recognize the difficulty of competing against Baltic grain, grown on extensive fields by servile labor, and to specialize instead in other products whose profit margins were higher. Dairy farming became the hallmark of Dutch agriculture; throughout the sixteenth and seventeenth centuries, herds increased in size as Holland became the cheese capital of Europe. Freed from the necessity of producing its own basic food grains, Holland skillfully exploited its limited land resources by developing an exportable, high-value surplus that could earn the balances necessary for the purchase of imported cereals. Moreover, expansion of herd size and specialization in livestock husbandry encouraged a host of ancillary rural trades, so that a large, nonagricultural population came to coexist with the farmers in the rural regions and to supply them with the requisite goods and services for the marketing and transportation of the dairy products and with the manufactured necessities demanded by the specialized farmer.[9]

Demographic and monetary recovery exerted the same pressures on prices and the land in the northern Netherlands as elsewhere; land became ever more valuable and greed urged men to seek more of it whenever they could. Yet in the north, conditions were markedly different from those prevalent elsewhere. On the one hand, concentration on dairy farming entailed certain technological constraints as well as benefits. Such farming required heavy capital investment in barns, stalls, and associated equipment, an intensive application of labor, intimate and somewhat rigidly determined relationships between the farm household and the herds; it also yielded the abundance of manure that enabled small quantities of land to produce bountiful supplies of fodder and grass. Success called for heavy investment and great personal care on a regular and disciplined basis. Indirect management of vast fields, common to major wheat-producing areas, was thus alien to the Dutch rural economy. Partly as a consequence of such factors, the northern Netherlands were distinctive in the relative weakness of the nobility. Wars and feuds in the fifteenth century had reduced their numbers, but more importantly perhaps, technological factors indigenous to livestock husbandry limited the ability of noblemen to gain control of large areas of productive land.

As a result, when cheese and dairy product prices rose in concert with wheat and grain prices, the ensuing struggle for control of agricultural land was not fought so much between the old nobility and the peasant or between the state and the church – although the issue of ecclesiastical appointments was a major provocation in the early stages of the Dutch struggle for independence – but rather between the farmer and the sea. The economic returns from capital-intensive Dutch agriculture justified the even greater capital expense of reclamation and polder making as land was wrested from the sea. Once drained, the soil was already extremely fertile, but in Holland, the presence of large herds of cows assured abundant quantities of manure, and fertile pastures soon displaced the ocean. The persistent struggle against the sea added 1,474 hectares (2.5 acres per hectare) to the Netherlands' agricultural base each year between 1540 and 1564; political disruption then slowed the accumulation to an annual rate of 321 hectares between 1565 and 1589, but growth was restored in the final decades of the century, when the annual addition again averaged 1,448 hectares.[10] Over the entire period from 1540 to 1600, more than 150,000 acres, or roughly 240 square miles, of new land were recovered from the sea. This increment is nearly 2 percent of the total area of the modern Netherlands and in the sixteenth century before modern reclamations was an even greater proportional addition. Relatively small dairy farms whose high yields were sustained by heavy and intensive capital investment allowed Dutch agriculture to become perhaps the most affluent in Europe and to withstand, indeed to benefit from, the competition of cheaper grain from the Baltic. In the Low Countries, nourished by foreign grain and domestic specialties, urban and rural areas flourished together, population expanded, and the region became the major market and redistribution center for the cereals of central Europe.

Central Europe

The prosperity of the thirteenth century largely bypassed the central European lands to the east of Germany that suffered the brunt of the Mongol invasions, but, as if in compensation, the catastrophes of the fourteenth century fell less heavily on those regions. Plague appears to have been less virulent in Poland and Hungary than elsewhere, and in eastern Poland, migration and colonization of the land continued throughout the later middle ages. In Hungary and portions of Bohemia, the mines produced enough precious metals for regional needs and some would claim that the quantities were large enough to affect the trade of the entire west.[11] Structural changes in the balance of international payments affected central Europe favorably as well. The depopulation of the west, consequent on recurrent plagues, caused a substantial drop in the price levels of basic foods and thus permitted greater expenditures on luxury goods at the same time as the desire for show was enhanced by the imminence of death. Piety rose in parallel with display; expenditures on the goods of salvation soared as men fearful of death sought to save their souls. Donations to the church rose and legacies, made more frequent by plague, increasingly provided sums for the purchase of such goods as candles for commemoration of the testator's obit. Collectively these developments favorably affected the lands of central Europe during the late fourteenth and fifteenth centuries.

In this period, the primary exports of the Baltic countries were wax, which was used for ceremonial candles, in contrast to tallow, which sufficed for ordinary lighting, and furs, the major northern luxury good. Exports also included some amber, which, like fur, was employed in personal adornment. The balance of trade with western Europe appears to have favored the Baltic region, although a good deal of precious metal was transferred to Russia and more moved southward in search of eastern luxuries imported through Germany by way of Italy. Some German cloth also found its way north in this trade. Specie flows tended to enlarge the monetary stock, first of the Baltic countries and then of all central Europe as the money was dispersed southward. As a result, the entire region was drawn increasingly into a monetary economy and away from the traditional work–service pattern of earlier feudalism. The relatively slack demand for basic food grains encouraged this development, because there was little pressure to produce huge surpluses when depopulation had so reduced the market demand for grain.

Circumstances favored a relaxation of the constraints of serfdom and simultaneously spurred the development of crafts, industry, and urban life. In the late fourteenth and fifteenth centuries, Poland experienced its first hopeful glimpse of economic development and of entry into the modern world.[12] Monetary exchange flourished as towns developed and prospered, providing markets for regional agricultural surpluses and, in turn, producing inexpensive cloth for domestic consumption and the manufactured goods required by the agricultural sector. From the fifteenth century forward, progress in metallurgy was continuous as the rich iron deposits of Silesia and Little Poland were exploited; waterpower was increasingly turned to the energy needs of both metallurgy and cloth making.[13] As internal trade expanded, opportunities opened for merchants, retailers, and the many ancillary trades necessary to town economies; as they did, men moved from the land and the development process became self-generating.

So long as the demand for grain remained weak, these happy developments in Poland and central Europe met little resistance, but when population recovered and purchasing power grew throughout the west after the mid-fifteenth century, landlords found it in their interest to oppose further economic progress and to try to reverse that which had already occurred. Trade within the region was open to all and gave less advantage to the great nobles than long-distance trade, and by sustaining the towns, it deprived the large landlords of the labor necessary to expand their grain output and to capitalize on the rising demand. Thus, from the late fifteenth century, nobles persistently sought to regain control over the peasants and to reimpose feudal authority. In the years 1518–20, not surprisingly, since this was precisely the time when grain prices as shown on Graph 1 began their most rapid ascent, the Polish Diet reasserted the duty of peasants to spend at least one day a week on corvée labor and again issued a series of regulations designed to tie the peasants more firmly to the land.[14]

The physical characteristics of the Baltic region and its central European hinterlands gave the area vast agricultural potential and encouraged specialization in grain production. Bounded on the north by the Baltic, on the east by the Urals, and on the south by the Caucasus lies the great European plain, a wedge-shaped lowland area that originates in southern England and widens as it extends eastward into Russia and the Ukraine. The soil is rich and the rainfall is evenly distributed over the year. The prevailing wind is from the southwest, from the Atlantic; as a result, the region enjoys a temperate climate that allows a sufficiently long growing season for effective cereal crop rotations. A glance at the accompanying map (Map 1) reveals the presence of numerous rivers that flow northward through the lowland plain into the Baltic. The Oder, the Vistula, the Memel, and the Düna provide inexpensive water transport for bulky commodities, and since they reach deep into the heartlands of central Europe, they can tap the agricultural surpluses of a very extensive area. The Vistula basin, for example, alone comprises some 200,000 square kilometers, or more than 70,000 square miles.[15]

Geographical conditions favored specialization in cereal culture and provided an economic rationale for the repression of the peasants by the great landlords of central Europe. Where the law aided the landlords it was applied or bent to their purposes; where it did not, it was ignored whenever possible. The direct laws of 1518–20 and earlier were supplemented by more subtle restrictions; in Poland during the sixteenth century, the nobility, on the basis of privilege alone, won freedom from all tolls on the Vistula for agricultural and forest products grown on their demesnes.[16] By overlooking the final provision, which limited privileged treatment solely to products from their own estates, the nobles were able to buy at large, conceal the origin of the goods, and, by shipping them toll-free, undersell all nonprivileged merchants. In 1565, the landlords obtained further legal sanctions, which prohibited Polish merchants from exporting domestic products and confined the trade to foreign merchants.[17]

Such policies constituted a double blow to the nascent Polish economic advance. By tying the peasant more closely to the soil and by increasing the amount of unpaid corvée labor demanded from him, the laws reduced his monetary income and thus either destroyed or severely damaged the internal market for Polish goods. From the other side, those policies aimed directly at merchants – discriminatory tolls and export restrictions – eroded the economic base of the urban economy

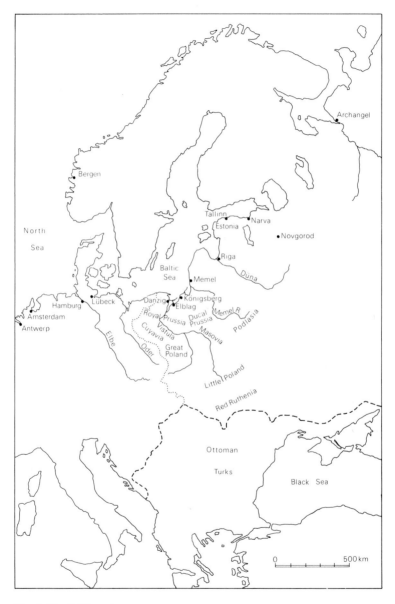

Map 1. The Baltic region

and rendered it almost impossible for a Polish townsman to earn his living. Out of self-interest the nobles successfully contrived to crush Polish economic development in order to reserve for themselves the rich grain trade and to assure adequate supplies of agricultural labor for the maximum exploitation of their estates.

The weakness of the Polish monarchy permitted the nobles to act without restraint in dealing with the peasants; indeed, in 1496, John Albert, the Jagiellonian king of Poland, was forced to buy support for his campaign against the Turks by allowing lords to reenserf the peasants, denying land-ownership to townsmen, and yielding much of his authority over taxes to the nobles.[18] Yet royal weakness was not devoid of beneficial effects. Casimir's 1454 campaign to wrest Royal Prussia from the Teutonic knights was bolstered by a royal promise to preserve elements of regional government and to maintain the traditional role of the Polish nobility in that area.[19] As a result of this concession, necessary to win local support, the towns of Royal Prussia were protected within a legal system alien to the rest of Poland, and the townsmen and merchants with legal representation in the General Diet were successfully able to oppose efforts to limit their trading rights.[20] Danzig and Elbing, located one on each of the two branches that form the mouth of the Vistula, retained their trading privileges and a dominant role in the grain trade; in 1579, 88 percent of the waterborne grain trade of Royal Prussia rested in the hands of nonnoble burghers.[21] Even the peasants of this region farmed larger holdings than were common elsewhere in Poland, and they retained their relative affluence and freedom until the wars of the beginning of the seventeenth century.

Elsewhere in Poland, however, the status of the peasants fell and the great landlords expanded their holdings. Between 1580, when figures are available for Cracow, and 1650, the portion of the land in the control of secular lords holding more than ten manors increased almost threefold, and when royal and ecclesiastical estates are included, the share of the greatest landlords rises to nearly half of the total area.[22] Even these figures understate the degree of market dominance of the large landholders, because the exportable surplus of grain came mainly from their estates. Cuyavia, eastern Great Poland, and Masovia, having the easiest access to the Vistula, predominated in the grain trade and supplied between two-thirds and one-half of the river-born rye during the second half of the sixteenth century. In Masovia, the secular nobles accounted for nearly 60 percent of that total, and the richest among them produced half of the nobles' share.[23] The combined effects of increased concentration of holdings and of low average yields per acre virtually guaranteed that surpluses would accumulate only in the granaries of the richest landlords. In bad years their market share climbed even higher, since only the largest estates could generate a surplus when the overall harvest was lean. Even though there had been some improvements in agricultural techniques during the fifteenth century, most notably the application of the three-course rotation, yields remained at medieval levels of 4 or 5 bushels per bushel sown. As a result, an enormous amount of land had to be cultivated in order to produce marketable quantities of grain after the subtraction of the following year's seed and the necessary sustenance for the agricultural laborers who tilled and harvested the crop. Some indication of the scale of the grain trade may be taken from the following figures in Table V.

Exports from the Vistula Basin constituted by far the greatest share – roughly 80 percent – of the Baltic grain trade, but one must add another 16 percent to the figures in Table V to include the exports from Riga, Königsberg, and Szczecin. It is also necessary to incorporate shipments from Tallinn and some of the lesser ports in Estonia, which may have reached 10,000 lasts per year, or some 800,000 bushels in the latter half of the sixteenth century.[24] Of the total grain exports from the entire Baltic region, rye comprised perhaps 85 percent, whereas wheat ran a poor second, at 10 to 15 percent.

Table V. *Annual average export of grain (metric tons)*

	Danzig	Elbing
1565	89,016	2,539
1585	33,244	1,489
1595	71,988	5,328
1618	186,571	13,211

Source: S. Hoszowski, "The Polish Baltic Trade in the 15th–18th Centuries," in *Poland at the XIth International Conference of Historical Sciences in Stockholm*, Warsaw, Polish Academy of Sciences, 1960, p. 135. Reprinted by permission of the publisher.

Although not on the Baltic, Hungary also contributed to the food supply of western Europe during the sixteenth century; little wheat or rye was exported,[25] but cattle shipments attained significant levels. In Hungary, as elsewhere in central Europe, the peasantry was repressed, but for the sake of expanding the outputs of cattle and wine rather than grain. Rents, which had been converted to monetary obligations during the later middle ages, were shifted back to payments in kind and arbitrarily increased. The nobles combined two wine levies, the tenth and the ninth, into a larger single levy, the fifth, and they greatly increased the burden of corvée labor. At Pozsony, for example, during the course of the sixteenth century, required labor service rose from an initial seven days per year to sixty days by 1574.[26] As in Poland, privileged status was used to oust nonnoble merchants and traders from the marketplace. The ancient wine ban, giving lords the exclusive right to sell, was reactivated in order to create a monopoly of wine sales, and in conjunction with heavy taxes on peasant production, it gave the nobles total control of both the buying and the selling side of the market. Privilege also freed the nobles from export taxes on cattle produced on their own estates, but again as elsewhere in the region, nobles simply claimed that all their exported cattle had been raised on demesne lands, even though most of the exports had been purchased from the peasants at monopsonistic prices. From the 1520s forward, large quantities of cattle were shipped to Vienna, southern Germany, Venice, and the whole north of Italy.[27]

It remains fashionable in the economic historiography of the west to condemn the so-called second serfdom and to castigate the backward-looking noblemen who subverted economic development, undercut the nascent town economies, and repressed the peasants. There is no doubt that the repression was common to central Europe and it is relatively easy to contrast the rising cities of the west, expanding commerce, increasingly sophisticated trading patterns, and the open opportunities for development and profit offered by early capitalism with the economic stagnation of eastern Germany, Poland, and Hungary. Sometimes, however, the contrast gives rise to moral and ethical judgments, as in the flood of literature that collectively is known as the Weber thesis, after Max Weber, who very carefully suggested a possible connection between the Protestant ethic and the spirit of capitalism.[28] Many of Weber's followers were far less cautious than their master and made the connection between Protestantism and capitalism a directly causative one, producing the unfortunate corollary that if Protestantism engenders the peculiar form of rationality required by capitalism, its absence is somehow to be condemned as the root of irrationality. The argument as presented by Weber himself emphasizes the "ethic" and the "spirit" and remains highly illusive as to the connections between the two, so that it is, in my opinion, virtually immune from empirical testing. His followers, to the contrary, are more blunt, and as a result, rather crude statistical comparisons among countries have been offered as proof of their version of the thesis. Countries with predominantly Catholic populations are shown to experience less economic growth than those with substantial numbers of Protestant inhabitants; one may note that heavily Protestant and economically backward Scotland is rarely incorporated into such loosely cast statistical arguments.

The application of such reasoning to developments in central Europe during the sixteenth century is at best one-sided and at worst a miscomprehension of historical forces. Urbanization was perhaps the most striking aspect of the century in western Europe, and it is only in urban areas that the phenomena that we collectively label capitalism or, more neutrally, economic development, could arise. Only in cities with large, diverse populations could sophisticated financial techniques, banking, and worldwide marketing mechanisms develop. Cities, however, require food, and in ever greater quantities as their prosperity rises. For this reason, it is perhaps more accurate to consider the affluent cities of the west and the agrarian regions of central Europe as an economic partnership instead of seeking the contrasts in their respective cultures. The figures in Table V are remarkable, not because they indicate the vast magnitude of the Baltic grain trade, but because they indicate the pitifully small surplus that could be extracted from the immense territory between the Oder and Estonia. The whole region from the Oder to Tallinn could afford to export only a little more than 100,000 metric tons, perhaps 3 million bushels, a year, and that would only be accumulated by brutally driving most of the inhabitants back to the land. Had Poland developed large cities and supported a substantial non-agricultural population engaged in trade and manufacturing, it is highly likely that Amsterdam and many other cities of the west would have starved. Further, it is by no means certain that increased urbanization in Poland would have achieved more than the internal consumption of its surplus grain. The classical economists' argument that demonstrates that each country should produce those goods in which it has the comparative advantage suggests that the central European specialization in cereals was appropriate and that such specialization would have maximized available income both for Poland and the world. Classical economics does not, of course, provide an apology for the manner in which that income was distributed once it reached Poland and the countries of central Europe. But even in this case, the classical proscriptions against monopoly and restrictive practices stand in censure of the distortions in income distribution introduced through privilege by the noble class. In any event, it was not a question of central Europe's refusal to emulate and follow the advanced techniques of western capitalism. Agricultural yields were too low to permit the growth of more than a few strategically placed cities; Amsterdam could not have survived without access to the 70,000 square miles of grain fields in the Vistula basin. Food, rather than ethics, spawned cities, and cities spawned capitalism and economic development.

Scandinavia

The sixteenth-century inflation of grain prices deeply affected the Scandinavian countries, although disparate historical and geographical legacies resulted in marked variations in the nature of the impact. Arable farming had always been marginal in Norway, because the climate was too severe and the terrain too rough for effective application of the three-field rotation, but the depressed world grain prices following the fourteenth-century plagues had caused Norwegians to become almost totally dependent on German grain imported through Lübeck. In return for grain, the Norwegians exported fish, which could be sold at a good price, since cheap grain allowed other Europeans to diversify their diets and to increase their intake of protein. Dependence on Hanseatic grain, however, was not entirely in Norway's interest; the merchants of Lübeck used their power to establish an extremely efficient monopoly of the trade at Bergen and to control the quantities sold and the price levels of fish through their monopoly of grain. As a result, German merchants dominated Bergen's foreign trade and came to represent a substantial portion of that city's total population.

As the sixteenth century progressed and grain prices soared, such advantages as Norway had obtained through specialization eroded and the terms of trade worsened continuously. More and more fish were needed to purchase the same quantity of grain, and with the exception of some timber and other forest products, few new commodities were developed to balance the accounts. One benefit for the Norwegians did ensue from the rise in grain prices, however. Since many more ships were involved in the expanding Baltic grain trade and since they sailed from a wider geographical area, competition inevitably grew and the Lübeck merchants were no longer able to sustain their monopoly at Bergen. Although the terms of trade disadvantaged Bergen and the commercial profits of the port declined, the Norwegians developed an indigenous merchant population toward the end of the century and were able at last to regain control of their own economic destiny.[29]

Unlike Norway, Sweden, at least in its southern portions, participates in the great European plain; consequently, it was able to devote a substantial amount of land to cereals and to maintain a position of near nutritional independence. The principal crop was barley, which seems to have been cultivated primarily under a two-course rotation, because of the severity of the Swedish climate in winter. Medieval farming methods persisted throughout the sixteenth century; strip farming predominated and yields were sufficiently low to make grain scarcity a matter of ongoing national concern. Oddly, the very scarcity of grain appears to have engendered an aversion to the use of arable for pasture both among government officials and among farmers themselves; the unfortunate consequence, of course, was to reduce the amount of manure available for the arable and thus further to reduce agricultural yields.[30] On the other hand, the proliferation of large herds of cattle, fed on wild meadows, in conjunction with the limitations on the Swedish population imposed by underfertilized and inadequate arable acreage created a surplus of cattle products, primarily butter and hides, that could be exported in return for such necessary commodities as textiles and salt.

The rise in world grain prices inflated the value of land in Sweden as elsewhere in Europe and provoked a struggle for control of the arable – a struggle that was deeply enmeshed in religious, legal, and political issues as well as .n the purely economic ones. When, as a result of the revolt against the Danes, Gustavus Vasa became king in 1523, he felt the Catholic church – entrenched, powerful, and rich in lands – to be an enemy and sought to reduce its power.[31] In 1527, after a carefull prepared campaign of propaganda largely derived from German Luthe anism, the Diet of Västerås, among its many other important action voted to confiscate "superfluous" church property and to return to th nobles all property that had been alienated since 1454.[32] The crow however, was the chief beneficiary.

Between 1527 and 1544, Gustavus Vasa's religious policies fluctuate sharply. At first, he supported Olavus Petri, who attempted to brin Luther's doctrines into the Swedish church and simultaneously in h other writings to revise and order Swedish legal practice.[33] Some el ments of Luther's writings – particularly those urging that in order t "keep the roads open, preserve peace in the towns, and enforce law i the land . . . the sword of the ruler must be red and bloody"[34] – ap pealed to the king, but Lutheran independence did not. Petri fell int disfavor, and, under pressure, the Diet of Västerås in 1544 created completely national Swedish church – an action followed closely b further confiscations of ecclesiastical land. The economic consequence of Vasa's religious reforms are apparent in Table VI.

The enormous gains made by the crown proved temporary; after th death of Gustavus Vasa in 1560, the alienation of crown lands ac celerated, and the aristocracy greatly enhanced its power. By the en of the Thirty Years' War, the nobility owned nearly three-quarters o the land in Sweden, while the combined royal and peasant holdings ha fallen to a mere 28 percent of the total.[35]

Table VI. *Land distribution in Sweden*

	Close of the middle ages (%)	1560 (%)
Crown	5.5	28.2
Church	21.0	—
Nobility	21.8	22.4
Peasants	51.7	49.4

Source: E. F. Heckscher, *An Economic History of Sweden*, trans. G. Ohlin, Cambridge, Mass., Harvard University Press, 1954, p. 67. Reprinted by permission of the publisher.

Germany and France

Economic historians, in analyzing Germany's agrarian history, customarily divide the country into two segments, one to the east and the other to the west of the Elbe River. The region east of the Elbe replicated the events in Poland and eastern Europe generally, pursuing the dismal pattern of peasant reenserfment, unmitigated expansion of labor service of all sorts, and concentration of the returns from agriculture in the hands of a powerful elite. Agrarian developments west of the Elbe are much more difficult to characterize. On the one hand, the political fragmentation of Germany – a perpetual problem for historians seeking general patterns – was reinforced by the religious fragmentation that sprang from the Reformation and was institutionalized after 1555 in the Peace of Augsburg, which allowed each petty prince to choose his own and his subjects' religious persuasion. On the other hand, economic realities did vary considerably within western Germany; as a consequence, crops, peasant status, and land tenure arrangements diverged markedly from one region to another.

One pattern – resettlement – emerges clearly, however. During the critical depopulation at the end of the middle ages, vast quantities of arable were simple abandoned, becoming *Wüstungen*, or uncultivated wastes, and even in some extreme cases reverting to forest, as happened throughout the Harz Mountain district.[36] With demographic recovery and the sharp rise in grain prices spurring the movement in the first half of the sixteenth century, the waste was quickly resettled and abandoned villages reconstituted. Once the waste had been reabsorbed into the cultivated areas and the remaining untilled land had become increasingly marginal or submarginal, continuing population pressure against limited resources drove up the value of the arable, and, in many regions, led to a reduction in the size of individual holdings.[37] In the southwest, where the peasants generally maintained their tenures, holdings became smaller through subdivision and inheritance; in the northwest, on the contrary, landlords were able to reduce many peasants to landlessness and to maximize their rents by quadrupling the holdings of others.[38] In the Harz Mountain region, perhaps because the land was less rich, peasants retained a considerable degree of personal freedom and control over their holdings, but in the more fertile southeast, ecclesiastical owners prevailed and their demesnes continued to be cultivated, at least in part, by bondsmen.[39]

The expansion in grain production that was required in order to nourish the growing German population was achieved primarily through the extension of the arable area, not through any significant advance in agricultural technology. Indeed, two factors tended to hold down agricultural yields as bread prices rose. Because basic bread cost more, consumers were compelled to retrench and to sacrifice the variety in their diets; while the absolute price of meat rose, its price relative to grain declined as demand was limited more and more to bread alone. This adjustment reduced the profitability of livestock raising and also the numbers of farm animals. The simultaneous extension of the arable acreage, spurred by the urgent demand for bread grain, constituted a direct subtraction from the wild pasture and from the acorn forests in which livestock and swine could find fodder. In tandem, these developments naturally led to a reduction in the available supplies of manure, which, in its turn, limited the yields on even the most fertile farms. But the lands that were incorporated into the arable during the swift recolonization and recultivation of the first half of the sixteenth century were not the best lands; they were the fields that farmers had chosen to abandon when depopulation had made it possible to do so, and consequently, they tended to be marginal, recalcitrant fields, more urgently in need of fertilization than those more naturally favored fields which had been kept under the plow. As the century progressed, the stress on agricultural yields became increasingly apparent. The price of rye, the standard bread grain, rose sharply in most regions until the 1580s, when the rise abated somewhat, although the elevated levels were maintained. Wages did not keep up, since labor was in surplus relative to land; the net result was a dramatic decrease in living standards for most workers. Expressed in rye-equivalents, the real wage earned by workers in a number of German regions was cut in half during the course of the sixteenth century.[40] The shortage of bread was further worsened by the diversion of land to such industrial crops as flax; between 1480 and 1624, flax production in the region between the Oder and the Elbe more than tripled.[41]

In France, the repopulation and reconstruction that followed the conclusion of the Hundred Years' War in 1453 also intensified the demands on limited land resources. At first, as elsewhere, the reincorporation into the arable of lands abandoned during the fourteenth and fifteenth centuries prevented too serious imbalances between food and men, but from 1500 on, population appears to have grown far faster than food production; inevitably, nutritional standards suffered. As in Germany, land that was brought back under the plow was often of marginal quality, and of equal importance, the manure cycle – more arable, fewer animals, less manure, lower yields – limited the potential crop. One may recall here that after the beginning of the sixteenth century, French grain could no longer be shipped in sufficient quantities to satisfy the demands of the cities of Flanders, and that after the mid-century, Flemish supplies came almost exclusively from the Baltic. By the 1520s, grain scarcity had become endemic in some regions of France; poor weather and overpopulation combined to produce veritable famine conditions in Languedoc, which, until 1500, had been a major grain-exporting region. Shortages were so pronounced that public officials promulgated a series of regulations forbidding the further export of grain.[42]

Rising population also forced alterations in land tenure arrangements, although no single pattern, common to all France, emerged. At the extreme, many men simply became landless; a cadre of sturdy beggars and vagrants peopled the countryside, living by their wits and intimidating the more fortunate, on whom they preyed. In Languedoc, arrests of vagrants and more brutal means of repression were sustained by royal edict in 1534.[43] Only a small step up the social ladder were those peasants who subsisted on inadequate holdings; their numbers grew once the recolonization movement was completed, because in the absence of new land, older holdings were progressively reduced through inheritance divisions. Smaller holdings sometimes led to intensification of culture as peasants tried to find a cash crop sufficiently valuable to pay for the equivalent grain formerly raised on larger plots, but the strategy was ultimately self-defeating. By devoting more land in the aggregate to olive or silk production, as in some regions in the south of France, peasants at once diminished the total grain crop, further raising its price, and elevated the supplies of the cash crop, holding down its price level and reducing the anticipated margin between the two commodities.

Parallel to the forces leading to the endless subdivision of holdings were those leading to the aggrandizement of a few, and to the reconstitution of great estates. Monetary and fiscal stimuli to the accumulation of land in the hands of a fortunate elite were supported and intensified by the increasingly widespread application of Roman law at the expense of custom. Starting in the reign of Louis XI (1461–83), when crown revenues trebled, French taxes climbed ever higher, and since they fell most heavily on small, nonnoble farmers, the fiscal burden grew more onerous. Division of land through inheritance and the highly variable, but always low, grain yields combined to render it nearly inevitable that small farmers would more than occasionally find it impossible to generate the cash required for the inexorable demands of the tax collector. When this misfortune occurred they were driven into the claws of the moneylenders. Foreclosure ultimately led either to the sale of the smallholder's land or to its transfer to the usurer for his own account. In either case, those with cash acquired land, and because cash was more readily available in the towns, the sixteenth century witnessed a remarkable expansion of bourgeois landholding. The same phenomena worked equally to elevate a class of rich peasant-bourgeoisie who, once they had risen a short way above their fellows, discovered that the economics of the time accelerated their further rise.[44]

Reinforcing the assault on small tenancies brought about by heavy taxation was the redefinition of the nature of property itself that followed in the wake of the sixteenth-century revolution in jurisprudence. Under Roman law, property by its very nature implied the existence of an owner. What, then, of the common fields and meadows shared under medieval law by all? French lawyers sidestepped this difficulty by inventing the fiction that the secular lord had originally owned the common but that he had allowed others to enjoy the use of it, although their claim was valid only when a fee was paid to recognize the lord's proprietary rights. Once this adjustment in the legal status of the common was accepted, the power of the secular lord was greatly enhanced. The lord, for example, gained the right to call for a division and enclosure of the common – a ploy that under French law of *triage* usually gave the lord absolute ownership of one-third of the common and allowed the peasants to use the remainder in return for a fee.[45] Needless to say, reduction of the common land and conversion of portions of it to private use made even more tenuous the survival of the small farmer whose personal land was barely adequate in good times. Stripped of the extra income once derived from grazing his animals on the common land, the smallholder became even more exposed to the vagaries of the marketplace and the extortions of the French fiscal system. By the same token, the jeopardy of loss of his holding to the moneylender grew.

As elsewhere in Europe, religious reform offered an opportunity to those who wished to despoil the church of its landed wealth, although the impact in France was less than that in Sweden or England. Still, a combination of Huguenot pressure and of the crown's fiscal embarrassment resulted in the expropriation of church lands in the second half of the sixteenth century. Partial confiscations of ecclesiastical property occurred in Languedoc in 1561, 1568, 1574, and 1576; subsequent land sales transferred the property primarily to citizens below the ranks of the true nobility but above the level of workers and artisans; the total quantities of land involved were not large, however.[46] The new owners of land, recently wrested from the unfortunate and from the church, and owners of long standing, where they were able to abrogate customary tenure arrangements, attempted to manage their holdings so as to protect themselves from inflation – the curse of the sixteenth century. Landlords had become keenly aware that rents fixed in money, a practice made common by the economic dislocations of the later middle ages, deteriorated over time and that their purchasing power fell progressively in the course of the century. Conversely, the survival, particularly in southern France, of large numbers of tiny holdings may be at least partially attributed to the beneficial influence that peasants derived from falling real rents. Inflation caused the interests of tenant and landlord to diverge even more sharply than normally; consequently, when traditional tenures could be overthrown, landlords renegotiated their contracts on the basis of *métayage*, the payment of rent in kind and usually at the rate of one-half of the total crop.[47] Such contracts amply protected the landlord, but they did so at the expense of the peasant; it was the pattern of the sixteenth century.

Spain and Italy

Whereas Sweden, France, and Germany were basically self-sufficient in cereal production, urban Italy and backward Spain, though for different reasons, were net importers of grain. In Italy, geographical limitations to the extent of the arable, low yields, and the intensity of urban concentration mandated the use of imported food supplies; in Spain, however, dependence on foreign sources was at least in part a matter of choice. Since the end of the thirteenth century, Castilian royal finances had been closely integrated with the Mesta, or sheep farmers guild; moreover, the expulsion of the Jews in 1492, by removing a major alternative source of funds, strengthened the relationship.[48] As a result, the crown habitually favored the Mesta at the expense of other forms of agriculture; in return, the sheep farmers were compelled to make generous payments to the royal fisc. A series of royal edicts in the late fifteenth century discomfited arable farming; in 1480, all enclosures that had been made after the reign of Henry IV (1425–74) were disallowed; in 1489, the *cañadas*, or sheepwalks, along which the sheep followed the weather and the grass from the dry southeast to the rainy northwest, were greatly expanded at the expense of ordinary farmers' lands; and in 1491–2, antienclosure legislation was applied to newly reconquered Granada.[49] Since adequate transportation was critical to the military endeavors of the Spanish crown, the carters' guild also benefited from special legislation passed at the expense of arable farming. After 1497, the carters had formal sanction for free passage through all jurisdictions on roads to be maintained by local municipalities; tolls were limited to those on the royal schedules; free grazing was authorized on any common pasture and water and camping rights were made universal along with the right to take wood from any woodlot; finally, all contradictory local ordinances were rescinded.[50] Though croplands were excluded from the incursions of the carters, the competitive use of pastures, woodlots, and water courses and the fiscal burdens of road maintenance disadvantaged the unprivileged cereal grower.

Under such governmentally imposed adverse conditions, it is not surprising that cereal culture did not flourish in Castile. By 1506, the country was already heavily dependent on imported grain, but the situation became even more serious. Grain prices climbed in Spain as elsewhere in Europe, but there, after 1539, the monarchy took direct action against the rise and established maximum prices for the sale of grain. Royal impediments to production were not alleviated; landlords could still legally reclaim lands and renegotiate leases at ever higher rates and the laws favoring the Mesta and the carters remained in force. The inevitable result of the ensuing cost–price squeeze was a flight from the land. Farmers simply gave up the struggle against the compounded difficulties born of mediocre soil and climate and of disastrous governmental policy. Displaced by economic and political forces, they fled to the towns to become beggars, or, more likely, soldiers; in either case, they were unproductive, net consumers of grain. By mid-century, largely because internal transportation was incapable of moving sufficient quantities of Baltic grain to the interior, famine became a regular visitor to Castile, yet by the end of the century, nearly a third of the farmland was uncultivated waste.[51]

Not all Spanish agriculture suffered during the century, of course; nodes of prosperity persisted and in some cases grew. Favored by governmental regulations and market conditions, sheepherding triumphed for a time; herds reached an average total of some 2.8 million sheep during the first fifty years of the sixteenth century. Thereafter, however, a worldwide financial crisis, market dislocations, the introduction of new woolen technologies, and inflation itself adversely affected Spain's exports of raw wool; by the 1560s, flocks had been reduced by more than eight hundred thousand animals.[52] Some specialized agriculture remained profitable; vineyards and olive groves expanded to meet an active demand and intensive farming, supported by heavy investment in irrigation, flourished. Unfortunately for the peasants, however, they lacked the capital requisite to such activities and the anomaly of Spain persisted. Famines intensified while fields went untilled, and irrigated oases rose richly from a land deserted by men who could find no productive work.[53] Income distribution was extremely uneven – the religious class represented only about 2 percent of the population but controlled nearly half of the national income[54] – and this inequality probably exacerbated the failures of Spanish agriculture in the second half of the sixteenth century. Whether it was lack of capital among the peasants, adverse government policies, an excess of power in the hands of the moneylenders with consequences similar to those in France, poor soil and dry weather combined with foreign competition, or the effective separation of arable areas from urban markets resultant on the inadequacies of internal transportation, Spanish agriculture was in disarray. Fernand Braudel, quoting the Spanish ambassador to Lisbon who in 1566 noted that the "country-side was profoundly ill," concludes that the disease in Portugal was only slightly more advanced than that in Spain.[55]

Italian agriculture virtually defies synthetic treatment, since Italy was, and remains even now, a collection of regionally disparate entities.

The urbanized north, for example, depended on imported grain, whereas the south was for a time the breadbasket of Europe. Yet a simple demarcation between north and south is far too crude a distinction to comprehend the political variations among the city-states and the geographical and topographical nuances of individual areas within either broad category. In the south, mountainous terrain and dry summers restricted farmers from introducing a three-course rotation based on a summer grain crop, and as a result, yields remained extremely low. During the fourteenth century, depopulation diminished the market for Sicilian – here southern Italy and the island of Sicily – grains; substitute crops more suited to the new patterns of demand enjoyed a brief period of prosperity. In the early fifteenth century, sweet wines and sugar were quite successful crops, but the swift development and exploitation of the Madeira and Canary Islands with cheap slave labor quickly reduced southern Italy's profitable monopoly of those luxuries and threatened to ruin the region's agricultural base. Happily, the growth of Spanish and Portuguese competition in sugar and sweet wine was coincident with the beginning of the demographic upsurge throughout Europe, a phenomenon that restored the market for Sicilian grain. True prosperity, however, did not follow. Although quantities of grain were exported from inland Sicily and the plains of Apulia, the surpluses were extorted in much the same manner as in eastern Europe. Low wages, repressive conditions, and low population density permitted grain to be exported despite low yields and the absence of any significant technological advances. Further, the concentration of land in the hands of a few assured the accumulation of surpluses in the granaries of those sensitive to the profit available in the northern markets. As late as the eighteenth century, the church remained in control of 65 to 70 percent of the land in southern Italy, whereas by the mid-sixteenth century in northern Italy, ecclesiastical control had been reduced to a mere 10 or 15 percent of the arable.[56] As is common in poor and underdeveloped lands, southern Italy found a viable economic activity in sheep farming.[57] This enterprise was aided to a considerable extent by the efforts of some northern towns, such as Venice, to develop industrial substitutes for the losses and dislocations that had been suffered in the more traditional sources of wealth through foreign commerce. On the whole, however, sheep farming did not signal affluence, and, particularly in the later sixteenth century, competition intensified in the world's wool markets and adversely affected Spanish and English, as well as Italian, profit margins. The Sicilian south remained an underdeveloped and poor land, sparsely populated by an impoverished and illiterate peasantry ruthlessly exploited by a few wealthy landowners.

North Italian agriculture was less volatile than that in the south, since the relationships between town and country made markets more dependable. From the twelfth century, northern Italy experienced a continuous and deepening urbanization, and urban demand quite soon outstripped the capacity of the *cantado,* or countryside surrounding the towns, to provide foodstuffs. Because urban markets devoured more than could be produced in their immediate vicinities, imported foods were vital for survival; by the same token, the added transport costs of imported foods provided a protective umbrella, guaranteeing the market for regional produce. Even the calamitous depopulation of the later middle ages proved insufficient to destroy the favorable market structure of the agricultural regions surrounding Italy's major northern towns.

Since local demand was greater than regional productivity, north Italian agriculture retained a good measure of prosperity despite the vicissitudes in population and in world markets. Consequently, when lands were being abandoned and the arable was reverting to waste in other areas of Europe, the flow of urban money into land continued and expanded in selected portions of northern Italy. There, much earlier than elsewhere, market conditions encouraged an assault on ecclesiastical property, and it is perhaps not an exaggeration to assign to this factor much of the responsibility for the early and effective subversion of ecclesiastical tenures and for the confiscation of much of the church's wealth in land. The same forces induced more creative acts of real investment in reclamation, drainage, and agricultural improvement – including intensification of land use through conversion to sericulture and other high-value products – that followed the transfer of land to urban entrepreneurs who sought to maximize the return on their investments.

Such measures, however, failed to protect the north Italian cities from the fluctuations of the international marketplace, and as grain prices rose in sympathy with population, the towns had to forage ever farther abroad to locate sufficient food supplies. As we have already noted, rising urban demand had repercussions as far away as Hungary, where central European magnates repressed the peasantry in order to gain control of the burgeoning export trade in livestock – a trade that served not only Germany but also the towns of upper Italy. By the same token, such coastal towns as Venice, Genoa, and, across the Adriatic, Ragusa were compelled to seek grain not only from Sicily, but also from more distant areas, such as Albania, the Dalmatian hinterlands, and even from the Turkish interior and the Black Sea region. Indeed, after the midpoint of the sixteenth century, a series of poor harvests, inclement weather, and perhaps soil erosion due to excessive timber cutting greatly increased Italian dependence on foreign supplies and produced a "boom for Turkish wheat."[58] The Turkish response was not dissimilar to that observed elsewhere in Europe; traditional tenures were violated, new property arrangements were imposed by the powerful, and great magnates reserved the grain trade to themselves at the same time as they extorted an exportable surplus from a miserable and underfed populace.[59]

For a variety of reasons, Turkey proved a fickle supplier of grains. On the one hand, the country's own internal problems restricted its capacity as an exporting nation. The early sultans in the period immediately following the conquest of Constantinople in 1453 had engaged in a policy of conscious urban development, seeking to restore the city's economic life and to resettle it with the faithful.[60] By the mid-sixteenth century, the efforts were visibly triumphant and the nutritional requirements of Constantinople were expanding at such a rapid pace that they directly challenged the export trade in grain. Prices of Turkish wheat rose steadily during the 1550s and 1560s. On the other hand, competition for control of the Mediterranean and its trade inevitably led to war between Venice and the Turks – a war that resulted in the dramatic but pyrrhic victory of Venice at the battle of Lepanto in 1571. There, Venice, at the cost of virtual exhaustion of her naval and timber resources, defeated the Turkish navy and created a power vacuum in the Mediterranean.

North Italian food requirements did not abate, but the sources of supply were diminished by this action and by the internal demands of Turkish cities. Urgent necessity drove the Italians to cultivate every acre that could conceivably be made to yield a crop, and since the desirable, level land had been pressed into service long ago and was, in any event, limited to a few valley plains and to the coastal regions, fields literally began to march up the mountainsides. Terracing, though not unique to the period, appears to have received an enormous stimulus from population pressure and from the shortage of food in the sixteenth century. The only other alternative, of course, was to search out additional supplies from new foreign sources, and during the latter part of the century, there was a marked expansion and development of the trade in Polish grain throughout the Mediterranean. The grand duke of Tuscany sent representatives to Danzig and endeavored to turn Livorno into an international port; English, German, and Dutch ships were soon regular visitors to the region. The Dutch ultimately triumphed in the struggle to supply the cities of northern Italy with Baltic grain as their commercial efficiency and maritime skills enabled them to capitalize on the Venetian victory at Lepanto that removed the Turkish menace without creating a truly victorious alternate naval power. Ironically, the Dutch, a land-poor people, became the provisioners of the world.

England

Rising population and monetary recovery after the late fifteenth century in England activated the same forces that we have already observed on the Continent. Fields that had been abandoned during the late medieval period of depopulation provided a temporary cushion against scarcity and the consequent inflation of grain prices, but they were quickly reabsorbed into the arable, and grain prices then rose inexorably. By the 1520s, Felix's price index of unprocessed agricultural products reads 132 on a scale where the price level in 1451–1500 equals 100; in the 1580s the price level rises to 262, and by the second decade of the seventeenth century, it exceeds 400.[61] Such increases in the price levels of agricultural products, of course, swiftly affected the value of land, but in England, more perhaps than elsewhere, industrial requirements for raw materials created an alternate use for land that was often directly competitive with the cultivation of grain. Cloth production flourished during the first half of the sixteenth century as exports rose from less than fifty thousand cloths per year to more than one hundred thirty thousand in 1550.[62] Demand for raw wool grew accordingly, and as a result of the dual pressures on agricultural land, English agrarian policy was markedly ambivalent during the sixteenth century. Periodically, in response to the counsel of those contemporary commentators who declared the sheep to be the most voracious of beasts, capable of devouring whole villages and depopulating the countryside, legislation restricting the enclosure of land was enacted; more often, perhaps because of the wool industry's dominant role in earning foreign bullion, such legislation was lightly enforced. Older agrarian histories of England viewed the sixteenth century as a period of substantial enclosure during which great numbers of smallholders were driven from the land to make room for vast herds of sheep, but this view has recently been somewhat modified.[63] Enclosures there no doubt were – they were extensive enough to cause mutations in the quality of the wool produced. Yet the movement has probably been overstressed by taking too literally the contemporary outcry. It remains to be seen whether enclosure will now be unduly underplayed in the enthusiasm of the recent debunking effort and by mistaking the absence of significant numbers of prosecutions for a similar absence of enclosures. It was, after all, one of the marks of English genius to apply laws that hindered prosperity laxly in most other areas and particularly in the manufacturing side of the profitable textile industry.

Although the extent of the enclosure movement in England remains undetermined, there is no doubt that substantial changes occurred in land tenures during the course of the sixteenth century. Perhaps the most spectacular shift was that caused by the dissolution of the monasteries in 1536 and 1539, and, somewhat later, by the dissolution of the chantries, both of which actions resulted in the transfer of church lands to the crown. Proffered explanations for these confiscations range from the insular and specific to the global. They may be seen as the immediate consequence of Henry VIII's marital difficulties, as the natural result of the English reformation, as a stage in the not unrelated, but still distinct, effort of the king to transform the monarchy and increase its power, as a response to the heightened demand for food induced by rising population and in particular by the startling growth of London, or, on an international scale, simply as the English version of the pattern, prevalent across Europe, of the use of political power to gain control of increasingly valuable land and land revenues as prices rose. All of these factors probably influenced the outcome, and, with the exception of the Tudor marital question, most affected the parallel developments in other regions.

In any event, the English case is especially interesting for what it reveals of the strengths and weaknesses in the legal fabric and in the correlative security of property titles. Henry VIII's divorce proceedings and his concurrent claim to be the supreme head of the church in England engendered the need for some form of legal justification; not surprisingly, an active propaganda campaign was conducted throughout the 1530s.[64] Sermons, royal rather than divine in inspiration, carried the doctrine of royal supremacy to the parishioners of England, and remote precedents were invoked to lend the sanction of time past to present necessity. Printing and the spread of literacy offered new means of political persuasion; new editions of some of the works of William of Ockham appeared during this period, and appropriately so, for Ockham had defended Ludwig of Bavaria against papal displeasure when he fell into marital difficulty in the early fourteen century.[65] More directly supportive of royal dominance over the church, however, was the *Defensor pacis* of Marsilius of Padua, and not surprisingly, it too appeared in a new edition. Translated by William Marshall under the subsidy of Thomas Cromwell, the king's secretary, it was duly published in 1535.[66] As will be recalled from our first chapter, this tract was a straightforward argument for the supremacy of the secular over the sacerdotal authority. Obviously, the argument served Henry's needs almost perfectly; where it did not, it was simply abridged. Such politically awkward passages as those that spoke of the "correction of the ruler" or called on the doctrinal authority of the whole body of the church were omitted from the sixteenth-century edition. So too was reference to the fourteenth-century papal ban on the work and the excommunication of its author. Marsilius's assertion of the dominance of secular authority has received far more historical attention than has been accorded to the theory of property contained in the *Defensor pacis,* but here too Henry could find substantial support. The book conceded to the *legislator humanus* – and by proxy to its agent, the secular prince – the right to "entrust to whomever it wants, and at any time, authority to distribute" property. The argument was all that Henry could wish for as he set about despoiling the church of lands that according to some, though perhaps exaggerated, estimates may have amounted to nearly a third of the total land of England.[67]

Henry VIII did not lack the energy to capitalize on the rent in the fabric of legal abstractions, and on the multiplicity of conflicting legal systems that had arisen during the later middle ages, but he was also a realist. Centralized earlier than most other regions of Europe, England, even by the sixteenth century, had developed a stronger tradition of rule within law, of custom, and of a monarchy limited by definite constraints with regard to person and property. These factors combined with the irregularities of the Tudor succession and perhaps with memories of the Wars of the Roses to render Henry circumspect and cautious about violating the property rights of large numbers of Englishmen. Indeed, one of the advantages of the takeover of monastic land was that it coincided with a secular shift away from demesne farming – a shift that had already motivated the monks to establish long-term leases of demesne lands to secular holders. Although the dispersal of lands through such leases may have been speeded by the impending dissolution, such contracts were honored by the crown as a matter of conscious policy, and every effort was made to avoid disturbing contractual tenures and thus arousing the resentment of the numerous holders of monastic lands.[68] Henry was both daring and astute enough to recognize the value of a propaganda campaign, calculated to exploit the confusions that had arisen in the theoretical abstractions of law and property during the later middle ages, as a device for forwarding his assault on church property. However, he was shrewd enough to bend before the power of English custom and the political realities within his kingdom. The same balance of forces and induced sense of royal constraint, persisting and developing as it did throughout the seventeenth century, has much to do, as I will attempt in part to demonstrate below, with the divergent paths of English and Continental mercantilism and in particular with the relative laxity of English industrial and commercial regulation and the consequent success of English economic development. Though not through greater wisdom or lack of desire, the English crown intruded less effectively in economic endeavor than its Continental counterparts.

Let us now, however, return to English agrarian history. Scholars generally agree that the output of England's agricultural sector increased markedly during the sixteenth century, but there is much dispute concerning the causal factors that gave rise to that expansion. Some argue that the crown's divestment of monastic lands seized during the Dissolution permitted purchasers to select those lands that could most efficiently be added to existing parcels or be made to form highly productive separate units.[69] Although such rationalization of tenures was perhaps one factor in raising output, its impact does not suffice to explain the total increment. A generation ago, historians would have broadly agreed with R. H. Tawney's thesis that the price revolution, by lowering the real rents of the aristocracy, drove them into financial distress and forced them to sell all or part of their lands. These sales, in conjunction with the crown's ongoing disposal of monastic properties, were conceived as a pivotal transformation that opened access to land to a group of rational, efficient, and market-conscious entrepreneurs who managed their new acquisitions with the same hard and rational methods as had already made them rich in the towns and in commerce. The new methods allowed them to squeeze an ever-growing surplus out of the agricultural sector. This view has been much debated and substantially modified in recent years, with the most striking challenge leveled against the supposed historical evidence for the impoverishment of the aristocracy.[70] If, in fact, the aristocracy did not fall precipitously and the gentry did not rise by transforming themselves into agribusinessmen, it is no longer permissible to predicate the explanation of England's increased agricultural output on such broad, and unfortunately rather vaguely defined, shifts in the social structure.

For the moment at least, it appears wiser to seek the causes of England's increased production in more humble interactions within the agrarian sector itself. Probably the single most important stimulus to output was simply the extension of the land under cultivation through drainage, reclamation of waste, and the conversion of pasture to arable. Second, the balanced nature of English market demand encouraged a balanced agricultural mix between grains and livestock that in turn allowed improved rotations and increased supplies of manure. Drainage and irrigation improved the yield of pastures, better pastures sustained more animals, expanded herds and closer care provided more utilizable manure, and, with more manure, crops were richer. In the words of Joan Thirsk, "improvements in arable and pastoral husbandry went hand in hand, each helping the other, and both serving to promote the specialization of regions."[71]

Overview

Across the length of Europe during the sixteenth century, population growth heightened the pressures on the food supply and intensified the demands made on the land. In all regions, more land was brought under cultivation, and in some – notably Holland and to a lesser degree, England – real gains were achieved in agricultural productivity, but the Malthusian pressures did not abate. Population grew faster than the food supply, and the inevitable consequence was a reduction in the nutritional standard of the European populace. Fortunately, the decline began at a time when the dietary level, artificially swollen as a result of the fourteenth-century depopulations, was truly gargantuan. Those few and dubious figures that remain to reveal the dietary habits of postplague and early sixteenth-century Europe suggest that a daily intake of between 4,000 and 5,000 calories was quite common, so a considerable reduction could occur without creating true hardship. Even so, nutritional standards fell precipitously by the seventeenth century, and in many cases, they stabilized at levels well below 3,000 calories per day.[72] A slightly different perspective on the same phenomenon may be gleaned from the surviving statistics for southern England. There, the real wage of building craftsmen during the years 1580–99 slid to exactly one-half the level that had been attained in 1451–75, and the fall was largely the result of a marked rise in the price of foodstuffs.[73]

The failure of the sixteenth-century economy sufficiently to increase agricultural productivity caused a general decline in the real wage rate; it was this decline that led Hamilton and others to speculate on the possible gain to industry that might have arisen from the lag of wages behind prices. Yet, as we have already noted, the wage rate lagged behind agricultural, not industrial, prices and was more a reflection of Malthusian pressures than a sign of improved manufacturing profitability or of enhanced capital accumulation. The industrial sector had its own rhythms, and before we can form tenable judgments regarding its profitability, it must be considered on its own terms and in more detail.

4

Industry: technology and organization

The forces that structured and influenced the market for manufactured goods during the sixteenth century were more complex and multidimensional than those that swelled the demand for foodstuffs. True enough, monetary recovery and the general expansion of population tended to raise the demand for the products of the artisans of Europe, but the connections between increased numbers and increased consumption were not direct. Since a certain minimal caloric intake is necessary to sustain life and since there are upper, though less definite, limits to the amount of food which even the most affluent human is apt to ingest, the demand of any given individual for foodstuffs is relatively inelastic. As a result, the aggregate demand for food closely follows demographic trends. The sixteenth-century demographic resurgence clearly heightened the pressures on the food supply. When output failed to keep pace with population growth, agricultural prices soared and real wages plummeted, but what of the demand for manufactured goods? It is a commonplace both of economic theory and of economic history – at least in regard to the behavior of an individual acting within the constraints of a limited budget – that when the cost of necessities increases sharply, the demand for luxuries and peripheral goods declines. In the postplague period of the fourteenth and fifteenth centuries, depopulation, by curtailing demand, lowered agricultural prices and thus enabled numerous consumers to offset their terror with wine, exotic foods, and the luxury manufactures previously available only to the very wealthy. Would not the converse have occurred in the sixteenth century when population once again rose and the most basic foods again became expensive?

One has but to consider the repression of the peasants and of the nas-

cent urban economies in Poland and central Europe, or the growth in
the numbers of beggars in Spain and elsewhere to give at least a partially affirmative answer to the preceding question. There is little
doubt that as bread prices rose, numerous Europeans were compelled
to retrench and to limit their purchases to the barest essentials. In
central Europe, the decision was not a matter of "free" choice, but
even in the west, where political repression was less pronounced, economic necessity forced many people out of the market for manufactured goods altogether and severely restricted the consumption patterns
of an even larger portion of the remainder. As these consumers withdrew
or were driven from the market, the potential aggregate demand for
manufactured goods contracted – a fact that provides one significant
element in the explanation of the relatively retarded rate of price ac-
celeration displayed by manufactured goods.

It is important, however, to distinguish between potential and absolute demand for manufactures. The failure of aggregate demand to keep
pace with population's growth did not mean that the market for
manufactures shrank, nor even that it remained stagnant. The remaining evidence is too frail to allow us to quantify the precise balance between the positive influence of population growth and the negative
impact of rising agricultural prices in shifting demand away from manufactured goods. It is probable, however, that some of our statistics
overstate the degree to which real wages fell, and therefore likely that
increasing population had at least some positive influence on the demand for all goods, even though that influence was muted in the manufacturing sector. The case for rising absolute demand for manufactures
is much stronger, however; monetary recovery and the concentration
of wealth in the hands of the powerful, in the context of the sixteenth
century, had an almost totally positive influence on the demand for
manufactures. The precious metals newly extracted from the mines of
central Europe and the New World represented a net increment to
European purchasing power, but, more importantly, the metal was not,
at least initially, diffused across Europe in such a manner as to allow
its expenditure to reflect the consumption patterns of the ordinary
man. Neither the king, nor the grandees, nor, for that matter, the adventurers and brigands who pillaged the New World modeled their
consumption habits after those of building laborers in southern England or of peasants in central Europe. They sought instead materials

of luxury and of war – in short, the products of the artisans of western Europe and indeed of the wider world.

Equally significant in influencing the demand for manufactures was the intensified concentration of wealth. The victors, who won control over land in the power struggle that had been engendered by soaring grain prices, benefited from substantially increased real incomes. In Poland and central Europe, where the nobility crushed industrial development and drove merchants and artisans back to the fields, internal demand for products of local manufacture, with the exception of some military supplies, virtually collapsed, but the nobles' requirements for quality goods imported from western Europe grew sharply. Similarly, the redistribution of church and peasant land in Sweden and its concentration in the hands of the nobility preserved and enhanced the market for imported cloth and other manufactures. Parallel phenomena occurred elsewhere in Europe as abandoned land was returned to cultivation and profitability and as landlords took steps to increase their rents and learned to protect themselves from the ravages of inflation at the expense of their tenants. Despite the fact that the rapid escalation of agricultural prices drove down the real wages of most workers, shifts in the pattern of income distribution during the sixteenth century generally favored the wealthy, and because food was a lesser portion of their expenditures, much remained for the purchase of luxuries and manufactures. While one may lament the inequities that resulted, it was as a consequence of the inequality of income distribution that the economies of the sixteenth century were able to sustain flourishing industries in spite of the thin nature of the market and the utter failure to generate an economic system based on mass consumption. Since the products of organized industry never constituted a major portion of European output during the middle ages and since their use, with minor exceptions, had always been confined to a narrow segment of the upper strata of society, a relatively slight increase in aggregate demand could call forth quite dramatic percentage increases in industrial production.

Only fragmentary statistical evidence survives to document the growth of industrial output in the sixteenth century, but Graph 2 furnishes some indication of the growth of the textile industry. Figures are presented as percentages of the maximum levels attained during the century in order to permit comparison among the relative

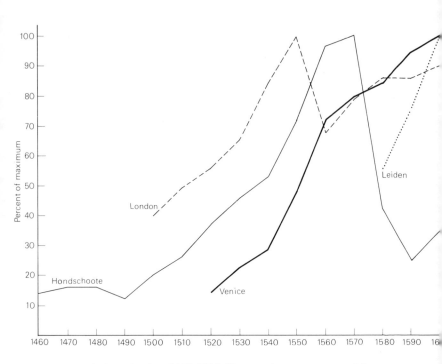

Graph 2. Cloth production, 1460–1600. (Expressed as a percentage of the area maximum during the time span for which statistics were available. Leiden, 1596–1605 = 100% = 58,500 cloths per year, London, 1546-1555 = 100% = 114,395 cloths exported per year; Hondschoote, 1566-1575 = 100% = 37,907 cloths per year; Venice, 1596-1605 = 100% = 22,515 cloths per year. *Sources:* London: F. J. Fisher, "Commercial Trends and Policy in Sixteenth-Century England," *Economic History Review,* X (1940) 95–117. Leiden: N. W. Posthumus, *Geschiedenis van de Leidsche Laken Industrie,* 2 vols., II, Gravenhage, Martinus Nijhoff, 1908, 1939, p. 129. Hondschoote: E. Coornaert, *Un Centre industriel d'autrefois: la draperie sayetterie d'Hondschoote,* Rennes, Les Presses Universitaires de France, 1930, pp. 487-90. Venice: Domenico Sella, "Les Mouvements longs: l'industrie lainière à Venise aux xvie et xviie siècles," *Annales: économies, sociétés, civilisations,* XII (1957) 29-45.

rates of growth in different regions. English figures record the export of traditional fulled woolen cloths from the port of London and clearly reflect a sharp increase in sales (250 percent) during the first half of the century. Although the Venetian increase, nearly tenfold, appears more spectacular, it is well to remember that the English series chronicles the development of a well-established major industry that had been developing since the middle of the fourteenth century. By contrast, Venice, at the beginning of the sixteenth century, was still nursing its incipient cloth industry, largely created in order to compensate for the revenues no longer forthcoming from its centuries-old Mediterranean commerce. The political disturbances in the Low Countries during the latter half of the century severely damaged most economic endeavor and caused deep and precipitous slumps in production, but despite the hazards, output was generally higher at the end of the century than at the beginning. At Hondschoote, cloth production rose from some sixty-five hundred cloths in 1500 to fourteen thousand by the end of the century, but it had grown to more than forty thousand cloths per year in the 1560s. At Leiden, annual output rose from some thirty-two thousand cloths to almost sixty thousand during the final decades of the sixteenth century.

Contemporary comment and other strong, if oblique, evidence confirm the industrial expansion indicated by Graph 2. Similar evidence documents growth in many more industries than textiles; cloth, however, retained the primary position among sixteenth-century manufactured goods, and in a number of regions not incorporated into the graph. Once it is accepted that rising output was common to a number of industries, particularly in England and the Low Countries, but also elsewhere, we are in a position to reopen and deepen our earlier discussion of Hamilton's notion of profit inflation.[1] As will be recalled, Hamilton argued that wages and rents lagged behind prices, thereby causing industrial profits to soar and permitting the very rapid accumulation of capital. Critics, in turn, observed that agricultural, not industrial, prices rose most sharply and pointed out that the inflation of raw material costs under such conditions would have had a detrimental effect on profits. We further noted that Hamilton's measurement of profit growth solely on the basis of the spread between the sales price of goods and the cost of the factors of production depends on an aberrant definition of profit, because what must in fact be calculated is the differential between total cost and total revenue – the quantity of goods sold times the unit price.

In the form in which he presented it, Hamilton's thesis is no longer tenable; yet the idea that economic conditions during the sixteenth century caused profits to swell and favored the accumulation of capital is not without merit. Our investigation of the nature and strength of demand for manufactured goods and of the consequent augmentation in output shows that, for many industries, at least one element of the profit equation – total revenue – rose markedly. Unfortunately, the evidence that would sustain such conclusions with regard to individual firms within a given industry is virtually nonexistent. As a result, it remains obscure in many instances whether expansion was achieved through the growth of existing firms or through the creation of additional firms, more or less identical to the old.

Sales prices of most manufactured goods rose moderately over the course of the sixteenth century. On a scale where 1451–1500 equals 100, English industrial products' prices were 116 in the 1550s and 150 by 1590; for textile products, the figures were, respectively, 121 and 118.[2] Woolen cloth, as distinct from the combined textile index, began the century with a price index level of 85 and finished at 80 – hardly an example of rampant inflation and certainly not one that lends credence to the Hamiltonian thesis of profit inflation. On the other hand, since exports of woolen shortcloths from London more than doubled over the same period, it is virtually certain that total revenues of the cloth industry as a whole increased sharply in spite of the relatively constant price level for goods sold.

Period statistics are too flawed to permit us to perform the economist's subtraction of total costs from total revenues so as to formulate precise estimates of the behavior of profits in the sixteenth century. Yet, since we can often be quite certain that total revenues rose, we may analyze specific industries on a qualitative basis in order to determine whether factors were present that tended to hold down total costs as output expanded. If favorable technological and organizational advances were made or if economies of scale were achieved, either within individual firms or within an entire industry, it is likely that revenues would have increased faster than costs and consequently that profits would have risen and that the accumulation of capital would have been accelerated. Let us begin our analysis with England, where sources are most readily available, and with the cloth industry.

Industry in England

During the early modern period in England, two quite distinct types of woolen cloth were manufactured: woolens and worsteds.[3] Woolens, the shortcloths whose export pattern is depicted on Graph 2, had been an ever-increasing portion of English overseas commerce since the middle of the fourteenth century. Worsteds, on the other hand, assumed a major role in English production only after the mid-sixteenth century and grew to dominance during the seventeenth. The prime raw material for the woolen industry was the clip from fine-haired, short-staple sheep; once this had been cleaned and the oil removed, it was stroked between two cards equipped with wire teeth in order to straighten the fibers and draw them into parallel. After carding, the wool was formed into a rough rope, called a roving, and then spun; the latter process simultaneously twisted the fibers together and drew out the roving until the wool was firmly interlocked and lengthened into the fineness desired for yarn. The next stage was weaving. Thereafter, the completed cloth was fulled, which required soaking the cloth in a foul mixture of fuller's earth and other noxious ingredients while simultaneously compressing the fibers together so as to mat or felt them into a single unit and to conceal the individual threads. Fulling was accomplished either manually by treading on the cloth while it was soaking or mechanically by means of a fulling mill where large wooden hammers, driven by a waterwheel, replaced the fullers' labor; such mills had been in operation in England from at least the twelfth century. After fulling, the cloth was washed, attached to the hooks of a tenter-frame where it was stretched – sometimes fraudulently overstretched, to the detriment of quality – to the appropriate or statutory size, and allowed to dry. The final stages of production were dyeing, then teaseling – lifting the nap by plucking the cloth with a burr, although mechanical teaseling by means of gig mills was known and largely rejected in the sixteenth century – and ultimately shearing or removing the nap so as to leave the cloth soft and smooth. The finished product was a highly expensive, luxury cloth, durable and virtually impervious to the elements.

The worsted cloth industry utilized a simpler technology. Coarser, long-staple wool was combed straight rather than carded, and when spun, the yarn drew its strength from the natural continuity of the fiber as well as from the twist imparted by the spinning wheel. Since the fulling process was omitted less wool was used per cloth. Worsteds, consequently, were not only cheaper than woolens, but the absence of fulling gave them other distinctive qualities that proved advantageous in some markets. More loosely woven and lighter in weight, worsteds were better suited for tropical or semitropical climates and thus found eager buyers in the Mediterranean and indeed in the New World. In addition, without fulling, the individual strands of yarn remained visible so that more complex and decorative patterns of both color and weave were possible. It was this factor, perhaps, rather than light weight that spurred worsted sales in northern markets, where climate was not a direct stimulant.

Few important technological changes affected cloth making during the sixteenth century. Even worsteds, referred to in England as the "new draperies," were old on the Continent and had been produced, although in small quantities, even in England long before they began their dramatic resurgence around the middle of the century. While technical advances in manufacture were minimal, deep organizational changes were necessary as cloth exports rose from miniscule levels in the fourteenth century to assume a major share of English overseas commerce in the sixteenth. The system that produced and exported more than one hundred thousand cloths annually could not have functioned on the same basis as that created two centuries earlier for the occasional marketing of a few thousand cloths.

Excessive emphasis in the literature of economic history has probably been accorded to the rather mechanical division of the progress of industrial organization into three parts: the guild system, where the worker owned both tools and raw material; the domestic system, where he owned the tools, but was employed by a capitalist to work up the latter's material; and the factory system in which the worker owned neither tools nor material. Yet while the origins of the domestic system are obscure and while the guild system persisted well into and beyond the sixteenth century, the concept of putting out raw materials to be worked into cloth at once describes the structure of

England's textile industry and reveals the way in which organizational changes could lead to increases in productivity.

In 1776 when Adam Smith praised the advantages of the division of labor and described the advance in productivity obtained in his famous, though hypothetical, pin factory where one worker specialized in drawing the wire, another in cutting, a third in pointing, and so on, he was focusing mainly on changes within the manufacturing process itself, and within a single factory.[4] The example is not really appropriate to the conditions of sixteenth-century textile manufacture, conducted under the domestic or putting-out system, because the actual manufacturing process continued to be performed in virtually the same manner that had prevailed for centuries. A variant of the concept of division of labor set forth by the Austrian economist Böhm-Bawerk, however, does provide a vocabulary, albeit somewhat archaic, and a conceptual frame for analyzing the achievements in the early modern textile industry.[5] For him, the levels both of capitalism and of productivity depended on the degree of "roundaboutness" of production, that is, on the production of goods by means of multiple intermediate stages over increasing periods of time. Few modern economists would find much of current relevance in Böhm-Bawerk's theory, yet the notion of "roundaboutness" captures the essence of the most significant structural changes in the advanced economies of sixteenth-century Europe. Everywhere throughout the more developed countries, middlemen proliferated, performing key functions of transportation and marketing in the interstices between the stages of true manufacturing, and contributing to the burgeoning "roundaboutness" of production.

As the putting-out system matured, the obvious inconveniences that an entrepreneur suffered by buying wool, having it first prepared, then spun, then woven, and finally finished by numerous specialists in diverse locations, were remedied by the increasing employment of middlemen. Under the primitive putting-out system, problems of venality and of quality control arose at every step. The many complaints by putters-out that they received back less spun yarn than the original weight of wool must be balanced against the spinners' claim that they often received short weight in the first place and could not spin more yarn than the raw materials allowed. Adulteration of the yarn with foreign materials appears to have been a common problem and to have wasted valuable manhours both in attempting to detect fraud and in repairing the damage done when the fraud went undetected. In response to opportunity, a class of yarn brokers emerged to serve as middlemen between the spinners and the weavers, putting out wool and selling finished yarn.[6] Fraud was not thereby vanquished, but regular connections between the clothier and his yarn broker and between the latter and his spinners balanced the benefits of preserving a continuing business relationship against the possible short-term gain from deceptive practice. That yarn brokers deepened their control over the spinners as the century progressed establishes their utility in the marketplace and suggests that the organizational "roundaboutness" that they represent led to improvements in productivity and reductions in cost.

Just as middlemen proliferated between the stages of manufacture, so too did they in the market chain that finally led to export. In the Welsh cloth industry, for example, the manufacturing process was completed in England either at Oswestry or, later, at Shrewsbury; the cloth was then sold to the drapers, a group that specialized almost entirely in buying and selling and whose members were involved only peripherally, if at all, in manufacturing. Much of the cloth purchased was subsequently sent to London, where a further group of specialists, the merchants of Blackwell Hall, saw to its export and sale abroad. The trip to London, however, was 140 miles and consumed a week's time by packhorse convoy, an arrangement required because of the high risk of theft along the border between England and Wales. Danger and the considerable transit time encouraged the evolution of a professional class of carriers who took cloths on consignment from the drapers and received payment upon proof of delivery at Blackwell Hall.[7] Once again the process became more "roundabout" and, once again, the fact that the market freely supported the carriers leaves little doubt regarding their economic worth in increasing convenience and in reducing overall costs within the textile industry.

Rapid expansion in the cloth industry permitted economies of scale, but such organizational change did not occur without creating internal tensions. As often happens during an evolutionary period, the older, vested interests turned to the state for protection against the innovative elements within the industry and sought regulation that would preserve their traditional monopoly. In response to their pleas, a series of legislative acts attempted to protect the old, town-centered industry from the competition of the countryside. In 1555, for example, the Weavers' Act limited the number of looms that a clothier might possess outside of the towns to one and restricted those of a weaver beyond the municipal borders to two. Exemptions granted in the immediately succeeding years largely vitiated the intent of the act, but similar efforts to control wages, to constrain competition, and to preserve the old marched in futile procession across the latter half of the sixteenth century. Neither economic rationality nor, in the long run, the interests of the crown were to be served by endeavoring to shore up an organizational structure whose time had passed, however, so the legislation was more effective in isolating the old centers of the industry than in preventing the growth of new competition. In addition, by the second half of the century, the woolen broadcloth industry no longer held the allure of dynamism. It made little sense for a state interested in maximizing its revenues and economic strength to harm the new draperies and the worsted industry, which were vital and growing, in order to attempt to restore health to the ailing woolen industry, whose prognosis during the 1550s and 1560s was at best uncertain.

Although the quantity of English industrial legislation was impressive, the failure to enforce it – either through wisdom, lack of desire, or simply the inadequacy of the bureaucracy – left disappointed those who hoped that the state would preserve their vested interests. The alternative was internal self-regulation through the guild structure, and, for a time, efforts were made to tighten guild requirements so as to exclude competition. Since the principal threat came from new enterprises beyond town limits, however, geography minimized the effectiveness of the traditional, urban guilds. Only action at a national level could have throttled England's industrial advance and such action was only narrowly averted. Legislative support for the reactionary guild hierarchies was forthcoming in the Statute of Apprentices of 1563, which sought to unify industrial organization and to place the positive sanction of the state behind guild efforts to formalize and preserve past practice. By recognizing and giving national legal sanction to the apprentice system, it sustained the power of the guilds, and by limiting the number of apprentices that each master might employ, it sharply curtailed the potential growth of any single firm.[8] Had it been strictly enforced, it would have severely restricted industrial growth, deterred innovation, and quite possibly have led to fiscal abuses similar to those that proved so detrimental in France and elsewhere on the continent. Happily for England, it was not well enforced; economic development and change were already too strong to be arrested, and since the legislation was primarily applicable to the older woolen industry, its impact was minor on new developments and on new areas of production.

Despite attempts, particularly under the Stuarts in the early seventeenth century, to infuse new life into the late medieval guild system and to use the guilds as part of a national network of industrial control, the English monarchy never gained the power over industry that the French, Prussian, and Spanish states won. In England, the role of custom and the tradition of rule within law retained their vitality and remained far stronger than on the Continent. They provided both a vocabulary of protest and a defense against royal incursions into industrial organization. Whereas in France a national guild system could be created, in theory if not in fact, by royal edict in 1581, the English experiment required an act of Parliament. The same forces that limited arbitrary enactment of guild regulations, limited arbitrary enforcement and protected the rights of those excluded from the guilds.

We have noted earlier the significance of Roman law in eroding the role of custom on the Continent and have also observed that Roman law had far less impact in England, where customary law retained a primary position in English jurisprudence. The point becomes important in guild history since custom frequently conflicted with the restrictive tendencies of the guilds. In London, for example, the custom of the city prescribed that no guild or company could exercise exclusive and restrictive control over any trade and further dictated that any competent member of any company with the freedom of the city could engage in any trade.[9] In the absence of defenders, customary law in this instance might possibly have been overridden by a determined national government, but instead the custom appears to have focused the energies of dissident innovators and entrepreneurs outside the guilds. Freedom to expand, to avoid national regulation, and to innovate were too important to too many rising entrepreneurs, and in the struggle between the vested interests and their challengers, custom was preserved and used to fend off effective economic control by the state in England.

A series of interwoven events, both on the Continent and in England itself, altered the very nature of the textile industry so rapidly and so radically as to render effective regulation extremely difficult, and in so doing lent support to those whose interests lay in resisting such regulation. The Treaty of Cateau-Cambrésis in 1559 had brought to an end French military involvement with Spain over the control of Italy and had allowed both the French and Spanish monarchies to turn to pressing internal matters. Philip II of Spain devoted himself to the eradication of heresy within his empire and his efforts at counterreformation seriously distorted economic stability within the Netherlands. After a sixty-year period of open trade for English cloth, the market at Antwerp was closed in 1562. The damage to the English broadcloth industry that resulted from the closing of its major Continental market was exacerbated by the prolonged effects of the revaluation of the English coinage in 1561. Whereas debasement during the 1550s had lowered the real price of English cloth on the Continent, revaluation and the strengthening of the currency had the opposite effect and artificially raised the cost to Continental buyers. The precipitous decline, visible on Graph 2, in English cloth exports during the 1560s was in large part the consequence of these two events. In turn, the decline may have contributed to an apparent lack of enthusiasm for the enforcement of restrictive legislation in support of the domestic industry.

Within the Low Countries themselves, economic and political conditions worsened with the progress of the Counter-Reformation; heresy was fought by means of torture and burning at the stake. After Alva assumed the governorship in 1567, repression was institutionalized in the Council of Blood, which had the arbitrary power to confiscate goods and to decree death.[10] In 1569, to ensure sufficient revenues for his continuing efforts and perhaps also to impose penance on a recalcitrant people, Alva imposed a 10 percent sales tax, modeled after the Spanish *alcabala* and levied on sales at each stage of the passage of goods through the market. The stern sanction of the Blood Council was necessary to force provincial acquiescence in the levying of the tax, because its impact in the commercially active Netherlands, where goods were sold many times before reaching their final market, was far more devastating than in agricultural and backward Spain.

Torture, confiscation of goods, penalty taxation, and the constant threat of death do not constitute an environment that fosters industrial production. Harassed at home, many producers sought safety abroad and many fled to England. Many of the immigrants were highly skilled in the textile trades, particularly in worsted manufacture, and these were warmly welcomed by a monarchy conscious of the desirability of expanding domestic employment and of earning gold and silver balances from abroad. Resentment of the prospering newcomers was inevitable, but royal protection was usually sufficient to mute the acerbity of lower-level protest and obstruction. Furthermore, since the immigrants did not normally settle in the centers of the traditional cloth industry, they were not immediately visible as a threat to the established textile workers.

The technology of the new draperies encouraged this geographical dispersion. It will be recalled that one of the crucial distinctions between worsteds and woolens lies in the fact that the former do not require fulling; this freed the worsted industry from dependence on water and waterpower for soaking the cloths and driving fulling mills. In consequence, the worsted industry did not need the swift streams of the west of England and could locate closer to the market, where transportation costs were lower and transit time was reduced. The industry grew rapidly in southeast England and soon new draperies were being manufactured in considerable quantities in a group of towns encircling and including London. The largest center was perhaps at Norwich, but Colchester, Canterbury, Sandwich, and Halstead all provided refuge, albeit sometimes reluctantly, for the clothworkers from the Low Countries.[11] Rye, on the south coast, became a sanctuary for French immigrants as the religious civil wars and especially the Massacre of St. Bartholomew in 1572 made existence in France intolerable for many skilled Huguenot clothiers.

Circumstance nurtured the new draperies. Skilled labor continued to flow in from abroad throughout the remainder of the century and freedom from dependence on waterpower allowed the new clothworkers to settle where houses were available and, at least for the early settlers, inexpensive. Even the sheep appear to have cooperated. When sheep are well cared for and protected from the elements, their wool becomes longer and less dense; there is some evidence that, partly as a result of enclosure and perhaps partly as a result of careless control of breeding, English wool in some regions was becoming more long-stapled and coarser as the century progressed.[12] Coarse, long-stapled wool was better suited for the manufacture of worsteds than woolens, because the natural length of the fiber gave strength to the warp, or longitudinal threads, of the unfulled cloth. It is probably not an accident that the "new draperies" centered about London, since by 1600 the entire region was rich in the production of coarse wool and since there was a particularly heavy concentration of long-staple wool in the countryside surrounding the textile towns of Norwich and Rye.[13] Whether the quality of the wool evolved accidentally or at least partially in response to altered demand is not altogether clear, but regional concentration and specialization had important consequences. The location of the new draperies in new areas, remote from the old textile centers and long-established guilds, gave the industry freedom both from national legislation and from restrictive guild practices.

It is inappropriate to make comparative judgments concerning economies of scale within the new drapery segment of the textile industry, since the industry was, in a sense, born fresh when it arrived in England. However, the growth of the new draperies affected and aided industrial organization both within the textile industry and across industrial divisions where their success stimulated other forms of economic activity. On the one hand, since the new draperies were marketed abroad by London merchants, their sale increased the volume of business of London export specialists; this, in turn, according to the principles of elementary economics, would normally have led to a reduction in the average fixed costs per cloth incurred by the merchants. If such was the case, it would have favorably affected both the new and the old draperies, and, by lowering costs, have permitted the more rapid accumulation of profits within the industry. On the other hand, since the new draperies were not directly competitive with the old, their export value constituted, almost in its entirety, a net increment in foreign earnings, and as this money was diffused through the economy, it created markets for other goods and worked to increase the scale of production in a number of other trades.

The concentration of the new draperies in southeast England reinforced a trend that had been evident for several centuries. From the early fourteenth to the early sixteenth century, the rate of growth of lay wealth in London and its surrounding region was substantially greater than the rates for most other English counties.[14] The new draperies supplemented the sources of wealth in the southeast, but they – along with the old textile industry when swift growth required new urban marketing techniques – became part of a dynamic interaction occurring within the city of London and its environs. Resident export merchants required housing, food, clothing, fuel, and a myriad of other goods and services, and they had the incomes to pay for them. Specialized carters, such as those serving the Welsh cloth industry, could not have functioned without accommodations within London for themselves and for their horses. Each terminus of the various roundabout chains that led to marketing in or through London obviously required the support of a host of ancillary persons and services and thus contributed to the increase in the city's population. Cloth alone was not, of course, responsible for the rapid growth rate of London's population – nearly three times the rate for the country as a whole over the course of the sixteenth century[15] – but it was a significant element in the pattern. Once underway, from whatever initial stimulus, the growth of the city and its impact on industrial development became self-sustaining. It is in the interaction between demographic concentration and industrial growth that one finds the most likely explanation for the profit inflation that Hamilton correctly identified but whose causes he misconstrued.

Expanding population, for example, obviously stimulated the building trades. Increased building activity and a shift in architectural style deepened the market for window glass and opened opportunities for an industrial transformation of glassmaking. One may note in passing that the change in taste favoring glass during the sixteenth century may have been forwarded by the marked improvement in cannon and explosives that made defensive fortifications ever more expensive and of dubious value. Since curtain walls offered small defense against cannon, the visibility and light provided by glass became increasingly attractive. In any event, demand for glass grew, and production expanded to meet the needs.[16] Until the sixteenth century, glassmaking was primarily a part-time activity for those who made their livings from work in the forests; it was in many ways similar to those textile activities conducted by farmers and farmwomen in the off season. As the process devoured huge quantities of wood and as the furnaces were quite simple, glassmaking remained a marginal occupation, located in the forests where wood and transport costs for wood were relatively inexpensive. Spurred by rising demand, however, the industry evolved into a full-time occupation for increasingly specialized workers at the same time as the political and religious dislocations on the Continent caused a number of highly skilled glassworkers to flee to England. French glassmakers from Normandy and Lorraine sought security in England, and, in 1567, Jean Carré, an entrepreneur from Antwerp, received official permission to establish a company for the manufacture of glass in London.

Increased scale and some technological improvements combined to lower the costs of glass production. As the manufacture became more specialized, the amount of rejected and waste glass appears to have decreased; manufacturers, now full-time practitioners, could select their raw materials with more care, and they became more skillful in adjusting and controlling their input mix. Fuel consumption per unit of glass produced fell, and because fuel was the largest component in the cost of glassmaking, the saving represented a significant lowering of costs. Technical advances in furnace design that allowed several related processes to be completed at a single heat source extended the fuel economies. In addition, the manufacture became more "roundabout" as manufacturers within London came to depend on intermediaries for their supplies of wood, sand, and potash. Improvements, both technological and organizational, allowed the price of window glass to fall from an index level of 100 at the beginning of the century to 77 in the final decade,[17] despite the fact that the price of wood had risen sharply. Once again, it would seem that the notion of profit inflation predicated on the differences between rising sales' prices and stagnant factor prices must be rejected. Yet since the cost of glass manufacture was lowered through advances in technology and organization as output increased, it is highly likely that ample opportunity existed for profits to rise and for capital to accumulate.

Industrial and demographic expansion and particularly demographic concentration within London and a few other major cities inevitably strained limited resources and caused cost increases that must be balanced against the economies derived from larger scale and more efficient organization. As cloth output rose, for example, there was a more than proportionate increase in dyeing as a bigger share of the cloth produced was finished in England. Dyeing, of course, requires the heating of the vats of dye, and both the manufacture of the vats and the subsequent boiling of the dye demanded the use of significant quantities of fuel. Consumption of firewood rose as dyeing increased, but the cumulative demand for wood was magnified by the very inter-action among industries that made London such a prosperous city. As clothiers grew in affluence, they bought the products of the glass-makers, whose industry consumed inordinate amounts of fuel. A single glazier in the early seventeenth century is reported to have burned two thousand wagonloads of wood annually while the average intake for a sixteenth-century glass furnace was 60 to 70 cords per month.[18] Housebuilding directly absorbed quantities of timber, but even when the construction was brick and the roof of tile, the kilns were fired with wood or charcoal. As naval power became ever more crucial for the commercial and political survival of states, the construction of ships claimed a disproportionate share of forest reserves, and timber became a highly strategic commodity. By the early eighteenth century, the construction of a first-rate warship required four thousand oak trees and 300,000 pounds of iron[19] – a commodity that was in turn smelted and refined over wood or charcoal fires. Nef estimates that the brewers of London alone may have consumed as much as twenty thousand wagonloads of wood in the year 1578 and notes the addi-tional consumption of the limeburners, saltpeter workers, tilers, pot-ters, sugar refiners, and soap boilers.[20] To this industrial usage, one must add the very considerable amount of wood burned for domestic heating purposes as the population of London rose from thirty or forty thousand at the beginning of the sixteenth century to nearly a quarter of a million in the early seventeenth century. The price of firewood soared with demand; from a price index level of 100 estab-lished during the last half of the fifteenth century, it climbed to 366 in the decade 1603–12.[21]

Rapid escalation in cost and awareness of the strategic importance of wood combined to persuade Englishmen that they must find sub-stitute energy sources and employ them wherever it was technological-ly feasible. Coal was an available and highly efficient source of heat, but there were limitations to its use. It could not, for example, be used in iron smelting until the beginning of the eighteenth century, when Darby's experiments at Coalbrookdale generated a process for smelt-ing iron with coke. A few other industrial processes frustrated those who would switch to the cheaper and more abundant fuel, but many industries – those that simply required heat where there was no danger of chemical reaction between the product and the fuel – could readily employ coal. Dyeing, salt making through evaporation, and soap boiling, for example, evinced no technical problems, and as the price of wood rose, reluctance to change over declined. The most general and direct substitution of fuels, of course, was in home heating; since all that was sought was warmth, there was no danger that the burning of coal would alter the final object of production. Londoners were not unaware of the smoke, soot, and foul air that resulted from the use of coal, but price and availability overcame their distaste for noxious fumes.

Rising demand led to sharply increased coal production. The trend was particularly strong during the late seventeenth century, when production was fourteen times greater than the 210,000 tons mined annually between 1551 and 1560, but the growth in production was persistent during the late sixteenth century as well.[22] Coal imports at London, largely from Newcastle, leapt from 10,785 tons in 1580 to 73,984 tons in 1606, a sevenfold increase within a quarter of a century. As in other industries, expansion led to increasingly roundabout methods of transportation, wholesaling, and retailing; in coal, it also led to extensive capital investment, however, since enhanced production required that mines be exploited at ever greater depths. During the middle ages, when population was relatively sparse and when wood sufficed for most industrial energy needs, coal had been mined primarily from outcroppings where it lay close to the surface of the earth. Mines rarely attained such depths as to encounter problems of drainage or ventilation, and when these limits were approached, the mines were usually simply abandoned as uneconomical. By the sixteenth century, however, the interaction between demographic concentration and industrial demands forced a more intensive exploitation of England's coal reserves and offered the market rewards necessary to encourage substantial investment. According to Nef, pit depths of 100 to 120 feet were common by the end of the sixteenth century; in such costly enterprises, particularly common in the north of England, he finds the beginnings of a major economic transformation in the development of capitalism and the capitalistic exploitation of mineral resources.[23]

While it is perhaps an overstatement to consider coal mining as the cutting edge of a protoindustrial revolution in the sixteenth century and while it is well to recall that many mines continued to operate at a primitive level and with few workers, large mines did entail intensive capital investment and advanced technology. The mining techniques that had been developed for the extraction of precious metals in Germany[24] had become economical for the extraction of coal as a result of the rise of energy prices during the second half of the sixteenth century. Elizabeth encouraged the immigration of German miners under the protection of her letters patent, and, in 1566, exercised personal care to assure their safety after a riot in Westmorland had resulted in the death of one of their number.[25] The infusion of German mining and metallurgical techniques raised the level of sophistication in English mining and, at the same time, created additional linkages to other segments of the economy. As mines became deeper, for example, greater quantities of timber were required for shoring up shafts and constructing drainage engines; coal transportation, whether by cart or by ship, again added to the demand for wood, thus placing upward pressure on its price and extending the market for more competitively priced coal. To some extent, the very mining of coal reinforced the demand for coal.

Similar interactions occurred elsewhere. The enlarged population of London required more food, and as greater expanses of English land were converted to arable, less acreage was available for timber production. The chain does not end there, however. The rise in the price of firewood, as we have already observed, encouraged the burning of coal for domestic heating, but this conversion entailed the use of iron coal grates in order to assure adequate ventilation for successful combustion.[26] The consequent increase in the demand for iron not only acted to stimulate production of that commodity, but, because iron smelting could only be accomplished with wood or rather charcoal fuel, contributed further to the scarcity of wood and thus led to an even greater dependence on mineral fuels.

Iron had been a scarce and expensive commodity throughout the middle ages. To economize on its use, tools were often merely tipped or edged with iron, and even the largest machines were primarily wooden, with only the bearing parts sheathed in iron to reduce wear. Fuel costs continued to limit the production of iron until the eighteenth century, but a major technological breakthrough was achieved in smelting toward the end of the middle ages. It was then that the bloomery – a device for heating iron over an open hearth until the metal was soft enough to allow the impurities to be hammered from the spongy mass – was replaced by the blast furnace.[27] With a tall enough chimney and a sufficiently powerful air blast, generated in most instances by means of tandem, water-driven bellows, temperatures could become high enough to liquefy the iron so that it flowed from the furnace with a purity that permitted direct casting. Production of wrought iron still required further hammering, but since the impurity and carbon content was diminished in the blast furnace, the hammering process was shortened. Iron output increased sharply; in Sussex, a late medieval bloomery yielded 20 or 30 tons a year, but after conversion to the new technology in the sixteenth century, output per furnace approached 200 tons annually.[28]

In the case of iron manufacture, we are fortunate enough to possess detailed records from a sixteenth-century firm, and are thus able to assess the question of profitability directly, although this single firm's price structure does not appear to reflect the overall experience of the industry. In 1546, at Sir William Sidney's ironworks in Sussex, a ton of finished bar iron cost 3£ 17s 2d to manufacture and sold for 5£ 18s, leaving the proprietor a 53 percent profit.[29] Since the firm's sales price continued to rise over the next decades, reaching 9£ per ton in 1571, there is some reason to concur with Professor Hamilton's analysis that the rise in prices led to an inflation in profits, in this instance specific to Sussex. Yet in reality, it was increased scale of production, technological change, and extensive capital investment, rather than lagging rents or wages, that made iron making such a profitable enterprise. Fuel, after all, was a major cost in smelting and its price rose far faster than the price of iron. Indeed, despite sharply rising demand, the supply of iron appears to have grown almost in proportion; from a price index level of 100 in 1451–1500, wrought iron prices rose only to 123 by 1613–22.[30]

Greater availability of iron naturally stimulated productivity in a myriad of other industries where durable materials were essential for bearing or cutting. Enlarged iron output also indirectly benefited those industries that supplied materials essential to the expansion; among these was the leather industry. The powerful bellows that provided the rush of air necessary to liquify iron in blast furnaces or to heat the metal in forges were fashioned of leather, as were those employed in glassmaking. Industrial sources of increased demand were reinforced by agricultural consumption of leather in harnesses, horse collars, and other vital equipment, by the carting trades for much the same materials, by the military for boots and harnesses, and by a wide variety of other users. Personal consumption of leather in the forms of shoes, boots, belts, gloves, purses, and clothing rose at least in proportion to the population, and perhaps a good deal faster as affluence encouraged decorative uses and permitted the acquisition of spare sets of items that had formerly been semiluxuries. Demographic growth and especially the concentration of population in London also affected the supply of leather and hides. Meat consumption in London yielded hides as a byproduct, since animals were driven to market on the hoof. One may note in passing that the availability of large quantities of animal fats aided the soap boilers by providing them with a steady source of raw material, and that this in turn may have raised the hygienic standards of the city and, by reducing disease, have reinforced demographic growth. In any case, the massing of population in London doubly favored the leather industry by simultaneously extending the market for leather goods and generating a ready source of hides for processing.

Leather making in the sixteenth century utilized two separate technologies to produce two essentially distinct types of leather.[31] Oil-dressing and tawing were short processes in which the skins prepared by smoking to remove the hair and then dressed with oil or certain chemicals, including alum, until they were clean and supple. Tanning, on the other hand, was an extended process, used to prepare heavy leather; it took many months and entailed considerable skill. Hides were first treated with a solution of lime to loosen the hair, scraped, soaked in dung, and finally placed in tanning pits for a period extending from six months to two years. The strength of the oak bark solution in which the hides were soaked was of critical importance, as was the duration of the immersion period. The wet hides required periodic turning and considerable skill was necessary at this stage to avoid damaging the soft and vulnerable skins. Once dried, the hides were sold to curriers, who replaced the oil lost in tanning and rendered the leather supple again.

The industry was clearly one that benefited from economies of scale. Because the tanning process was lengthy and required highly skilled workers, leather making was a prototype of the sort of industry in which rising output allowed the more efficient use of expensive labor. One man could supervise numerous tanning pits and the number of hides per pit was upwardly flexible; as scale increased, labor costs per hide diminished and profits grew. Meat consumption in London assured an adequate supply of hides at the same time as the city's shoemakers – nearly three thousand of them by the early seventeenth century – guaranteed a ready market for the finished product.[32] These factors, rather than lagging rents or wages, were responsible for the high profitability of leather making, especially since the major investment was in inventory in process. Economies of scale reduced labor costs, but proximity to London held down inventory costs and permitted rapid sale of the completed product. Together these influences furthered the accumulation of capital and fostered healthy growth.

Eastern Europe

There are two reasons for the foregoing emphasis on English industry and our discussion of several industries in detail. On the one hand, we have pursued the Hamiltonian thesis of profit inflation as an analytical theme, and have sought to test and ultimately to reject it on the basis of the English evidence from which it arose. On the other, the history of English industry during the sixteenth century is the history of success and provides a basis for contrast with countries that achieved less. From the position of a relatively backward nation – technologically retarded by comparison with Italy, Germany, or the Low Countries – England developed into the most sophisticated industrial state in the early modern world. Although Holland grew richer than England, its wealth was drawn from international commerce, finance, and intensive agriculture; manufactures, though important – especially in the seventeenth century – played a relatively minor role in the generation of its overall wealth. Shipbuilding became a major industry as the United Provinces came to dominate world trade, but it was commerce that supported the industry and earned foreign balances even though some ships were sold abroad. In most other regions of Europe, the contrast between Continental stagnation and England's industrial growth is even more striking.

In eastern Europe, for example, we have already noted the nobles' use of their relatively unbridled power to drive artisans, small traders, and urban dwellers back to the land. Forced specialization in the production of food for export naturally afflicted industry in a variety of ways. Most directly, of course, artisans who were compelled to become farm laborers could no longer contribute to the production of manufactured goods, but, indirectly, the redistribution of income implicit in reenserfment constricted demand for domestically produced manufactures and simultaneously worked to increase demand for luxury imports. Laws that prohibited Polish merchants from exporting Polish goods and restrictive legislation that set prices below the levels needed to recover costs exacerbated the effects of the contraction in demand already caused by the redistribution and concentration of income.[33] The conscious assault pressed by the nobles against town and village economies precluded the development of such economies of scale and of such industry-fostering interactions between growing urban communities and expanding industries as occurred in the vicinity of London. Similarly, the destruction of a goodly portion of the class of small domestic merchants virtually eliminated the possibility of productivity gains from the employment of more roundabout methods of manufacture.

This is not to say that Poland utterly failed to develop industries; some of the very factors that prevented balanced and integrated growth favored the founding or expansion of certain crafts. Heightened disparities in the distribution of income permitted those crafts that catered to the thin luxury market to thrive; the building crafts, the goldsmiths, and a few other low-volume industries flourished.[34] For a time, the domestic iron industry expanded as the demand for farm tools swelled in response to the reenserfment of the peasants, but, ultimately, reenserfment was directed against the industry itself. In the late sixteenth century, the iron makers were driven back to the land while the nobles seized the furnaces, ran them with corvée labor, and directed the output toward armaments rather than tools. The industry virtually collapsed in the seventeenth century. The bleak record was partially brightened by the origination and survival of an indigenous paper industry, but the general pattern traced by Polish manufacturing during the sixteenth century was that of a downward spiral. The ebullience and energy so apparent in England was not to be found in central European industry. The absence was largely the result of the calculated specialization in grain production, imposed by the nobles and the powerful for their own self-interest and in response to the market conditions created by the worldwide surge in population.

Spain

Elsewhere in Europe, the causes of the failure to match England's performance were more complex than those that retarded growth east of the Elbe. Spain would at first glance appear to have possessed all the economic stimuli necessary for industrial growth. The flood of gold and silver from the New World came first to Spain, Spanish population growth was swift, and, as a result, consumers were not only more numerous, but they were affluent as well. The monarchy did not consciously seek to repress industry, but rather seems to have attempted to encourage its growth. Even so, Spain failed to generate a successful industrial sector. What was her potential and why did she fail?

At the beginning of the sixteenth century, Spain seemed ready to expand its industrial production. The Castilian textile industry, centered in the north at Segovia, Toledo, and Cuenca and in the south at Cordoba, benefited from ample, indeed overwhelming, demand and from the easy accessibility of supplies of raw wool.[35] In Catalonia, cloth production recovered sharply from its depressed fifteenth-century levels as the full power of the Spanish monarchy was employed to guarantee a Catalonian sales monopoly in Sardinia, Sicily, and Naples.[36] Iron was manufactured in sufficient quantity to sustain an export industry in Vizcaya in the far north, and once the reconquest was completed in the south, the silk industry of Granada prospered for a time. Lesser industries produced luxury leather goods and fine weapons.

The royal effort to assure Italian markets for Catalonian cloth serves to document the Spanish monarchy's interest in fostering industry; it is well to keep this fact in mind, however, since many of the royal attempts along this line seem misguided, if not consciously counterproductive. Under Ferdinand and Isabella, for example, the Ordinances of Seville were promulgated; these were 119 laws designed to unify the textile industry of Castile, to preserve a common standard of quality, and to do so by imposing at the state level in Castile the system of internal self-regulation that had developed in the Catalonian–Aragonese portion of the kingdom.[37] In its Castilian manifestation, however, the system was tempered neither by the constitutionalism of Aragon nor by established tradition. The prime effects of the ordinances were to freeze the organizational structure of the Castilian cloth industry at the development level that it had reached in the late fifteenth century and to prevent innovation. The dynamic organizational changes and increasingly roundabout methods of production that did so much to forward prosperity in England's textile industry were, in effect, illegal in Spain. In the same vein, the royal decision to maintain separate economic regions within the Iberian peninsula restricted the stimulation that might have arisen from economies of scale. Partly in order to prevent the export of Catalonian and Aragonese constitutionalism to that unspoiled region, the trade of the New World was reserved to Castile, and though the protected Castilian cloth industry flourished briefly as a monopoly, it failed to become competitive in European markets. Weakness became painfully obvious when, in 1548, the crown, ambivalent between the conflicting interests of consumers and producers, temporarily permitted the entry of foreign cloth and prohibited the export of the domestic product, save to America. Although the export ban was quickly rescinded, Spain lost its traditional and protected markets, and by the latter part of the sixteenth century, its cloth industry was rapidly approaching bankruptcy.[38]

The very power and apparent invincibility of the Spanish imperial crown contributed to a worsening of the economic substructure of Spain in at least two ways. On the one hand, illusions of indomitability nurtured the impossible dream of reversing the progress of history and of eliminating heresy through counterreformation. The effort was as futile as it was expensive, but taxes are rarely proportional to accomplishment. We have already noted Dutch resistance to Alva's imposition of the *alcabala*, or sales tax, levied at each intermediate stage of production or marketing, and observed that such a tax was devastating to a developed commercial country; yet this was the main source of Castilian revenue in the fifteenth century. Happily for the early progress of Spain's economy, the *alcabala* had been effectively compounded into single lump payments by the beginning of the sixteenth century so its impact on commercial development and the use of roundabout methods of production was minimized. This beneficial change was not, however, achieved without further cost.[39] Rising, indeed limitless, expenses combined with the creation of an upper bound on receipts from the *alcabala* to force the crown to seek additional revenues elsewhere and to institute the *servicios*. Nobles were exempt from these subsidies to the crown, and, as a result, the tax fell most heavily on the economically productive classes and on the southern portion of Castile where there were fewer *hidalgos*, or knights. Distortions in the incidence of the tax were worsened as the receipts proved inadequate. Massive loans were required to support imperial delusions, and even when the loans were sound they absorbed and misallocated capital; when, as in 1557, 1575, and 1596, the crown defaulted, such loans destroyed capital.

Periodic government default and the overall nature of the tax structure were factors that affected Spain's industrial establishment in its entirety, but there were also specific discriminatory taxes and arbitrary laws that brought harm exclusively to certain industries. The silk industry, for example, was one of the truly prosperous enterprises native to the Iberian Peninsula, and one that was ideally suited to capitalize on the conditions created by the increasing inequality in the distribution of real income in early modern Europe. During the first half of the sixteenth century, the production of silk fabrics rose sharply; a flourishing export trade developed, and Spanish silk graced the rich and elegant consumers of Italy and the Mediterranean. Unfortunately, the industry was located in southern Spain at Granada and to some extent in Toledo and Valencia – regions recently within the Moslem tradition. Partly because of this perhaps, but more likely because such action was prevalent throughout Europe as a device for controlling international payments, Ferdinand and Isabella, in 1494, promulgated a set of sumptuary laws limiting the domestic use of silk; the laws were reissued and strengthened in 1534 and 1586.[40] So long as the export market remained rich, little damage was done, but during the 1550s, when the Inquisition was becoming ever more active and was supporting itself through massive confiscations of the property of both Jews and Moriscos, an export ban was imposed on silk fabrics.[41] It remains unclear whether the silk export ban was specifically directed against the Morisco population or whether it simply paralleled the cotemporal ban against the export of woolen cloth, but the draconian increase in the taxes levied on the silk industry of Granada after 1561 constitutes circumstantial evidence that the former motive was significant.[42] In any event, the constriction of the domestic silk market through sumptuary legislation and of the foreign markets through export controls combined with the increased demands for taxes to end the prosperity of the silk industry by the end of the century and to reduce it to the same sad state that had befallen the woolen industry.

Much of the literature concerned with the economic history of Spain during the sixteenth century seeks to find evidence of economic growth. This was, after all, Spain's age of gold, and historians, like others, are reluctant to discover that they have been deceived and that what they took to be gold was merely brass. The evidence, however, is in fact mixed; both the silk and the cloth industries, for example, enjoyed an early upsurge that aborted and turned to decay before the century was over. Prosperity appears to have varied with geography as well as with time and this further compounds the difficulty of forming straightforward judgments. The only Spanish city whose rate of urban growth approximates the rates of Amsterdam (3.19) and London (2.82) during the sixteenth century is Zamora, a city in northwest Castile far from the southern centers of the bullion trade, which registers an urbanization index level of 2.43.[43] The index level is high enough to suggest that at least some of the favorable impact rapid urbanization produced elsewhere might be found in Zamora, and, indeed, there is considerable evidence of interaction among industries and, though weaker, between demography and growth. From the fifteenth century forward, the town was a marketing center for the wines produced in the Duero valley between Valladolid and Zamora itself.[44] Zamora's natural geographical advantage, derived from its location on the Duero River, an important east–west waterway, was supplemented by the artificial advantage of its position on one of the three main *cañadas*, or sheep routes. The Zamora *cañada* ran from Leon, through Zamora, and south to Toledo. Because one of the principal deterrents to economic growth in Spain was the utter inadequacy of inland transportation, location on the *cañada* was of critical significance. Where villages, towns, and regions were isolated from each other, little positive economic interaction could occur, but when as was the case in Zamora, the sheep route coincided with a favorable distribution of natural resources and commodities, carters were able to follow profitably the paths of the migratory herds. Cloth, produced at Zamora and collected from other towns in the Duero valley, and the abundant harvests of wine from the region made the city a natural marketing center; as the carters descended toward the Atlantic coast, they could add the iron of Vitoria to their cargoes.[45] On the return trip, they carried to the interior the salt that was produced by evaporation along the warm, clean shores of the Bay of Biscay.

The interrelated commerce in cloth, wine, migratory sheep, iron, salt, and such other commodities as moved inland from the northern coast of Spain was sufficient to sustain Zamora and to make it a city of major commercial importance during the sixteenth century. After Salamanca and Toledo, both incidentally affected by the Zamora *cañada*, Zamora was, at the end of the sixteenth century, the third largest city in Castile and the one whose rate of demographic growth had been most rapid.[46] Unfortunately for Castile, the combination of the *reconquista*, completed in 1492, and of the influx of bullion through southern Spain made it seem for a time as though the destiny of the country lay to the south. During the sixteenth century, a persistent internal migration occurred as the inhabitants of the north sought their fortunes in the regions below the Tagus River and particularly along the banks of the Guadalquivir, where agriculture prospered by catering to the demands of newly enriched Seville.[47] Affluence temporarily favored the southern region, but it was built on bullion flows from exhaustible mines rather than on real and enduring economic foundations. By transferring people from the north, migration hindered economic growth in that region and constricted the economic interaction and economies of scale that might otherwise have benefited the most promising area of Spain. In so doing, it appears to have contributed to the impoverishment of the country when the mines ceased to produce and when the absence of firm economic foundations became manifest.

France

If Spain's economic performance during the sixteenth century ultimately proved to be a disappointment, the most obvious alternative candidate for the role of competitor with England ought to have been France. The latter country was, in many ways, the most richly endowed in Europe, as its mercantilist pamphleteers incessantly reminded their readers, and it shared some of the structural advantages that spurred English growth. France's population was perhaps six times as great as that of England during much of the sixteenth century, and, in Paris, it had a capital city far larger than London at the beginning of the century and still comparable in the closing decades. A rich agricultural land, served by splended inland rivers and waterways and blessed with numerous fine harbors on both the Atlantic and Mediterranean coasts, France possessed all the physical attributes necessary for leadership in the sixteenth-century quest for economic growth.

Progress was indeed forthcoming. The great expansion in Europe's naval resources that resulted from the rapid development of the Atlantic economy and from the exploitation of the African coast and the Far East sharply enhanced the demand for sailcloth. At the same time, climatic conditions in the tropical New World, in the Atlantic islands, and in Asia favored the utilization of lightweight fabrics for dress. The linen industry of Normandy flourished in response to these demands and Rouen became a center for the world export of sailcloth and other linen fabrics.[48] The canvas industry of Brittany benefited equally, and by the seventeenth century, it produced nearly four-fifths of the sails that powered English ships.[49]

The region of most aggressive French growth in the sixteenth century was not in the north, however, nor even in Paris; it lay further to the south and east, in Forez and the area surrounding Lyons. Like contemporary London, the latter city welcomed immigrants and enjoyed a rate of demographic increase that, at least during the first six decades of the century, far outstripped the level attained by the rest of the country. In the period from 1470 to 1520, the population of Lyons rose from around twenty thousand to a figure between sixty and eighty thousand; in subsequent years, immigration accounted for half of the increase and nearly one-fifth of the immigrants were foreign nationals rather than Frenchmen from the countryside and neighboring towns.[50]

The initial stimulus for the growth of Lyons – beyond the obvious benefits that arose from the retreat of the plague and the end of the Hundred Years' War – came from Louis XI's efforts to develop the city as an international fair and thus to ruin the Geneva fairs and to restore French prosperity. By denying Frenchmen access to Geneva by royal edict and by granting important privileges to Lyons, Louis was successful in channeling commerce through his pet city. With international trade came the bankers to finance it; the most important were the Bonvisi from Lucca, but there were forty other banking houses by 1575 and the city served as a truly international center of finance.[51] Neither banking nor international commerce are properly industries, but their presence appears to have provided the climate in which industry could flourish. The printing industry began in Lyons when the first press was installed in 1473, and by mid-century, there were over one hundred presses at work in the city.[52] Silk manufacture, which had been founded by Louis XI in 1466 at Tours and carefully nurtured thereafter, was introduced in Lyons in 1536. Initially the industry was mainly engaged in working up silk thread imported from Italy and the Po valley, but by the end of the century, Italy's monopolistic control of the secret of the mechanical silk mill had been broken, perhaps as a result of the French invasions of Italy, and French silk mills spread through the Rhone valley.[53] The Forez district, immediately to the west of Lyons, was rich in timber, iron, and coal, although the latter did not attain much significance in sixteenth-century French industry. The abundance of firewood, however, sustained an important group of heat-intensive industries in the region and St. Etienne became a center for iron goods, tools, and especially arms. Indeed, there is some evidence that, under the stimulus of military demand for artillery, the number of ironworks in France as a whole rose from about 50 in 1500 to some 450 by mid-century.[54] Firewood resources in the Forez also provided the basis for a fairly active glass manufacture, although this remained a peripheral forest product industry during our period.

Other areas of France also experienced growth and recovery during the sixteenth century. Languedoc was an active producer of cloth, particularly inexpensive cloth that found a ready market as the population of southern Europe and the Mediterranean expanded. Paris, like Lyons, was a major center of the French printing industry, and, in addition, a prime factor in the manufacture of luxury goods. Indirectly supported by court consumption and directly aided by royal subsidy, privilege, and efforts to entice skilled artisans from the entire European world, the luxury manufactures of Paris became world renowned. Under the last Valois kings but especially during the reign of the first Bourbon, Henry IV, Paris attracted numerous highly skilled luxury workers whose output was more artistic than commercial. The latter monarch made the Louvre into a veritable workshop for painters, sculptors, clockmakers, goldsmiths, and engravers.[55] Even so, Lyons and the Forez region constituted the most active industrial area of

France during much of the sixteenth century. It was there that one might have expected to find the kind of interaction among industries and increasing roundaboutness of production that we have already noted as a prime component of England's – more specifically, London's – swift economic growth. Rapid population growth, an influx of immigrants, a number of important industries with broad markets were all present in Lyons and suggest a parallel with the experience enjoyed by London and southwest England, but unfortunately for France, the interactions did not occur and growth failed to become self-sustaining.

To some extent this failure was simply the result of bad luck and historical accident as, for example, the plague of 1564, which carried off nearly a third of the population of Lyons and ended the interval of demographic increase.[56] Another external and at least as damaging destructive force was religious war. France had barely set aside her ambitions for military dominance in Italy by accepting the terms of the Treaty of Cateau-Cambrésis when bloody civil war erupted between Catholic and Huguenot factions. In 1562, Duke Francis of Guise discovered a group of Protestants at worship in Vassy and led an assault on their church; 30 Protestants were killed and perhaps another 120 wounded. The massacre led to war throughout France as Protestant armed against Catholic, and peace did not return until Henry IV issued the Edict of Nantes in 1598. Shortly after Vassy, Lyons fell to the Protestant forces serving under Condé. Even though the Protestant troops appear to have been well disciplined during the early years of civil war, some disruption of commerce was inevitable, and, in any case, discipline soon succumbed to the temptations of pillage. Lyons' troubles continued. In 1572, when the Guise forces dominated the weak Charles IX, they engineered the St. Bartholomew's Day Massacre. Thousands of Huguenots were slaughtered in Paris and the disaster spread almost simultaneously to Troyes, Rouen, Lyons, and much of the countryside. We have already noted the advantages that England drew from the skilled artisans who fled France at this time and sought political security in the vicinity of London, but it is perhaps worth repeating here that England's gain was France's loss. Although it cannot be estimated, further damage to French industrial development undoubtedly resulted from French inability to attract skilled immigrants with essential industrial skills during a period of intense turbulence. If epidemic disease, massacre, and war were not in themselves sufficient to frustrate economic growth, the taxes necessary to finance war constituted a further negative element. Tolls proliferated on the Rhone; in 1581, duties were imposed on all goods entering the kingdom; and in 1590, a tax of two écus per bail was levied on all goods leaving Lyons; the tax was doubled in the following year.[57]

The religious wars obviously limited the power of the crown and temporarily aborted the further growth of economic absolutism; France could not immediately follow the disastrous economic policies that were being implemented across the border in Spain. This was not for lack of desire, however, and civil war in the long run enhanced state domination of economic activity. By its very nature, civil war represented a breakdown in the legal structure; its essence was the commission of violent acts by one group of citizens against another and such acts in and of themselves withdraw from their perpetrators any further claim to ordinary protection under the civil law. Once a town, for example, has denied the monarch's authority through rebellion, it can no longer seek his protection on the same terms as it enjoyed before the revolt. The force of custom and the validity of prior grants of immunity and liberty are undermined, and when civil order is restored it will inevitably be established under new terms, set by the victor and dependent on his will under the rules of conquest rather than those of past law or custom. To the same end, the very dislocations of civil war – migration, swift change, lack of stability – lessened the credibility of appeals to immemorial custom and thus reduced the power of law to act as a conservative and constraining force over the monarch.

At the same time as the legal order appeared to be crumbling in sixteenth-century France, the need for order and stability became ever more pressing. Men wearied of personal insecurity, massacre, and lawlessness and they became willing to seek peace at any cost. It soon became apparent that the only hope for an end to the time of terrors lay in supporting a strong monarch. It was the desire of the growing party of the *politiques* to do just that and to assert the necessity for stability and royal strength over the claims of religious faction. Difficulties arose, however, when thoughtful men sought to exalt royal authority without limiting personel liberty. How could one simultaneously strengthen and constrain the king? When confronted with the choice, theorists of the *politique* party generally opted for royal strength and hoped for a benign monarch. Jean Bodin was a *politique* and his inconsistent writings reflect the temper of his age; as a civil lawyer committed to the integrity of contract and of private property, he yet maintained that the prince was absolute, not bound by his own laws, and empowered with the right to unlimited taxation if it was justified by necessity as defined by the prince. In Bodin's eyes, the proper role of the corporations of France was to act as tools of the monarch, and their proper posture was kneeling before the king.[58] Political disruption, weariness with war, and political theories more assertive of royal power coalesced in the late sixteenth century and served to increase royal control over economic endeavor.

The first steps had been taken as far back as the early fourteenth century, but the reign of Louis XI (1461–83) witnessed a major increase in effective government involvement with industry. Scores of guild charters were issued during the reign, and with the charters came the power to control, to appoint officials, and to set regulatory standards of quality. Equally came the power to extract fees for registration and for granting exceptions from guild rules. As the economic recovery from the Hundred Years' War broadened, royal influence over guild affairs continued to expand, and it was employed to support and nurture some industries through privilege and subsidy, on the one hand, and to sustain an ever more voracious royal treasury, on the other. The degree to which the one policy dominated the other may perhaps be measured by the remarkable relative success of Lyons in attaining economic leadership in France. Until the end of the sixteenth century, that city preserved its freedom from guild restrictions and to a great extent from royal regulation that had initially been granted to it by Louis XI during his campaign against the Geneva fairs.

In any event, the royal impact on industrial development was only temporarily diminished by the Wars of Religion, and when peace returned, all the old regulations were still in place and the old policies were enforced by a far stronger monarchy. The voices of opposition were muted as a result of the preceding civil turbulence, and while the vocabulary of royal control had waxed through the efforts of such absolutist political theorists as Bodin, the vocabulary of opposition and constraint waned with the loss of prestige suffered by the old legal abstractions and by customary law. It is against this background that we must view the two major pieces of industrial legislation of late sixteenth-century France.

In 1581, Henry III, in an edict prefaced by the formulaic obeisance to his role as the good father of his family seeking justice and fairness for all, ordered all the artisans of France to group themselves into regulated guilds.[59] Parisian masters were permitted to practice their skills throughout France, whereas all others were limited to their own districts, save those from Lyons. The importance of the latter city justified an exception allowing Lyonaise masters to practice everywhere but Paris. Fees and the methods of payment were established in additional clauses of the edict. In 1581, the monarchy was still too weak to enforce such a sweeping piece of industrial regulation, but by 1597, when Henry IV reenacted and strengthened the same laws, the crown was in a position to impose its authority with vigor.

The deleterious consequences for French industrial progress were pervasive.[60] The industrial regulations had multiple intent: to preserve quality; to raise money for the royal fisc; to compete in international markets; to avoid importing luxuries that required the export of precious metals; and to foster an armaments industry so the country would be independent in time of war. In practice, luxury production was subsidized and the profits of strong and expanding industries were diverted to uphold the weak; capital accumulation was thus retarded and the growth of truly vital industries slowed. As state-ordained monopolies grew, so did the fees charged by the state; fiscal motives led government to develop a system in which the profits of artificial monopolies became a regular source of royal revenues. Under the guise of protecting quality, especially in the seventeenth century, inspection fees became an ever-increasing burden and sales of the titles of inspector were guided by the needs of a voracious treasury. Even before this stage, however, efforts to control quality exerted a negative influence on the economy. Quality was usually measured against the state of the art at the time regulations were introduced. Thus, a survey of a given industry would be made, proper standards and methods of production would be determined, and then the findings would be formally transcribed and immortalized in government regulations. By so doing, the French government, in effect, legislated the opportunity for product improvement out of existence and made certain that the advan-

tages of those increasingly roundabout methods of production that had
proved so effective in England could not occur in France.

Italy

Although it is dangerous to refer to Italy as a unit during this period,
and although it is necessary to temper even the most cautious general-
izations by noting the exception of Venice, political history linked the
economic fortunes of France and Italy in an inverse relationship during
the sixteenth century. In general, however, it is fair to claim that while
the French enjoyed a reasonable measure of domestic prosperity during the first half of the century, they caused widespread destruction
and catastrophe in Italy, which they invaded in 1494. Dislocation and
sporadic warfare persisted until 1559, when the French abandoned
their Italian dreams and withdrew under the terms of the treaty of
Cateau-Cambrésis. At that point, Italian fortunes recovered while
France itself sank into the morass of religious war.

During the first half of the century, the French invasions initiated
an international conflict, entangling both Spain and the Empire and
devastating much of northern Italy. Industrial centers such as Como,
Brescia, Bologna, and Milan were ruined; the population of Pavia fell
from sixteen thousand inhabitants to less than seven thousand over the
first three decades of the century.[61] Production fell even faster than
population; in Florence, population fell by one-sixth, but the number
of woolshops decreased by three-fourths between 1500 and 1540.[62]
Not all of the population decline may be attributed to the apocalyptic
events of war, famine, and plague, however. Many men simply fled to
more secure areas of the country. One such region was Venice, which
remained free from invasions, and perhaps even more importantly,
remained relatively well supplied with provisions and raw materials
as a result of its powerful navy and extensive colonies.

As a curious consequence, Venetian industry prospered during
Italy's darkest period.[63] Traditionally, however, the wealth of Venice
had been drawn from the sea and from long-distance commerce; thus,
it is well to bear in mind that much of its industrial endeavor was
undertaken to compensate for the loss of trade caused by Turkish expansion in the eastern Mediterranean and by the discovery of alternate
routes to the spices and exotic commodities of the East. In any event,
as shown in Graph 2, the production of woolen cloth soared from

small beginnings to something more than twenty thousand cloths annually during the course of the century. Growth in the silk industry paralleled that of wool; between 1493 and 1554, the number of silk weavers in Venice climbed from five to twelve hundred. Glassmaking and the subsidiary art of mirror manufacturing at Murano attained perhaps their highest reputation and relative share of world markets during the first three-quarters of the century. A number of lesser industries – soap making, lace, leather working, candle manufacture, and jewelry production – complemented the earnings from larger industries. Printing in Venice developed so rapidly as to make it one of Europe's major book-producing cities, along with Paris, Lyons, and Antwerp, where the Plantin–Moretus establishment, with its sixteen presses, was possibly the largest printing house of the era.[64]

The most remarkable industrial enterprise in Venice was the Arsenal – the navy yard charged with the responsibility of maintaining the naval supremacy of the republic.[65] With the expansion of the Ottoman Empire, and after the early fifteenth century, the concomitant danger of naval attack, the Arsenal doubled in size; at its peak, it occupied more than 60 acres and employed as many as three thousand men. Iron foundries and rope walks within the walls supplied the ancillary material of shipbuilding and an ample lumberyard provided seasoned and selected varieties of timber. Because the Arsenal was required to maintain a reserve fleet – more than one hundred galleys after 1540 – it was necessary to experiment with standardization of parts, both in production and in subsequent assembly. Reserves of masts, spars, oarsmen's benches, and weapons were stored separately and could be used interchangeably from ship to ship.

For a time, Venice was the greatest industrial center in Italy, but its prosperity proved fragile. Since her success was, at least in part, attributable to the misfortune of the rest of northern Italy, the termination of the French involvement in that region reduced her relative advantage. The late sixteenth century witnessed a resurgence of industrial growth in the cities that had suffered most at the hands of the French, and woolen cloth output expanded rapidly and in competition with Venice. Bergamo's output more than tripled from 7,000 or 8,000 cloths annually in 1540 to 26,500 in 1596; Florentine output grew from 14,700 cloths in 1553 to 30,000 in 1560.[66] One may note in passing that this "Indian summer" of Italian industry probably did not recapture past prosperity; Florentine production had exceeded 70,000 cloths in the early fourteenth century. By the late sixteenth century, others had mastered such skills as mechanical silk making, and northern Italy could no longer claim its former dominance in luxury manufactures. Despite competition, Venetian production continued to expand, but, as may be seen on Graph 2, at a lesser rate as competitors returned to the market and as immigration to that city became less attractive. The fragility of Venice's ascendance was further emphasized in 1575–7, when plague struck and carried off perhaps a third of the population – a disaster that led to an additional reduction in the rate of growth of the woolen industry. The potential for economic interaction associated with urban growth was at least temporarily undermined by disease, and although population recovery was fairly rapid toward the end of the century, Venice did not enjoy the almost uninterrupted expansion that made London such a dynamic stimulant for England's manufacturing sector. Resources of another, but equally crucial, type also became scarce; the magnificent effort mounted against the Turkish challenge at sea assured the Venetian victory at Lepanto in 1571, but it accentuated the timber shortage that had plagued the city of St. Mark since the fifteenth century. In defeating the Turkish navy, Venice and its allies opened the Mediterranean to others, especially northerners, who had greater access to abundant naval stores and who were capable of building larger, more efficient ships more cheaply. Increased foreign competition diminished Venice's maritime commerce; the temporary resurgence of the Mediterranean spice trade leveled off after 1590, and by the first decades of the seventeenth century, both commerce and manufacturing fell into a state of decline. This trend was only reinforced by increasingly restrictive guild practices and by a commitment to protectionism that prevented Venetian merchants from adapting to changing patterns of international trade.

Germany

We have already considered central Europe's early, dominant role in metal production, but it is worth noting here that between 1460 and about 1540 that region and Germany in particular were the leaders in heavy capital investment and in the application of new techniques and large, albeit by our standards primitive, engines. Ore crushers, trip-hammers, winches, and elaborate water-raising devices formed the core of an industrial complex with worldwide ramifications. More modest in scale and, as an unfortunate result, of less interest to many economic historians was Germany's role in the textile industry of Europe. The Hanseatic cities of the north generally drew their wealth from trade rather than industry, but in so doing, they supplemented the native supplies of flax and carried substantial quantities of that commodity from Poland through the port of Danzig. Such materials, normally fabricated into cloth in southern Germany, became the basis for a profitable export industry; in a good year during the first half of the sixteenth century, Munich alone might produce as many as six thousand linen cloths and export the greater part of them to Venice.[67] Production of linens was carried on in a number of other towns as well, several of which could boast as many as two hundred weavers during the middle years of the century. Perhaps even more important than linen in the Bavarian region of south Germany was the manufacture of cheap, coarse woolens or lodencloths; between 1500 and 1620, the number of Munich masters of this trade rose from 70 to 114 and collectively they employed more than three thousand souls throughout the countryside to workup the material.[68] In contrast to the vigorous growth of the coarse woolen industry, one must note the almost total demise of Bavaria's production of fine cloth; the latter succumbed to pressures from foreign competition, from the higher quality of imported cloth, and ultimately to the disasters caused by the Thirty Years' War. In Augsburg, the center of the Fugger enterprises and of the central European metal trade, and to a much greater extent in Cologne, a silk-weaving industry developed, drawing its raw materials from Italy and the Levant.[69] Also dependent on imported materials was the fustian industry of Ulm and much of the rest of southern Germany; cotton for this cloth, a mixture of cotton and linen, was largely imported from Sicily.

Bavarian forests supported several heat-using industries. Salt evaporation produced a valuable export good since the salt itself was the essential preservative for the fishing industry. Wood, both in the form of charcoal and of potash, was plentiful enough to sustain a fairly active glass manufacture; cheap glass beads were shipped to Venice in substantial quantities for the production of rosaries.[70] More importantly, increased agricultural prosperity in the late sixteenth century contributed to greater demand for window glass and the output of Bavarian furnaces found its way to Nürnberg, Leipzig, and Stuttgart. Luxury glass was for the time beyond the capacity of the region, but proto-mercantilist efforts were made during the latter part of the century to attract highly skilled artisans from Belgium and Venice in order to domesticate the art and to avert foreign exchange losses.

Despite considerable natural resources and some promising achievements, however, Germany remained essentially an agrarian land. Political instability arising from the Reformation and Counter-Reformation limited economic growth by subjecting the country to revolution and war for much of the sixteenth century, and even when a certain degree of calm was restored by the Peace of Augsburg in 1555, the consequences were not entirely positive. The famous formula *cuius regio, eius religio* permitted the local rulers to determine the religion of their districts, but since there were a great number of small principalities, the effect was to institutionalize and render permanent the political fragmentation of Germany and thereby to limit potential regional economic support for urban centers. German cities remained small – Augsburg and Nürnberg began the century with only some 20,000 inhabitants, and Munich only expanded from 13,400 dwellers in the early century to about 22,000 a hundred years later.[71] The cities appear to have retained a provincial and defensive posture, suspicious both of innovation and of immigration. Even Cologne, which had been one of the most important medieval cities, declined both in economic and demographic significance over the course of the period. No single German city attained the economic role held by London, Amsterdam, or even Lyons; thus urbanization could not act to stimulate industry or to enhance productivity through increased roundaboutness in the manufacturing process. When mining in Germany and throughout central Europe began to lose its vigor after 1530, the economy lost its most dynamic sector, and, with the limited exception of silk weaving, reverted in the main to the production of inexpensive goods, manufactured on a small scale by producers dispersed throughout the countryside. As the greatness of the Fugger faded, so too did the importance of Germany in the world economy, but before that occurred, as we will observe in the discussion of international trade, German silver funded world commerce and German copper, both raw and manufactured, had considerable impact in world markets and particularly in Africa.

5
Trade patterns in the wider world

During the course of the fifteenth century, the geographical limits that had contained the European economy for centuries were finally and irreparably shattered, and, as a result, there arose what one recent historian has chosen to call the "European world-economy."[1] The change was not simply a new awareness of the broader dimensions of the earth; medieval men had already colonized Iceland, touched America, traveled to China, and made some progress in the economic exploitation of the Atlantic islands, especially the Canaries. It was rather a new permanence, a regularization of contacts, and the development of a technology capable of sustaining wider geographical and economic probes. Ship design improved rapidly; building on ideas long available but ultimately original in combination, shipwrights produced vessels capable of withstanding the vagaries of the Atlantic weather patterns and of covering the vast distances between continents. The initial challenge of substituting sails for manpower and oars had been overcome in the fourteenth century, and marine technology developed further during the fifteenth, when the single-masted, square-rigged ship was brought to a high degree of sophistication. Crew size contracted sharply while cargo space rose concomitantly; geographical range was enhanced by the increased capacity to carry food supplies for smaller crews at the same time as the economic potential of such vessels rose with the expansion of available cargo space. By the late fifteenth century, additional improvements in rigging and hull design had been mastered. Ships grew longer in relation to their beams, and longer, thinner ships proved more suitable for ocean sailing. The square rig of the north was combined with the lateen rig of the south and of the Mediterranean to capitalize on the advantages offered by each. With two masts – the foremast square-rigged and the mizzen lateen-rigged – the pointing ability of the lateen sail could supplement the effectiveness of the square sail for sailing before the wind. Further, since by the end of the fifteenth century, ships employed several square sails per mast, such rigging permitted easy and swift reduction of the sail area when the winds were full and the seas heavy. Such ships and subsequent improved versions proved ideal for the conquest of the Atlantic, and when mounted with cannon during the fifteenth century and, from the beginning of the sixteenth century, with cannon on the lower decks firing through gun ports, they were well suited for that curious blend of piracy and commerce that formed the essence of sixteenth-century international trade.[2]

The Portuguese adventure

The initial steps were taken by Portugal, which began its inexorable march along the West African coast after capturing Ceuta in 1415.[3] By 1434, Cape Bojador had been reached; by 1448, a permanent warehouse had been established at Arguim. A temporary setback occurred in 1471, when Fernando Po, sailing eastward in the expectation of rounding Africa, discovered that the coast shifted from its east–west orientation and followed a due south course for hundreds of miles. The island named Fernando Po commemorates the location of its discoverer's disappointment, but despite this a second Portuguese establishment, founded to the west at Elmina in 1482, proved to be a highly successful commercial colony. This warehouse-fortress, while west of the furthest exploratory advance, became the center of an active trade in slaves, ivory, gold, and a coarse variety of West African pepper, which, though inferior to that brought overland from the Malabar coast of India, did much to disrupt the Italian spice monopoly and to upset pepper prices in western Europe. Gold exports from the region, although not massive – approximately 410 kilograms, or about 0.45 ton, annually from 1500 to 1521[4] – were rendered more significant by their appearance early in the century, before the full impact of central European and American precious metals had been felt in western Europe.

The initial stages of the Portuguese expansion in Africa were more closely comparable to conquest and raiding than to commerce, but regular trade soon superseded pillage and a regional economic system emerged. The Treaty of Alcáçovas, in 1479, gave Portugal a nominal monopoly of the African coast and of the Atlantic islands, with the exception of the Canaries, which remained Spanish; together with Hungary and southern Germany these possessions formed a trading region. The Atlantic islands were extremely fertile and well suited for the cultivation of sugar and sweet wines, commodities in high demand throughout Europe. Plantations were soon established in the islands, and with such agricultural exploitation there arose an ever-increasing need for cheap labor. The African coast was an obvious source of manpower, and with the encouragement of the Portuguese crown, which from 1433 extracted one-fifth of the value of all slaves captured or purchased, the slave trade expanded rapidly. Nearly 40 percent of the total export trade in slaves – some one hundred thousand souls – between 1450 and 1600 was directed to the plantations of the Atlantic islands and São Thomé.[5]

Slaves in such numbers could not simply be captured by loosely organized raiding parties, and so the Portuguese were compelled to seek out some commodity that could serve to balance this unfortunate commerce. Copper was the answer since it appears to have been even more highly valued than gold among the West African peoples. Throughout the fifteenth century, Portugal had been a purchaser of copper in Flanders, largely for use as a monetary metal, but with the heightened intensity of the slave trade such purchases became larger and more regular. The exploitation of the African coast coincided with the technological revolution in the central European mining industry and provided a ready market for the copper that was produced as a by-product of the amalgamation technique of extracting silver from argentiferous copper ore. The economies of Hungary and central Europe were thus closely linked to West Africa and the Atlantic islands via Portugal.

Spurred by the success of their African ventures, the Portuguese pressed on in their exploration of the southern coast. Bartholomew Dias rounded the Cape of Good Hope in 1487; a decade later, in 1497, Vasco da Gama set out with a fleet of four ships and fulfilled the centuries-old dream of finding the southern route to India. Da Gama returned, his ships laden with pepper and a variety of other spices, after some early difficulty in finding a cargo, and thus initiated the Portuguese domination of the Cape spice trade that was to endure until well into the seventeenth century. From the standpoint of European geography, Lisbon was a rather isolated outpost and remote from major trade routes. To some extent this was an advantage as it freed Portugal from excessive involvement in European wars and political entanglements, thereby granting her security and stability to pursue overseas exploration. From a commercial viewpoint, however, Lisbon was poorly located. Under the stimulus of the growing spice trade, Portugal consequently sought a more centrally situated European city as a base for handling the new trade; in 1499, Antwerp was chosen as the European entrepôt for the Eastern goods imported by the Portuguese.

The choice was not arbitrary. Bruges and Antwerp together had considerable economic contact with the south Germans and their copper supplies, but by the beginning of the sixteenth century, Bruges was declining as a trading center while Antwerp was drawing to herself the former prosperity of the older medieval city. With the spice trade and, as we will later observe, the English woolen trade, the city quickly rose to preeminence throughout Europe; between 1500 and 1550, Antwerp's population doubled, reaching nearly one hundred thousand by the latter date.[6] Let us return for the moment to the sugar–slave–copper economy of the African littoral and focus on the metal supply. Copper arrived in the West and in Lisbon by several routes; initially a good deal was exported by way of Venice, but as the century progressed, the river-born traffic to the north of Europe grew dominant. Table VII illustrates the importance of Antwerp as a copper market.

The figures in Table VII are admittedly only partial for they represent the output of but one firm. The Fuggers, however, were the greatest of the south German mining and banking families during the early sixteenth century, and because their business was such a large share of the total, their activities may reasonably be taken as representative of overall trends in copper trading. Note that the decline in the level of exports to Venice coincides with Portugal's selection of Antwerp as its permanent European entrepôt and its challenge to the traditional Mediterranean spice route. Portuguese demand for copper on the Antwerp market appears to have coopted the metal that might otherwise have been shipped to the East via the Levant. Actual figures for copper purchases by Lisbon are less certain than those shown in Table VII, but the Portuguese historian Magalhães-Godinho estimates that the average export from Antwerp to Lisbon in the period encompassing the

Table VII. *Hungarian copper exports by the Fugger (expressed in U.S. tons)*

Years	Total exports (annual average)	Exports to Antwerp via Danzig and Stettin		Exports to Venice and Trieste	
		Annual average	% of total	Annual average	% of total
1497–9	1532.7	7.3	0.48	492.5	31.12
1500–3	1532.7	370.6	24.18	492.5	32.12
1504–6	—	—	—	—	—
1507–9	1627.9	802.3	49.25	217.7	13.33
1510–12	2484.4	1363.0	54.80	78.1	3.14
1513–15	1392.7	870.7	62.50	58.8	4.22
1516–18	1497.3	755.2	50.43	5.2	.29
1519–25	1581.8	538.6	34.05	73.6	4.65
1526	985.1	476.8	48.40	29.4	3.00
1527–32	1281.1	742.6	61.00	68.3	5.60
1533–5	1041.0	503.3	48.35	159.6	15.33
1536–9	1331.4	653.9	49.12	165.9	12.46

Source: These figures are derived from H. Van der Wee, *The Growth of the Antwerp Market and the European Economy*, Louvain, Publications Universitaires, 1963, Appendix 44/1, pp. 522–23. Note: my figures differ from those in C. Cipolla, *Guns, Sails and Empires*, p. 26, since his appear to be expressed in long tons.

late fifteenth and the first half of the sixteenth centuries amounted to some 10,000 quintals or the equivalent of 647.6 U.S. tons annually.[7] Since the average Fugger exports to Antwerp each year between 1500 and 1539 amounted to 703.2 U.S. tons, this estimate would imply that 92.1 percent of the Fugger share of the copper brought to Antwerp eventually found its way either to West Africa or, through the spice trade, to the Malabar coast of India.

Not surprisingly, the export of so much copper to a relatively primitive society had considerable economic impact, and, primitive or not, the West African economy soon experienced serious price inflation. The price of a slave near the Rio Cestos rose from two copper barber's basins to four or five during the course of several early sixteenth-century years; in the Niger delta, slave prices escalated from twelve copper manillas to fifty-seven over the first seventeen years of the century.[8] The research remains to be done concerning the economic consequences of such a rapid rise in labor costs to the sugar industry in the Atlantic islands, but it must surely have been substantial. On the other hand, the increase in commodity prices that resulted from the vast augmentation in central European silver production may have compensated for heightened labor costs.

Substantial quantities of the copper purchased at Antwerp were shipped around Africa in support of the Portuguese spice monopoly; Godinho estimates the amounts to be on the order of 225 U.S. tons annually in the early sixteenth century; 560 tons annually from 1520 to 1526; and quantities varying from 356 to 485 tons per year during the early 1540s.[9] Where did this copper go and what trade did it maintain? The papal divisions of the world during the late fifteenth and early sixteenth centuries gave Portugal title to the undiscovered regions of the eastern half of the world, and this, plus perhaps the Spanish perception that their self-interest lay in the rich mines of America and the west, gave that small nation time to seek its commercial interests in India and the Spice Islands. Trade was not new to the area. For centuries, Chinese and Arab merchants had exchanged goods throughout the East, and the land and water routes using the Persian Gulf and the Red Sea had connected this vast trading area with Europe and especially with Venice. The Portuguese latecomers had little to offer that could gain for them commercial supremacy in the region, but they were the beneficiaries of superior military and naval technology and it was by these means that they rose to preeminence in the spice trade. As military governor, Albuquerque established by force warehouse-fortresses at Sokotra (1503), Goa (1510), and Hormuz (1515). A glance at Map 2 will reveal the strategic significance of these sites; Sokotra, an island at the mouth of the Red Sea, and Hormuz, at the southern entrance to the Persian Gulf, were bases that together permitted an effective sea power like Portugal to constrict the trade routes that had long carried the European spice trade. Control of Goa gave Portugal command of the commerce of the entire Malabar coast – the source of the finest pepper, the commodity most important in volume of all the spices. Having at least temporarily seized the power to close the ancient trade routes to Europe, it remained for Portugal to seek out the riches of the East and to win access to the diverse goods that the West demanded. The extension of the

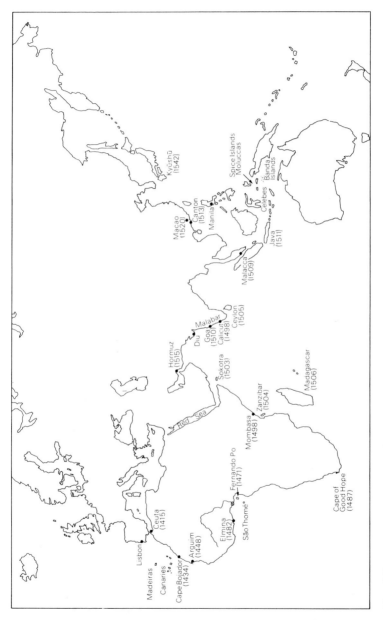

Map. 2 Portuguese overseas expansion

spice empire was swift. Malacca, Java, the Moluccas, and the Celebes were all reached by 1512; Canton on the Chinese mainland was visited by 1513, and by 1520, the Portuguese had a trading station in China at Macao. By 1542, the explorers had touched the southernmost island of Japan.

Commercial success came swiftly to Portugal, but it proved fragile. From the Spice Islands came cloves, an extremely valuable commodity, and from the Bandas nutmeg and mace were shipped to the West. Ginger and silk from China, Indian pepper and cotton cloth, and finally rubies, emeralds, and sapphires from Tibet, India, and Ceylon supplemented the output of the Moluccas and enriched Portuguese merchants. The quantities involved were not large by modern standards. At the height of Portuguese control of the Eastern trade, between 1500 and 1520, the Cape route yielded the following annual amounts of spices: pepper, 7,260 to 8,250 tons; ginger, 330 tons; cinnamon, 165 tons; mace, 126 tons; nutmeg, 1,540 tons; and cloves, 1,276 tons.[10]

Portugal never attained a complete monopoly of the spice trade, and even her partial monopoly was soon threatened. On the one hand, the demographic and economic resources of that small nation sequestered on the western corner of the Iberian Peninsula were simply inadequate for the task of ruling half the world. As the century progressed, it proved impossible for the Portuguese even to maintain the ethnic identity of the crews on the merchant ships, and more and more sailors whose loyalty to a country they had never seen was dubious at best were drawn from the indigenous population of the East. On the other hand, within India, the Spice Islands, and the other widely scattered trading posts, native competition became serious and frequently resulted in violence, both political and piratical. The expansion of the Ottoman Empire into Egypt in 1517 confronted Portugal with a powerful and unified challenger to its ability to close the Red Sea route to Europe. In order to win help from the Shah of Persia in the struggle against the Turks, the Portuguese were compelled to reopen the spice routes through Hormuz.[11] This, plus venality and incompetence among the Portuguese agents charged with enforcing the blockade of the traditional spice routes, rendered ineffective all efforts to constrict the old routes and thus permitted a brief resurgence of Venetian trade. It is this fact, perhaps, that explains the increasing share of Fugger copper that was shipped to Venice after 1535.[12]

Challenges to Portuguese dominance in the East came from other quarters as well. The arbitrary line dividing the world between Spain and Portugal had been drawn north–south in the Western Hemisphere, but it left the division in the other half of the world open to considerable dispute. Magellan's expedition, sailing westward, reached the Spice Islands in 1522 and sharp controversy arose regarding the respective rights of each power to that rich commercial prize. Competition for trade was intense for several years, but the Spanish, pressed for money and at war with France, relinquished their dubious claim to the Moluccas in return for a substantial cash payment from Portugal.[13] Spain, however, reasserted its claims and returned to the islands during the 1540s, and again, this time more strenuously, after 1570, when her interests and appetites had been sharpened by the establishment of regular trans-Pacific trade between Mexico and Manila and between Manila and the Asian coast. Ten years later the failure of the Portuguese royal line resulted in a brief conflict in which Spain overwhelmed an irresolute Portugal and united the crowns of the two nations. The Iberian Peninsula was unified from 1580 until 1640, but instead of increasing the strength of Portugal, the union drew all of Spain's numerous enemies into conflict with the Portuguese empire and against her tenuous control in the East. In both European waters and in the East itself, the political climate shifted against Portugal. India, which had been split between Muslim and Hindu factions early in the century, slipped increasingly under Muslim control and Portugal's leverage as a balancing agent was thereby lessened.[14] Closer to home, the disastrous defeat of the Armada in 1588 at once weakened Iberia's capacity to defend distant trade routes and encouraged interlopers from England and Holland to try their hands at wresting the spice trade from Portugal. The survival rate of Portuguese trading vessels fell precipitously: from 1500 and 1580, 93 percent of Portuguese ships reached harbor safely; during the period from 1580 to 1612, the figure declined to 69 percent.[15] Portuguese trade with the East persisted, but the dreams of unlimited riches proved elusive.

The New World

The catalogue of goods imported from the East – silks, spices, precious stones – in itself reveals the essential difficulty of that trade. Return cargoes for the voyage to Portugal from the Indies were light and, with the possible exception of pepper, small in bulk; they were also extremely valuable. What could the West send in return for these expensive goods? Copper, of course, served to make up a part of the balance, and the Westerners capitalized on their technological superiority in a few items such as firearms, but these were utterly inadequate to settle the international accounts. Regional trade was of some help. Moroccan copper, for example, supplemented supplies from central Europe, and by the end of the sixteenth century, East African gold production at Mozambique had risen sharply, outstripping the West African exports from Elmina.[16] In the Far East, once Japan had been reached in 1542, regional trade developed between China, India, and Japan; Portugal gained from the carrying trade. Indian wares were shipped to Macao in return for silk, porcelain, and gold; Chinese goods and Western muskets were subsequently traded in Japan for silver, and the silver in its turn helped to finance the purchase of more goods in India.[17]

Despite valiant efforts at developing interregional trade, however, the value of the commodities sent from East to West greatly exceeded that of the goods shipped in the opposite direction. It was always necessary for Portugal and later Western interlopers to ship silver bullion eastward in order to balance the commercial accounts. As a consequence of the East's voracious appetite for silver, the Atlantic trade that brought the mineral riches of Potosi and Mexico to Europe was indispensable for the continuance of the Eastern trade. Indeed, although no firm records remain to document the bullion shipments from Europe to India, one recent historian has attempted a correlation between the number of surviving Mogul coins by mint year and the total bullion imported annually from the New World by Europe.[18] After allowing for a certain time lag to permit the silver to pass through the trading system, the correlation is remarkably close; it is even more precise during the seventeenth century when it becomes possible to compare ingot shipments by the English East India company and the survival levels of Mogul coins. While one may reasonably harbor reservations concerning the precision of correlations between bullion shipments from America and the survival rate of Mogul coins preserved in European museums as an index of coinage levels, there is no possible doubt concerning the overriding importance of American bullion shipments in sustaining the trade with the East. The quantitative dimensions of this trade have already been described in Table III.

Although it is certainly true that bullion shipments from the New World's mines represent the most important element in the eastward transatlantic trade of the sixteenth century, it is well not to lose sight of the other components and of their impact on the European economy. Equally significant, of course, is the flow of goods from Europe to the Americas, but, for the moment, let us consider the nonmetallic constituents of production in South America. The papal divisions of the world and the Treaty of Tordesillas, created at least partially in geographical ignorance, conferred upon Portugal the Brazilian coast, and since during this early period no precious metals were discovered there, the Portuguese endeavored to exploit the agricultural wealth of their new territory. In the first half of the century, brazilwood was the most profitable export from the Portuguese colony, and as European tools became more prevalent, increasing the productivity of native labor, a sizable export trade developed. Wood arriving in Lisbon was transshipped to Antwerp or Amsterdam where it was processed into dye and distributed to the cloth industries of Europe. Brazilian dye was supplemented by cochineal and indigo from Mexico.

Far more important in the long run to the New World's economy was sugar. Arabic in both name and origin, sugar during our period migrated around the world and became inextricably linked to the African as well as the transatlantic trades. During the population crisis of the late fourteenth and early fifteenth centuries, grain prices fell sharply and farmers in Sicily, once the breadbasket of Europe, sought to maintain their incomes by planting luxuries such as sugar and sweet wines. The opening and colonization of the Atlantic islands ended these dreams, for the Madeiras soon displaced the climatically less favored Mediterranean sugar centers. Between 1508 and 1570, sugar exports from the Madeiras rose from 1,134 U.S. tons to more than 3,239; the West African island of São Thomé, also a major producer of sugar, yielded 324 tons in 1580 and 648 in 1600.[19] The migration of sugar culture did not, however, cease in the Atlantic islands, but continued on to Brazil, where production became so great during the late sixteenth century as to force alteration in the economic structure of the island producers themselves. In 1570, Brazil's sugar production was roughly 2,915 tons; ten years later, it was 5,668 tons; and by 1600, it had risen to some 19,434 tons.[20] In the face of such intense competition, production at São Thomé stagnated after 1600, while that of the Madeiras plummeted during the last decades of the century and became insignificant by its close. In the latter archipelago, land was diverted to the production of sweet wines; in the Azores, too far north for successful competition in sugar, efforts were made to produce enough wheat to supply a relatively overpopulated and newly hungry Portugal.

Sugar production, as noted, implied plantation economies, and these, in turn, were closely tied to the slave trade. Table VIII, which gives slave imports by various regions, reveals the shifting patterns in that trade.

It seems clear that slave imports were closely related to sugar production. The late-century decrease in imports to São Thomé and the Atlantic islands corresponds to the reduction in profitability of their indigenous sugar economies, while the steep increase in Brazilian imports is cotemporal with rapid growth in that territory's sugar exports. In passing, one may note that the brisk augmentation of imports to Spanish America in the latter half of the sixteenth century corresponds with the somewhat more humane treatment of the surviving native Indian population on whose behalf the church had long struggled.[21] From a strictly economic point of view, however, the slave trade was more than simply a means of satisfying the labor demands of the ruthless few who were exploiting the vast lands of the New World. The sale of slaves provided Portugal with a means of earning silver for use in the Indies commerce. In addition to earnings from these sales to Spanish America, regulated through the *asientos*, or

Table VIII. *Atlantic slave trade by importing region*
(in thousands, 1451–1600)

	1451–75	1476–1500	1501–25	1526–50	1551–75	1576–1600
Europe	12.5	12.5	12.5	7.5	2.5	1.3
Atlantic islands	2.5	5.0	5.0	5.0	5.0	2.5
São Thomé		1.0	25.0	18.8	18.8	12.5
Spanish America				12.5	25.0	37.5
Brazil					10.0	40.0

Source: P. Curtin, *The Atlantic Slave Trade: A Census*, Madison, University of Wisconsin Press, 1969, Table 33, p. 116. Reprinted by permission of the publisher.

licenses to import slaves, the trade provided a cover for smuggling western goods to the New World in return for silver. The *asientos* themselves may have been less profitable than previously was thought, but by reducing the volume of slaves and thereby increasing the cargo of western manufactures, the holder of the *asiento*, normally a Portuguese, could substantially increase his profit.[22]

One of the peculiarities of the eastward trade from Spanish America, as distinct from that of Portuguese Brazil, was the almost total specialization in precious metals. In 1594, for example, 95.62 percent of the cargo to Europe was treasure, 2.82 percent cochineal, 1.16 percent hides, 0.29 percent indigo, and 0.11 percent other small articles; in 1609, treasure still accounted for 84 percent of the cargo officially recorded and carried in the annual Spanish convoy.[23] Especially curious is the virtual absence of recorded copper. Since German mining engineers, brought to the New World for their expertise, knew the secrets of refining by amalgamation, and since one possible byproduct of that process is copper, one might expect that a substantial amount would have been available, as it later was, in proximity to the rich silver mines of Spanish America. Early in the century, copper was an indispensable metal for the production of bronze cannon. It was crucial for ship fittings, was necessary for sheathing hulls, and, as the century progressed, became increasingly significant as a coinage metal. As we have noted, it was a critical item in both the West African and Indian trades. Nor does copper appear to have been in oversupply in Spain; indeed, there is evidence of shortage. In 1551, for example, the cost of copper limited the supply of fractional coinage in Spain, and the problem remained manifest a decade later.[24] In the 1590s, Spain was strategically weakened by dependence on northern supplies of copper for the manufacture of ordinance and the Dutch gained commercial advantages through their role as provider.[25] Despite what seems to have been urgent need, however, very little copper was produced in the New World during the sixteenth century. It was not beyond the technological capacity of the times to smelt the metal. Small amounts were exported during the sixteenth century, and, by 1621, the metal served as a fraudulent filler for the centers of false gold ingots.[26] In 1643, a cargo of American copper arrived at Seville to restock the Spanish mints.[27] More research is required before an explanation of the lack of copper production can be asserted with confidence, but perhaps silver was simply so abundant in the New World that mining costs, both economic and psychological, were driven to such heights as to render uninteresting the refining and transportation of a mere base metal like copper. This hypothesis would concur with the timing of the known shipments of copper in the seventeenth century, when the silver mines had passed their peak and silver output was falling.

The Baltic trade

There are striking similarities between the Baltic and the East Indies trades during the early modern period. Although the Indies trade was primarily composed of luxury goods, while that of the Baltic consisted of bulky and relatively cheap commodities, both regions were hard-currency areas and both adversely affected the balance of payments of western Europe. Many of the goods from the Baltic region – Poland, Prussia, Russia, Estonia, Finland, Livonia, and Scandinavia – were indispensable to western economies. We have already noted the critical significance of the grain trade in the survival of the burgeoning cities of Europe and, in Table V offered some estimate of its magnitude. Grain was by far the largest component of the export trade of the Baltic, attaining levels of some 80 percent of the total volume in most years, but it was by no means the only regional product that was vital to western states.[28] Timber products were shipped from the entire region. Specialty woods included barrel staves, split oak for shipbuilding, and masting timber from Riga and Scandinavia. Tar from Poland and Prussia found its way to the shipyards of all Europe, and wood ash, often refined into potash, was a chemical essential to many industrial processes. We have already observed the utilization of Baltic potash in the south German glass industry; it was also widely employed in soap boiling, in textile dyeing, and in the manufacture of gunpowder.

The rapid growth of world shipping, associated with demographic and economic revival and with the discoveries, assured a brisk market for Baltic flax and hemp. Russian, Livonian, and Polish flax, once made into sailcloth, powered the world's ships; hemp, from roughly the same regions, provided the rigging, ratlines, and hawsers that supplemented domestic manufactures throughout Europe. Tallow for ordinary lighting and wax for religious and ceremonial purposes were supplied through Estonia, Livonia, and portions of Russia extending inland as far as Novgorod. Skins and leather were exported from the same area, and highly valuable furs, perhaps the only real luxury good from the Baltic hinterland, were capable of bearing the cost of transportation over far greater distances. Novgorod was a long-established fur center, but the most important sixteenth-century route lay along the Düna River from Ustjug, where fur shipments were assembled from lands as distant as Siberia.[29] Salt fish from the Baltic was also sold throughout Europe, although the relative share of these fisheries declined during the century as those of the North Sea rose to preeminence. Toward the end of the century, Swedish copper assumed a major role in the economic structure of the west.

The unique qualities of Baltic goods had sustained an active trade for many centuries and had contributed significantly to the recovery of the European economy after the Viking invasions. The north German cities of the Hanse had grown wealthy in this trade; Lübeck served as a prime collection center for Baltic goods that were subsequently transshipped to Hamburg and thence to a number of western cities, but especially to Bruges. During the fourteenth and fifteenth centuries, depopulation and depressed grain prices permitted the Germans to undersell all competitors, particularly those in Scandinavia, and to drive even the farmers out of agriculture. The resultant dependence on German and Polish grain was exploited by the Hansards to bend the terms of trade in their favor, but although this policy was successful in the short run, it convinced a large segment of the Baltic's population that their self-interest lay in breaking the German monopoly. When Dutch merchants began to prowl the Baltic after the mid-fifteenth century, they were enthusiastically welcomed as a challenge to the Hanse. The Dutch route, by sea around Denmark and through the Danish Sound, bypassed Lübeck and forced that city to relinquish its medieval prosperity. Bruges attempted to maintain its ancient control over northern commerce, but the effort degenerated into narrow restrictionism. This, the silting of its harbor, and, among a number of other factors, the Portuguese decision to make Antwerp their European spice entrepôt caused Bruges to fail and gave the ascendancy to Antwerp. During the first half of the sixteenth century, Amsterdam ran a close second; by the end, however, it was triumphant. Political events conjoined with shifts in the trading patterns to weaken the Hansards. The capture of Novgorod by Ivan III in 1478 and the subsequent expulsion of the merchants of the Hanse virtually ended Hanseatic dominance of the entire region; termination of German control allowed new centers to form and greatly contributed to the prosperity of Narva, Riga, and Reval.[30]

Failure to preserve discipline among the Hanse towns, resentment of prior German success, political change in the Baltic region, and even the disrupting impact of the Reformation in Germany weakened the organizational structure of the Hanse and its ability to act in concert. Whereas Lübeck alone had accounted for 31 percent of the vessels visiting Danzig during the late fifteenth century, its ships constituted less than 2 percent of the total in 1530; even with the addition of the entire North Sea coast, Prussia, and all Wendish towns, German shipping in the latter year was only 34 percent of that serving this prime grain port at the mouth of the Vistula.[31] By contrast, 954 Dutch ships out of a total of 1,657 paid tolls on departing from Danzig in 1530; in 1583, Dutch departures from Danzig numbered 2,534 out of a total of 4,044 for ships of all nations. The Dutch commanded 62 percent of the entire trade; it was, of course, this remarkable achievement that permitted a nation so limited in land resources to become the granary of Europe.

In return for the goods of the Baltic, the Dutch and other nations carried a number of commodities northward. Salt was a major import to the region, especially during the early part of the century, before the herring fisheries had yielded their prime place to those of the North Sea and the wider Atlantic. French bay salt moved north to Antwerp or Amsterdam for transshipment to the Baltic. The location of the Netherlands was such that these two cities were favored by climate and by the duration of sixteenth-century sailing voyages. Slow transit and a short sailing season denied time for salt and eastern species that arrived in the Low Countries to go on to reach the Baltic before winter; the same was true in reverse for northern goods destined for southern ports, so Antwerp–Amsterdam was a geographically favored site for an entrepôt where goods from diverse regions could be exchanged.[32] Spices, southern fruits, wine, silk, velvet, and certain metals and metal wares were also shipped eastward, but cloth was probably the most important item in terms of aggregate value. The *Magnus Intercursus,* a commercial agreement concluded in 1496 between Henry VII and Archduke Maximilian of the Netherlands, established Antwerp as the continental staple town for the sale of English cloth. These cloths were the traditional unfinished white broadcloths described statistically in Graph 2. Rapid expansion in the export trade of such cloths contributed heavily not only to the prosperity of London but also to that of Antwerp, and they played an important role in balancing the commercial accounts of the west with the Baltic region. Swift growth of cloth exports, both English and Netherlandish, however, appears to have been offset by the equally remarkable growth of the northern commerce. Despite the sharp increase in the earnings of the textile industry, the balance of trade with the Baltic registered nearly the same degree of adversity at the end of the century as at the beginning. Imports to the Baltic between 1550 and 1650 were approximately 30 percent of the total trade, while exports remained fairly close to 70 percent.[33] The Baltic trading area thus enjoyed an export surplus equivalent to nearly 40 percent of the total value of the annual commerce. These figures are somewhat crude in that they measure only the recorded values of the commodities trade. Precision would demand an allowance for the smuggling of easily concealable goods of great value – precious stones, silks, some spices – but as smugglers rarely leave records of their activities, their significance in balancing the commercial accounts remains moot. Equally unknowable, although probably much more important, is the role played by carrying charges and shipping fees. The immense proportion of the commerce carried in Dutch bottoms during the sixteenth century represented a shift from earlier practice, and the earnings generated by the west in this fashion must have helped in meeting the visible trade deficit. No plausible estimate of such invisible items in the trade, however, suggests that such earnings were sufficient to balance the accounts; as a result, substantial quantities of coin and of precious metal in ingot form found their way to the Baltic and to the Russian hinterland.[34] Like the Indies, the Baltic remained a drain on the money supplies of the nations of western Europe.

The winners

In the fierce competition for the trade of the world during the sixteenth century, political events became inextricably enmeshed with commercial achievement. The trade of the Indies, the New World, the Baltic, and the Mediterranean cannot be fully comprehended without mastery of the political history of every state and principality from

Mexico to the Moluccas and the Far East; it might be added that the converse is equally true: The history of politics rests on economic power. Such comprehensive knowledge is patently beyond the capacity of any individual, yet a modest effort along these lines is essential in order to understand the forces that permitted some nations to achieve competitive success while others, often those that seemed dominant in the early century, failed. Antwerp, at the mid-century mark, for example, was a golden city with the riches of the entire world flowing up the Scheldt to its harbor and a level of affluence that made its rapidly expanding citizenry the envy of Europe, yet the prosperity of Antwerp proved fleeting. Hanseatic, Portuguese, and English politics; the success of German mining and the resultant power of south German financiers; Spanish financial exigencies; and geological accident coalesced at the turn of the century to allow Antwerp to eclipse Bruges and to focus the world's trade on its port. Similar factors – political, financial, and geological – contributed to Antwerp's decline.

The Treaty of Cateau-Cambrésis of 1559, in freeing Philip II of Spain from his Italian entanglements with the French, permitted that monarch to pursue more vigorously his efforts at counterreformation.[35] In the Low Countries, numbers of new bishops were created at the expense of the local nobility, who had come to view episcopal positions as family sinecures. Resistance led first to protest, then to rebellion, and the rebellion was reinforced by the duke of Alva's attempt to repress it and to introduce the punitive *alcabala*, or sales tax, on all transactions. As resistance mounted, Spanish forces were marshalled against Holland, but luck rescued the tiny state in 1575, when Spain suffered its second major backruptcy of the century. Unpaid mercenaries turned against their masters and sacked the town of Antwerp in 1576; their barbarous acts of murder, rapine, and pillage have earned the historical soubriquet of the "Spanish Fury." In 1579, the seven northernmost of the seventeen provinces of the Low Countries entered a formal union, and, two years later, solemnly declared that they had deposed Philip II. Small numbers of French and English troops sporadically aided the United Provinces, but their intervention met with limited success; in 1585, Antwerp fell to the Spanish and the ten southern provinces were separated from the north. The following years were portentous. Spain's misguided attempt to invade England in 1588 led to the disaster of the Armada and greatly re-

duced the global threat of Spanish and, because the crowns had been
united in 1580, Portuguese sea power. The assassination of Henry III
caused war between France and Spain and brought the dynamic figure
of Henry IV to the French throne. By the end of the century, France,
England, and the United Provinces were together arrayed against a
bankrupt and exhausted Spain. The financial failures of the silver giant
in 1596 and 1607 protected the United Provinces and led, in 1609,
to an eleven-year treaty that gave the Dutch permanent control over
the mouth of the Scheldt and thereby denied Antwerp access to the sea.

Political and religious insecurity drove many of the most energetic
members of Antwerp's economic community north to Amsterdam,
while the closing of the Scheldt destroyed the former city's advantage as an entrepôt. Refugees from the religious wars in France and
from such incidents as the St. Bartholomew's Day massacre also swelled
the population of Amsterdam. By the end of the sixteenth century,
Amsterdam was all that Antwerp had been and more; the brief, but
spectacular, prosperity of the Brabantine city receded into memory.
In the absence of competition, Amsterdam flourished; population
rose from some thirty thousand in 1567 to more than one hundred
thousand in 1622.[36] The luxury trades that had formerly enriched
Antwerp found their way in large measure to this well-defended em-
porium in the northern Low Countries and supplemented the already
legendary earnings from the Baltic trade; from the 1570s until well
into the seventeenth century, Dutch ships carried more than half of the
cargo passing through the Danish Sound.[37] Even the herring appear
to have conspired to increase Dutch wealth; toward the end of the fifteenth century, their spawning grounds shifted from the Baltic to the
North Sea, giving the fishermen of Holland the advantage of proximity
to this valuable source of protein in an increasingly hungry world. The
Dutch were not laggard in capitalizing on their advantages; specialized
shipping was designed and built for the fishing industry. Ships with
holds open to the sea preserved the freshness of the fish until they
could be salted ashore; experimental innovation led to the flute ship, a
capacious, inexpensive, but extremely efficient cargo vessel that could
undersell all competitive shipping at the end of the century. Finally, in
the 1590s, the Dutch devised a mechanical, rotary sawmill that drastical-
ly reduced their ship construction costs and perpetuated the competitive advantages derived from Dutch design.

The importance of the United Provinces in fishing and the Baltic trade gave the tiny country a strategic significance unparalleled in six-teenth-century Europe. Even Spain and Portugal, virtually irrational in their resistance to and resentment of Protestant heretics, were compelled to modify their behavior with regard to Holland. The failures of Iberian agriculture, accelerating during the latter decades of the century, com-bined with rapidly rising population to make the peninsula increasingly dependent on imported grain. During and after the revolt of the Nether-lands, Dutch ships retained access to Spanish and Portuguese ports, and despite the embargoes against Dutch trade in 1585 and 1595, some of the commerce persisted, and, directly or indirectly, Spanish agents continued to purchase in Amsterdam.

Dutch dominance in the Baltic and the economic demise of Antwerp conjoined with events in the Mediterranean further to enrich the United Provinces. Population growth in the Mediterranean littoral, particularly during the second half of the sixteenth century, sharply increased the demand for food grains and fish; in the 1550s and early 1560s, scarcity created boom conditions for Turkish wheat sales in Italian markets.[38] Turkish success in developing and repopulating Constantinople,[39] however, soon created sufficient internal demand to consume the exportable surplus of Anatolia, and war between the Italians and the Turks in the early 1570s provided political cause for a cessation of the now strategic trade. Venetian success at the battle of Lepanto simultaneously reduced Turkish naval power, opened the Mediterranean to outsiders, and limited the capacity of timber-short Italy to replace and maintain modern fleets. Strenuous efforts to ex-pand domestic grain output, to substitute inferior grains, and to increase imports of central European cattle prevented the ensuing food shortage from becoming critical for a while, but grain from Poland and the Bal-tic inevitably proved essential for the survival of Mediterranean cities.

Imports of grain in small quantities from the Baltic were continu-ous from the 1540s, but the amounts grew rapidly toward the end of the century. Cosimo de' Medici, after becoming grand duke of Tuscany in 1547, had endeavored to develop the port of Livorno, and further efforts were made by his successor, in 1577, but it was Ferdinand I who took the critical steps in 1593. In that year, he declared Livorno a free port, open to all nations without regard to religion or political status.[40] The port soon emerged as a distribution center for northern goods and served the entire Mediterranean. In 1593, some 16,000 tons of Baltic grain arrived at Livorno; from 1590 to 1594, more than 2 million écus were transmitted to Dutch, English, and Danziger suppliers.[41] By 1619, over two hundred Dutch ships entered the Mediterranean annually.[42]

Holland's success was not limited to the Baltic and Mediterranean trades. Indeed, the very efforts of the Spanish to ruin the Dutch and to exclude them from Iberian ports through the embargoes of 1585 and 1595 spurred the tiny republic to undertake compensatory excursions to the colonial empires that were the source of the wealth from which they were now barred. From the beginning of the revolt of the Netherlands, Dutch ships had challenged and harassed Spanish shipping; William of Orange had regularized the practice by issuing letters of mark during the 1570s, so the concept of a blow aimed at Spain's colonial empire was only a short additional step. The conjuncture of the embargoes and of the destruction of the Armada, then, inevitably led the Dutch to Spanish America and to the Portuguese Indies. Regular voyages to the Caribbean were an established routine by the early 1590s.[43] Dutch and, as we shall see, English attacks on Spanish shipping seriously disrupted the schedules of the treasure fleets at the end of the century, while more peaceful commercial endeavor captured a portion of the trade that Spain was coming to depend on as the silver mines became more difficult to work and the extraction process more expensive. The real success of the Dutch during this period, however, lay to the east, in the Portuguese segment of the combined empire.

The migration of people skilled in a variety of disciplines from Antwerp to Amsterdam made the latter a center of technological diffusion and exchange. Jews, financiers, merchants, navigators, and geographers lived in close proximity, providing each other with mutual stimulation while reinforcing their individual knowledge of the wider world. Specific information regarding Portuguese trade routes was increasingly accessible, and in 1595, the geographical survey of Linschoten was published, providing a navigational handbook for the journey to the Spice Islands.[44] In the same year, four Dutch ships, carrying the manual, set forth for Java and, despite the fact that they appear to have alienated the initially friendly Sultan of Bantam, returned safely, with a modest profit. Before the end of the century, more than sixty Dutch vessels had undertaken the long voyage and found that the profits more than justified the risk and expense of the difficult passage. By 1601, the Dutch had established themselves at Bantam in Java, and in the following year, they organized themselves into the Dutch East India Company in order to control the trade through a single corporate body without internecine competition. Subsequent incursions into the Portuguese spice empire were swift and effective. Portugal lacked the resources of men, ships, and armaments to resist the more efficiently organized intruders from the United Provinces. By 1602, the Dutch had sent a fleet of fifteen warships to the East; two years later, twenty-three more joined the task force and set about attacking and coopting Portuguese and Spanish trading bases with cruel efficiency.[45]

Military force was the key to the Indies trade, but, in itself, it would have proved insufficient, because no amount of determination could have enabled so small a nation as the United Provinces to control the entire East. The Dutch, however, benefited from a balanced trade throughout the world, and from this circumstance, they derived a commercial edge in the Eastern trade that they were not slow to exploit. As the principal carriers of the vital and strategic Baltic trade, they earned large quantities of precious metal throughout Europe. Some of the metal was, of course, required for the trade itself, but that was recouped when the products of the Baltic were resold in the West. The remaining earnings were net, and consequently, though without mines itself, Holland became more affluent in silver than any other country in western Europe. In the long run, Dutch silver was more important than military force in winning the commerce of the Indies and in allowing the Dutch to attain the dominant position that they held in that trade during the seventeenth century. Cannon remained important, but even there Dutch access to Swedish copper and their role in Swedish industry made them the armament kings of all Europe during that century of war.

The English too benefited from and contributed to the disruption of the Spanish empire during the second half of the sixteenth century and, as a result, were able to expand greatly their commercial hegemony. As in the case of the Dutch, crisis pushed them to greater exertion in the quest for markets. The religiopolitical turbulence in the Netherlands during the early 1560s and the closing of the Antwerp market to English merchants in 1562, partly in reaction against Elizabeth's religious beliefs, were only temporarily harmful to the English cloth industry, which had for decades utilized that city as its Continental marketing center.[46] By 1564, in fact, an alternative market was in operation at Emden, from whence it was subsequently transferred to Hamburg, at the mouth of the Elbe. The new staple cities offered the English merchants access to north German markets, eased the mid-century crisis of overproduction, and enabled English cloth exports to enjoy a hearty recovery for the remainder of the century. The northeastward migration of the cloth staple and the nearly simultaneous suspension of Hanseatic privileges in London (1552) enticed English merchants into the Baltic in increasing numbers during the second half of the sixteenth century, and although the Muscovy and Eastland companies were never truly competitive with the Dutch, the profits were significant and the commodities themselves aided England in developing a broader entrepôt trade. From 1564 to 1574, fifteen English ships a year, on average, visited Narva.[47] Thereafter, trade with that city declined, but trade with Archangel in northern Russia appears to have compensated for the decrease in Narva; from 1564 to the end of the century, just under ten English ships per year sailed to Archangel, where they were virtually free from French or Dutch competitors during those decades.

Although the English East India Company was founded in 1600, two years before the equivalent Dutch company, it did not so rapidly achieve the same striking financial success.[48] On the one hand, it was initially far less tightly knit in its financial structure and, consequently, less well organized for permanent trade; on the other, whereas the Dutch during the late sixteenth century confronted a weakened and irresolute Portugal, the English were competing with the powerful Dutch themselves. The long-run viability of the company ultimately contributed to the founding of the British Empire and to its vast wealth, but during our period, success was limited. Some voyages to the Spice Islands were effective, some trading posts were established, but the trade with the Malabar coast, less threatened by the Dutch, remained England's most profitable Eastern market through the first half of the seventeenth century.

English involvement in the spice trade during the sixteenth century followed more traditional patterns and was supplemented by English industrial sales in the Mediterranean. The Portuguese efforts at severing the spice routes through the Persian Gulf and the Red Sea, as we have already observed, were ineffective; as a result, during the middle years of the sixteenth century, there occurred a resurgence of the Mediterranean commerce in spices brought overland to the Levant. For a time, Venice dominated this trade, but after Lepanto, in the final quarter of the century, northern interlopers, the English among them, began to make inroads in this active trade. The English signaled their return to the Mediterranean by visiting Livorno in 1573 under much the same stimuli that had impelled the Dutch to traverse that sea, but circumstance here favored the English. England was rich in tin and had for centuries supplied the European world with that metal; the growing importance of artillery, both on land and at sea, combined with the superior quality of bronze cannon gave the English a strong bargaining tool for prying open the Levant trade. In 1578, the Turks granted trading concessions in the Levant in return for tin, and in 1581, the English Levant Company was granted a royal charter to exploit the trade at Constantinople, Smyrna, and Aleppo.[49]

Through these cities, the English gained access to the overland spice trade and bypassed that conducted by means of the Cape route. Spice prices in Europe, however, were highly volatile, and it was partly fear that the Dutch could ruin English spice markets by oversupplying European outlets that led to the formation of the East India Company.[50] Even more important to the English than spices, however, was the Mediterranean trade in more basic commodities. The fall of Constantinople in 1453 gave the Turks control of the Phocean alum deposits and resulted in a precipitous rise in the price of that vital industrial raw material. Happily for the West, alum was discovered on the papal estates at Tolfa, but the papacy sought to exploit the find through the exercise of monopoly power and even went to the extent of placing an interdict against the Turks' "infidel alum." Considerable quantities of Tolfa alum were shipped to England, mainly in Italian and French ships, during the early sixteenth century, with the peak years falling between 1566 and 1578.[51] Thereafter, imports of papal alum declined while those from Turkey increased; perhaps even more significantly, the carrying trade reverted to English ships. During the first six decades of the century, no English vessel is recorded as carrying papal alum, but from 1566 to 1578, twenty-one such ships plied the trade, and that level was maintained throughout the century.[52]

Alum was a prime raw material in both the textile and leather industries, each a major component of England's manufacturing sector, and
easier access to it under new and less monopolistic terms must have
enhanced industrial opportunity in that country. Further, the fact that
alum was shipped primarily in English bottoms during the latter half of
the sixteenth century meant that transit costs were recovered and that
such earnings could simultaneously contribute to England's capital
formation and general prosperity. Within the textile industry itself,
shifts in manufacturing techniques, in the nature of the product produced, and in marketing areas served reinforced and interacted with the
gains from England's newly opened trade routes in the Levant. By the
latter half of the sixteenth century, the old woolen cloth industry recovered and then stabilized, but it had passed its zenith of vibrant
growth. Northern markets in Germany and the Baltic absorbed much
of its output, and, as we have observed, were more than able to pay for
the cloth imports through the export of naval stores, grain, furs, timber, and a variety of other goods, including linens and fustians. The
latter, being light in weight and ideally suited for wear in warm climates, became a staple of English cloth reexports from the Baltic to
the Mediterranean. Just as climate had encouraged the transit trade
in linen and fustians from Antwerp–Amsterdam to Africa, the New
World, and the East, it urged the resale of light cloths in the Mediterranean basin.

Within England itself, moreover, the sixteenth century was a period
of rapid change in the textile industry. As will be recalled, the exodus
of refugees from the Continent under the stimulus of religious repression and religious war brought a multitude of highly skilled cloth
producers to the vicinity of London in the decades following 1560. The
swift growth of the "new drapery" or worsted industry dates from this
era, and unlike the older, unfinished white broadcloths that earlier
formed the bulk of England's export trade, the new cloths were often
woven with colored yarns in decorative patterns. Because the yarn itself was dyed, the demand for alum, used as a mordant, increased, and
indeed the records indicate that substantially more papal alum was
shipped to England during the latter half of the sixteenth century
than had been the case earlier.[53] Moreover, as we have noted, this
alum was supplemented by Turkish supplies after 1578. The properties of the "new draperies" – more loosely woven, lighter in weight,

less expensive, and more brightly patterned and varied – commended them to Mediterranean markets, where they joined with German fustians in providing England with valuable exports and helped to balance the trade with that region. Spices, alum, silk, and other luxuries could be had from the Levant in return for northern goods and English cloth without the risks entailed in the Cape route around Africa and without the need for exporting large quantities of silver. The trade in "new draperies" continued to grow after that in woolens leveled off, and in the seventeenth century, the dynamic worsted industry first equaled, then surpassed the older textile trade. The latter fell into a deep depression, partly as a result of misguided royal policies and partly in consequence of the disruption of northern markets during the Thirty Years' War. The success of the "new draperies" was reinforced by another development with major ramifications in subsequent English industrial history; the later sixteenth century witnessed an experimental interest in the domestic manufacture of cotton fabrics in Lancashire based upon raw materials imported from the Levant.[54] Relatively insignificant during our period, the cotton industry ultimately became the giant of England's eighteenth-century industrial revolution and the foundation stone of England's industrial supremacy during that country's period of greatest glory.

Though not properly included under the rubric of international trade, it will perhaps be permissible to mention in passing the statistically shadowed world of smuggling, piracy, and privateering. The Spanish and Portuguese monopoly of the New World was simply too valuable an asset not to tempt the greater portion of seafaring Europe, which had been excluded by treaty and papal decree. Throughout the sixteenth century, French, Dutch, and English adventurers offered their illegal but often welcome services to colonists hungry for European supplies. Where commerce failed, piracy filled the void. Sir John Hawkins, for example, apparently intended to trade peacefully in the New World when he set out in 1562 with a cargo of slaves for the West Indies, but though his initial voyage was successful and his reception friendly, Spain tightened its restrictions in order to prevent a repetition of the English incursion. On his second voyage, in 1567, Hawkins's fleet was trapped and only two of his five ships returned. Thereafter, English expeditions to the New World were mainly concerned with piracy and privateering. The exploits of Sir Francis Drake, although occasionally very profitable, as in the case of the capture of a caravan of Spanish bullion in 1573, were more closely akin to naval warfare than to ordinary commerce.

The problems posed by trade: perceptions and solutions

Geographical discovery, commercial expansion, and the casting of exploratory probes to the most distant reaches of the globe tend to obscure the very real difficulties associated with the vibrant exchange economy that developed in Europe during the early modern period. Concomitantly, our own post-Enlightenment consciousness renders the task of recapturing the thought processes of sixteenth-century theorists and policy makers more difficult, and understanding their acts and recommendations in context becomes a matter of considerable complexity and intractability. The immediate problems confronting contemporary observers of international trade are fairly straightforward, however, and by simply dividing the world into trading regions, they become quite visible.

As we have observed, two of the major trading zones in the early modern world, the Baltic and the Far East, were hard-currency areas that exported more than they imported and thus demanded precious metals in return for the excess value of the goods shipped to Europe. The Baltic trade entailed the most strategically important goods, since naval stores, rope, and sailcloth were vital commodities in an age increasingly committed to naval warfare, and since the expanding cities of western Europe – the centers of commerce, banking, and government – could not survive without northern grain. Even so, the East Indies trade, though primarily concerned with spices and luxury goods, could claim some political importance in the context of the sixteenth century. On the one hand, spices were not merely luxuries, since they performed a useful function as preservatives for a portion of Europe's food supply. On the other, the shifting patterns of income distribution and the concentration of wealth, as a result both of more extensive commerce and of changes in land distribution consequent on the sharp rise in grain prices, meant that those most desirous of consuming Eastern luxuries were growing in economic and sometimes political power as the century progressed. The voices in favor of the Eastern trade, therefore, were not easily muted.

Two trading areas – the Mediterranean and the West African coast – were essentially neutral from a balance-of-payments point of view; the one because the states of northwestern Europe could offer sufficient goods in return for those purchased and the other because the principal unit of currency was copper, the export of which posed only a marginal threat to monetary stability, and that only at the level of the fractional coinage. The fifth trading region, Spanish America, in the eyes of sixteenth-century men was, of course, the prize, because it offered few manufactured or agricultural goods and was at once able and compelled to export vast quantities of precious metal in return for European goods. If, as the economic and political cliché of the period went, money was the sinews of war, money in abundance was only to be had from the Spanish mines in the New World. As a result, much of the economic thought and commercial policy of the sixteenth century, and indeed of the seventeenth, urgently addresses the problem of acquiring bullion, drawing it into one's own country, and preventing its departure.

Considerable historical precedent was available in most European states for direct action to regulate specie flows. The bullion crisis that arose in the fourteenth century as a result of the inadequacies of mining technology was exacerbated by the demographic and economic dislocations caused by the century of plague after 1350; in response, most states had introduced legislation to control and limit specie exports.[55] Although the prosperity of the central European mining industry and the discovery of precious metals in the New World did much to alleviate absolute bullion scarcity, the peculiarities of sixteenth-century trade patterns perpetuated imbalances in the international accounts and hence encouraged the further proliferation of bullionist regulations. In Spain, bullion imports were carefully monitored through the *Casa de Contractación;* a sailor caught smuggling bullion into the country for his own account was liable to receive two hundred lashes and ten years in the galleys.[56] Illegal export of bullion or coin was punishable by death for the first offense until 1480, when the penalty was softened slightly to death for the second offense; in 1552, bounties were offered to those who informed on their compatriots engaged in the illicit bullion trade.[57] In France, sumptuary laws designed to prevent the export of specie as payment for frivolous luxuries were passed with dreary regularity in 1486, 1532, 1543, 1549, 1554, 1560, 1561, 1563, 1565, and so on.[58] In England, the export of bullion was consistently discouraged by a variety of regulations, and in 1581, a new law revived direct prohibitions against bullion export.[59] Associated with such laws in almost all countries were efforts to enhance the strength of the merchant navy in order to capture earnings from the carrying trade, to develop domestic industries that could provide substitutes for imported goods, to stimulate the formation of companies that could either find new sources of treasure or break the Spanish monopoly, and to assure the effective utilization of the domestic labor force as a means of acquiring increasing amounts of foreign exchange.

There is little doubt that policy makers during the sixteenth century were virtually obsessed with bullion flows, but it is reasonable to question whether such concerns were rational. The economist Keynes set forth a defense of mercantilist policy as a stimulant to employment, and given economic conditions early in the sixteenth century, such a case can be made. At that time, Europe had not yet recovered from the monetary crisis of the preceding century, resources were still underemployed, and much land remained waste, not yet drawn back under the plow. Given these circumstances, an increase in the money supply would have stimulated production and encouraged employment up to the point where resources were utilized at full capacity and inflation, rather than increased production, began to absorb the incremental money. Although this argument is patently the result of Keynes's reasoning by analogy from personal observation of his own era of economic depression, it is not without merit, at least for the early part of our period. It is efficacious, however, only at a very general level of abstraction, where the question posed is simply that of the consequences of an infusion of money into a depressed economy suffering from insufficient purchasing power. It does not justify the specific policies devised by sixteenth-century legislators to augment the supply of bullion. Nor does it account for the persistence of such policies long after the influx of bullion had begun to have embarrassing effects on price levels.

The policies themselves ranged from the blunt, Draconian efforts to halt precious metal exports that we have mentioned, to more subtle, but equally misguided, actions, all with a heavy element of voluntarism. Louis XI's edict of 1466, decreeing the formation of a silk industry in France, is only a case in point; for several centuries thereafter, French officials attempted almost by fiat to control trade patterns, to establish companies for state ends, to initiate or terminate, as in the case of Lyons, economic undertakings without regard to their innate profitability, and even to insist that precious metal be mined domestically without serious prior consideration of the existence or non-existence of ore deposits. When bullion did flow into France and prices rose in accord with the laws of modern economics, legislative steps were taken to hold down wages and to reduce prices in order that more goods could be sold abroad so as further to increase the bullion supply. When such legislation inevitably failed in its purpose, new laws were enacted and enforcement was strengthened. When artificially created industries foundered, they were subsidized at the expense of those less favored branches that flourished. France may have been an extreme case, but even in England, efforts to invigorate the merchant marine were implemented through legislation enforcing the consumption of fish on specified days of the week.

The history of mercantilism is essentially the history of failure; most of the policies that are grouped under that very general rubric were either counterproductive or such as to limit real economic growth in areas not favored by the state. How can we explain why policy makers repeated their mistakes and failures with only minor variations over the course of several generations? One might call attention to the absence of a developed science of economics and thus appeal to ignorance as the excuse for unwise policy makers, but this is not entirely convincing. By 1568, Jean Bodin had already articulated the quantity theory of money and observed that increases in the money supply caused prices to rise.[60] Yet, as we have noted earlier, he failed to draw the obvious conclusions from his own brilliant work and subsequently recommended the usual sterile policies of manipulating the customs duties so as to favor exports and discourage the import of all but raw materials from abroad.[61] Contemporary economic theory, in my opinion, was sufficiently sophisticated to have allowed the emergence of the correct formulation of the price–specie flow mechanism – that when bullion enters the country and is monetized, prices rise; that this causes exports of goods to decrease while imports increase as foreign goods become relatively cheap; and that the net result is an outflow of bullion until prices and bullion supplies are balanced among all countries. This conclusion was not, however, reached during the sixteenth and seventeenth centuries.

Two factors, one practical, the other abstract, may have contributed to this and related failures of perception. At the practical level, the price–specie flow mechanism only operates when the mutual trading partners monetize bullion imports, and by allowing the metal to circulate, permit prices to rise. Hoarding, which precludes circulation, existed to some degree in the Baltic region and to a greater degree in the Far East, although the evidence of correlation between Mogul coinage levels and bullion shipments to the East suggests that considerable monetization occurred in India.[62] The existence of hoarding might have supported, at least partially, a rationally argued case against depending on the price–specie flow mechanism to distribute bullion supplies, but the argument never became that sophisticated. The failure of perception appears to have arisen at an earlier stage and, if I may be permitted to speculate, to have been embedded in the voluntarist philosophical assumptions and absolutist leanings of the period. If the existence of universals was in doubt, as it had been since the fourteenth century; if natural laws were only those general precepts enacted by the state; if the abstractions quintessential in all forms of law were in question; if even the physical sciences were enduring a period of turmoil during which older systems of classification and formally accepted theorems were overthrown before substitutes were adequately formulated; and if the Lord himself, freed from the comfortable Catholic dogma of orderly hierarchy, had begun to appear more and more like the inscrutable and ferocious God of the Old Testament, what would have led men to assume that economic phenomena were governed by regular laws that would permit them to foresee the inevitable consequences of economic policy? In short, why should sixteenth-century man have assumed that his will was more limited in economic than in other matters? Sully, finance minister to Henry IV of France, describes in his memoirs a conversation with Henry and the queen. Henry turns to the queen and observes that, according to Sully, "no one dare to give me the least offense and it depends only upon myself to give law to all the world"; Sully responds, "It is true, Sire, and so you may whenever you please."[63] Without placing too much weight on a mere anecdote, one may note that the attitude implicit in Sully's response seems at best inconsistent with our modern search for the constraints of economic laws.

Now mental attitude – mindset, if you will – and the conceptual framework against which empirical evidence is evaluated have a great deal to do with the final interpretation of the empirical evidence itself. At first inspection, it seems odd that misconceived policies and actions that generally yielded counterproductive results would be constantly reenacted and repeated. The dreary regularity of French sumptuary legislation is but one case in point; examples could be almost endlessly multiplied of the reiteration of efforts to legislate price levels, to control trade patterns, to prevent specie outflows, and to create by governmental fiat companies, both national and international. Not all such endeavors failed, but lack of success was so general that a modern mind finds it difficult to conceive causes for the stubborn refusal of sixteenth- and seventeenth-century policy makers to learn from their mistakes. It was not that the failures themselves were obscured, but rather that in searching for the causes of failure, the wrong conclusions were reached. Given a fairly generalized premise of voluntarism, and the concomitant incompatibility of viewing the world, in this case the economic world, as governed by immutable laws, the only logical explanation of policy failure lay in faulty administration. Once it was assumed that a soundly conceived policy yielded negative results because of the shortcomings of subordinate administrators, no amount of empirical evidence documenting those negative results would lead to reconsideration of the basic policy. Instead, such evidence would encourage precisely that behavior which we are apt to find so puzzling – repetition of laws, exhortations for stricter enforcement, and increasingly Draconian penalties directed against malingering subordinates and the unfortunate souls subject to the laws. It is perhaps this peculiarity of attitude, more than specific policy measures or theoretical economic propositions, that constitutes the essence of mercantilism and accounts for the remarkable durability of that much maligned term in the historiography of early modern Europe.

6
Finances: private and public

That sixteenth-century policy makers were obsessed with bullion flows is beyond doubt, yet even if many of their recommendations and policies appear irrational to us, some very real and pressing problems demanded resolution. The bullion shortage that depressed the European economy during the later middle ages seems progressively to have worsened during the first half of the fifteenth century and then to have been alleviated with the opening of the central European mines and the consequent increase in the amount of precious metal available to the mints. The impact of shortage on contemporary thought is self-evident, but implicit in this terse précis of monetary history, simple enough on the surface, lies a more complex and difficult problem that vexed early modern financial administrators and unsettled European monetary systems. In the modern world, the connection between bullion and the money supply is tenuous indeed; most countries have long since abandoned the least pretense that the domestic money supply is in any way related to the amount of bullion held in reserve or contained in the coinage. In the later middle ages, however, this was not the case; the money supply was virtually identical to the bullion supply and this identity was perpetuated despite the efforts of almost all the monarchs of the period. It is this congruence that simultaneously makes it possible to speak of a long-term monetary shortage and that rendered the problem so intractable.

Confronted by the inadequacies of state revenues in a time of rising expenses and urged on by the public clamor for sufficient circulating specie, princes almost everywhere debased their currencies during the last two centuries of the middle ages. Yet aside from the uncertainties thereby introduced into fixed contracts and long-term rents, the real monetary impact of debasement appears to have been negligible. A cautious public, justifiably wary of royal motives, persisted in weighing the coin, even though the practice was usually punishable by severe penalties, and in adjusting prices so as to receive the same quantity of precious metal for goods and services sold as was the case before each successive debasement. With higher prices, the increased number of intrinsically less valuable coins received in payment contained the same amount of bullion as a lesser number of older and better coins.[1] While these practices produced nominal inflation and disrupted fixed contracts until defensive measures were devised, they minimized any real impact of debasement by tying the money supply directly to the bullion supply.

As a result of this identity between money and bullion supply, the importance of bullion flows was increased, but there were further consequences. On the one hand, since substantial shipments of bullion to both the Baltic and the Far East continued throughout the century, the total European stock of metal grew far less rapidly than the levels of bullion imports would suggest. Even in Spain, the initial recipient of the massive influx, exports appear to have exceeded imports, with the paradoxical consequence that the richest country in Europe experienced periodic scarcities of circulating medium.[2]

To comprehend the significance of the money supply in the sixteenth century a brief digression into the world of the economists is essential, and although there are many relevant models, we shall select that set forth by J. R. Hicks in explication of Keynes's *General Theory*.[3] Briefly, Hicks's model entails two curves: the *IS* curve, along which investment equals savings, and the *LM* curve, along which the desired amount of money equals the actual money supply. The coordinates are, vertically, the interest rate and, horizontally, the gross national product. At the intersection of the two curves, the interest rate and the gross national product are simultaneously determined. No claim is made here that such a model can be directly or mechanically applied to sixteenth-century economic phenomena, but it is useful as a device for identifying the relevant variables and for estimating the possible effect and direction of historical change. At the most obvious level of application to sixteenth-century events, the model indicates that when an influx of bullion increases the money supply and thereby shifts the *LM* curve to the right, interest rates will fall and gross national product and employment will increase as long as full employment levels are not yet attained. It is this sequence that led Keynes to express sympathy for some of our period's bullionist spokesmen.

Other relationships may also be derived from the model. If the number of investment opportunities increases or if technological change enhances investment profitability – economists would speak of a shift in the marginal efficiency of capital – the *IS* curve would shift outward, with a consequent expansion in gross national product and, in this instance, with upward pressure on interest rates. Within the historical reality of the sixteenth century, some technological change did occur, and even more significantly, the organizational mutations, which we have referred to as "roundaboutness" in Chapter 4, were prominent aspects of the period. Together they would have acted to increase the marginal efficiency of capital and thus to shift the *IS* curve outward. In this case, upward pressure on interest rates emanates from the desire of entrepreneurs to acquire more money to commit to increasingly profitable investment opportunities and from their willingness to compensate those with ready cash to loan in return for their consent in surrendering control over liquid sums of money. In simpler terms, this means that more credit is required in an expanding economy and that, collectively, the economy is willing to tolerate certain inconveniences in order to win access to ready money. Converting these theoretical notions to a historical context, we may observe that since bullion flows only partially met the growing needs of trade during the sixteenth century, when exports of bullion persistently reduced the net effect of imports, considerable pressure developed for the substitution of credit for circulating specie.

This same tendency was reinforced by another factor, not usually incorporated into those hypothetical and instantaneous periods within which monetary economists so often circumscribe their models. As we have already indicated, population growth was rapid during much of the sixteenth century, and in some regions, urbanization was even more swift. Under the conditions prevalent during our period, demographic growth led inexorably to increased output of goods and services, and this in turn augmented the requirements for transactions cash necessary to conduct the larger amount of business that ensued.[4] Urbanization intensified the need, because urban life is by definition a more market-oriented existence. The separation and specialization of those social functions that might be undertaken by a single individual in a rural environment generated many more cash transactions in accomplishing the same ultimate ends in a town. Even though highly developed marketing arrangements were more efficient, they placed heavier demands on the money supply and consequently stimulated the desire to alleviate monetary insufficiencies by devising alternative credit mechanisms.

Developments in a number of quarters heightened the pressure to institute a more flexible money supply and to expand the use of credit. Shifts in industrial organization and technology enhanced investment opportunities. Population expansion and urbanization elevated the demand for transactions cash, while periodic shortages of specie emphasized the urgency of generating a money supply that was elastic enough to support the burgeoning activity of international trade on a world scale, without suffering intolerable bouts of monetary feast or famine. From governments themselves came the need to meet the exigencies of increasingly expensive military and military-commercial endeavor on a scale never envisioned by medieval man; with this need came the desire to expand the money supply so as to borrow at reasonable rates of interest.

Taken together, these pressures constituted a compelling force for freeing the money supply from dependence on bullion stocks through the introduction of a fiat currency. Europe in the sixteenth century was not yet ready for a total separation of the two, as, for example, through the issuance of paper money, but a middle stage could be attained if the public proved willing to accept the royal valuation of bullion, to receive coins at par, and to forego efforts to maintain the intrinsic value of payments received by raising prices in response to debasement. Convenience and economic rationality dictated that the royal valuation be accepted, but who would take the first dangerous step along this path? Some generalized guarantee that the coin would be taken at par was requisite before any individual could be persuaded, save through force or royal threat, to accept coin at par without regard to bullion content. For some centuries, governments throughout Europe had issued edicts, laws, and regulations specifying the circulation value of coin and declaring its legal tender quality, yet their efforts do not seem to have become fully effective prior to the sixteenth century.[5] What guarantee could governments offer for the coin? It was clearly fatuous to promise redemption in bullion, because the coinage already contained precious metal and because an offer to exchange coin for greater quantities of bullion than the coin's intrinsic value would simply have resulted in a return to bullion as the single determinant of the money supply. What was needed was certain assurance that the coin could be spent at par, either for the pleasurable and desired amenities of life or for some obligatory payment; since states are rarely in a position to offer the public pleasurable opportunities for spending money, the requisite guarantee took the form of obligatory payment. Governments through time have ever been ready and eager to impose taxes and to insist on payment. Further, because they were motivated by self-interest, it was highly unlikely that governments would refuse to accept payment of taxes in the coin of the realm. Taxation thus served as a guarantee that coin would ultimately be accepted at face value. If a citizen knew that he was responsible for a tax payment that he could not avoid and that was specified in coin at face value, there was no reason for him to exchange his coin at less than face value anywhere else; in addition, he would presumably be willing to hold coin in amounts equal to his tax obligation without regard to its intrinsic value.

Now for taxation to serve a guarantor of the circulating value of the coinage, it had to be sufficiently broad and extensive to touch the lives of significant numbers of people. In short, there appears to be some critical level to which taxation must climb before its impact is sufficiently widespread to persuade all men to accept and hold coin at par. The sixteenth century was a period of great stress on government budgets everywhere. War, defense, and overseas adventure strained traditional revenue sources and forced governments to seek out new and higher taxes, extending ever more deeply into the lower levels of the body politic. Graph 3 gives some impression of the growth of crown receipts in France, Spain, and England, but a word of caution is necessary here. The figures are somewhat impressionistic and will not bear the weight of close analysis; they are strongest for England, less reliable for Spain, and most dubious of all for France, where the expected revenues, which these figures represent after 1483 and before 1610, were almost certainly reduced by the upheavals and civil disruptions prevalent during the latter half of the sixteenth century.[6] Despite their flaws, however, the series may be trusted to reveal general trends; in all three cases, there is a precipitous upward sweep in

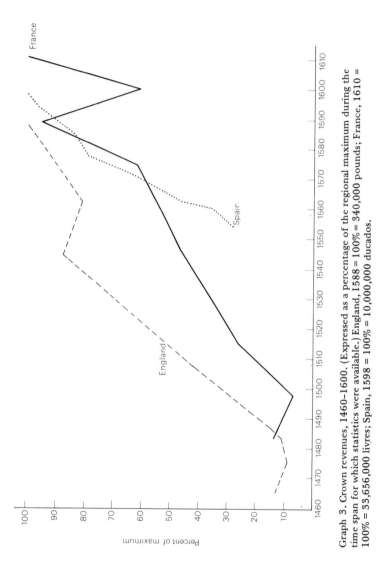

Graph 3. Crown revenues, 1460–1600. (Expressed as a percentage of the regional maximum during the time span for which statistics were available.) England, 1588 = 100% = 340,000 pounds; France, 1610 = 100% = 33,656,000 livres; Spain, 1598 = 100% = 10,000,000 ducados.

revenue levels. The rise greatly exceeds any plausible estimate of population growth, and supported by direct evidence of tax assessments and incidence, permits us to conclude that increasing numbers of people were subjected to heavier levels of taxation over the course of the sixteenth century.

Given the growing political power of government in most countries and the evident need for more flexible money supplies induced by demographic and economic causes, rising levels of taxation may be presumed to have acted as guarantee for the integrity of the par value of the coinage and to have finally broken the direct link between the money supply and the bullion supply. Precision with regard to the dating of this event in any single country is at best an elusive goal. Severe problems resulting from international arbitrage based on differences in gold–silver ratios among countries, however, provide oblique evidence that money was generally accepted domestically at face value by mid-century in much of western Europe. If coins had not been taken at par, arbitrage could not have occurred, since if all coins were treated as bullion, only one world bullion ratio would have prevailed, and consequently, international differences in legislated gold–silver ratios would have had no economic relevance. Equally supportive is clear evidence of the operation of Gresham's law – bad money drives

---

Sources (Graph 3): France: The figure for 1483 is taken from R. Gandilhon, *Politique économique de Louis XI,* Rennes, Imprimeries Réunies, 1940, p. 295. Figures for 1498 to 1589 are taken from C. Leber, *Collections des meilleurs dissertations, notices, et traités particuliers rélatifs à l'histoire de France,* VII, Paris, G. A. Dentu, 1838, p. 466; the numbers in which I do not place great confidence purport to be regnal averages and are plotted in the final year of the reign. Figures for 1600 and 1610 are taken from D. Buisseret, *Sully and the Growth of Centralized Government in France, 1598–1610,* London, Eyre & Spottiswoode, 1968, p. 77.

England: Figures are plotted as the middle year of periods of varying length for which statistics are available. Figures for 1461-70, 1471-80, and 1481-5 are taken from A. Steel, *The Receipt of the Exchequer, 1377-1485,* Cambridge, Cambridge University Press, 1954, pp. 446-54. For 1485-90 and 1504-9 the source is F. C. Dietz, "English Government Finance, 1485-1558," *University of Illinois Studies in the Social Sciences,* IX (1920) 186. Dietz (pp. 138-40) is also the source for 1540-7 and (p. 216) for 1556-9. Figures for 1587-8 are taken from S. Dowell, *A History of Taxation and Taxes in England from the Earliest Times to the Present Day,* 4 vols., I, London, Longmans, Green & Co., 1884, p. 167.

Spain: Figures are taken from F. Braudel, *La Méditerranée et la monde méditerranéen à l'époque de Philippe II,* 2nd ed., II, Paris, Armand Colin, 1966, p. 33. Braudel cites the unpublished work of Alvaro Castillo Pintado.

out good – since the distinction between "good" and "bad" money depends on the coin circulating at face value despite variations in the intrinsic values of the units of account. The dating of the shift from a a bullion to a metal-fiat monetary system depends on subtle and highly technical arguments; the view expressed here will not pass without opposition from a number of historians who would place the emergence of a metal-fiat coinage farther back in the fourteenth or fifteenth centuries. Since that view, however, demands that its proponents produce some explanation of the inability of late medieval princes to alleviate monetary shortage through debasement, and since the proponents have not complied, I believe that the argument in favor of ascription to the mid-sixteenth century remains the most persuasive.

Direct governmental borrowing

Acceptance of governmental valuation of the currency and the consequent establishment of a more flexible money supply could, under certain circumstances, act to stimulate economic growth. Within circumscribed limits, the newly won flexibility could result in an expansion of the money supply, a decrease in borrowing costs, greater investment, and an increase in both employment and the output of goods and services. Overdone, monetary expansion could generate disastrous results, including rapid inflation, low economic growth, and, ultimately, rejection of the legal tender dimension of coin in favor of a return to the security of bullion, which remained immune from irresponsible, expansionary acts of ambitious princes. Such a situation developed in Spain during the seventeenth century after the monarchy severed all ties between bullion and the copper vellon coinage.[7] In general, however, somewhat greater flexibility was desirable in the money supplies of European states, and the development of monetary systems, especially in France and England, based at least partially on the faith and credit of government, probably aided economic growth.

Counterbalancing the positive effects derived from refinements in the monetary system and a more ample money supply was the withdrawal of funds from the private sector in the form of taxation. Although reasonable taxes might guarantee the integrity of the currency, it is obvious that excessive taxation could stifle capital accumulation and impede trade. We have already observed these negative influences on the manufacturing sector of Spain, where the *alcabala* and the *servicios* retarded industrial growth, and in France, where heavy taxes and gild exactions forestalled the retention of capital within profitable businesses and limited commerce in such cities as Lyons.[8] Indeed, it is not difficult to discern a correlation between retarded economic growth and excessive taxation. In Spain, where tax revenues rose most swiftly, real industrial growth was the slowest among the three countries depicted on Graph 3. In France, where the per capita tax level was substantially higher than that in England, economic growth was markedly less rapid, although the comparison is damaged by the differences in the political stability of the two countries during the late sixteenth century. Positive effects could emerge from the tax structure only when the harmful consequences were limited and carefully balanced against the favorable impact of taxation in supporting a flexible currency.

Now the receipts shown on Graph 3 consist only of those that passed through ordinary revenue channels (i.e., the income that governments drew from taxation). Another, and often far more important, source of revenue was the issuance of public debt, and that derived from various alternate types of borrowing, either freely proffered or forcibly extracted from a reluctant public. Public borrowing was an ancient practice with roots far back in the middle ages; indeed, some Hanseatic privileges dated from the loans that German cities offered for the ransom of Richard I of England in 1194, after the Third Crusade. The incentives for borrowing – rising expenses, military costs, inadequate revenues, and delays in their collection – grew relentlessly with the coming of the early modern world and public debt increased at an exponential rate. During the sixteenth century, Spain was not only the most bullion-rich state in Europe, but the world's largest debtor as well. The diverse empire that Charles V ruled was in fact purchased on time, and the Spanish monarchy was never free from crushing levels of debt and debt service.

Early in the sixteenth century, Charles V's efforts to win election as Holy Roman Emperor placed him in direct conflict with Francis I of France, who also sought that goal. The competition between two of the most powerful monarchs in Europe enabled the imperial electors to demand immense sums in return for their ballots; as a result, the power struggle for the once glorious imperial title quickly degenerated into a test of the credit worthiness of the two monarchs. In large measure, the outcome had been predetermined by the economic events of the late fifteenth century. The affluence of the central European mining industry enriched the merchants of southern Germany, particularly the Fugger family of Augsburg, whose roots may be traced back to the fourteenth-century cloth industry in that city. For a variety of reasons, Augsburg was a node of prosperity during the economic decline of the later middle ages; this lucky circumstance, combined with their innate business skill, permitted the Fugger family to acquire and preserve a very considerable fortune.[9] Using this capital as a base, the family was able to extend its activities beyond the textile trades and to advance money to needy princes, such as the archduke of Tyrol; in return for the loans, the recipients granted liens on the output of the central European silver and copper mines.[10] Further loans deepened Fugger control of mineral production throughout Hungary and the Tyrol, while rising levels of output and more sophisticated technology enhanced the value of the mines. Portugal's choice of Antwerp as an entrepôt for the Eastern spice trade and the soaring demand for copper induced by the West African slave trade linked the commerce of more than half the world to the central European mining industry and assured the growth of the Fugger family's wealth. Profits averaged 54.5 percent annually from 1511 to 1527, and that generous rate of return permitted Fugger capital to rise from a substantial 196,791 florins to a spectacular 2,021,202 florins over the same period.[11]

Rapid capital accumulation and the Fugger's loyalty to Hapsburg interests at once allowed and induced the Fugger to support Charles's election as emperor in 1519. Of the total of 851,000 florins that were needed to bribe the electors, the Fugger family alone contributed 543,000; the Welsers, another south German banking family, put up 143,000; and the Genoese and Florentines financed the remaining 165,000 florins.[12] German and Fugger involvement with Spain and the new emperor diminished for several years following the election, but their role as financiers to Spain grew rapidly after 1524 and continued throughout the remainder of the century. In that year, the Fugger's direct financial interest in Spain was heightened when they became tax farmers to the king for the revenues of the three great ecclesiastical orders of Spain.[13] This farm, known as the lease of the Maestrazgos, was, like all such tax farms in Europe, predicated upon an advance of money to the crown in return for the right to collect the revenues leased. From the crown's point of view, the farm offered the convenience of certain and immediate collection; from the farmers', it promised a handsome return, because the amount paid for the lease was, in normal times, much less than the revenues were worth. Initially, the arrangement was extremely profitable for the Fugger since there was a certain element of fiction in the earliest advances. The money received by the crown was used in part to repay money previously borrowed for the imperial election, so it may be assumed that the Fugger were in essence paying themselves and receiving the crown revenues as collateral for the service that they so graciously provided.[14]

The dominant role of German financiers in funding the election of Charles V is standard fare in the political histories of western Europe, and perhaps for this reason, German participation in Spanish imperial finance has been somewhat overemphasized in the literature of economic history. In fact, with the exception of the few years surrounding the imperial election, Genoese bankers were a more significant factor in imperial finances than were the Germans. Of the total loans extended to the crown between 1519 and 1556, the Flemish granted 3,542,916 *ducados*, the Germans 13,414,090, and the Genoese 14,937,287; Spanish bankers, often acting with silent Genoese partners, lent a further 7,476,727 *ducados*, for a total from all sources of 39,371,020.[15] The Genoese share, at 38 percent, was the largest.

The Genoese had long been active merchants in Spain. They possessed commercial privileges in that country dating back to the mid-thirteenth century, yet their numbers remained small until the latter half of the fifteenth. Turkish military success in the Levant and the fall of Constantinople in 1453 severely damaged Genoa's overseas commerce; statistics reflecting the value of Genoa's international trade indicate a steep decline after 1300 and one that continued until the late fifteenth century, when a moderate recovery began. With the loss of the Levant, the Genoese devoted more attention to Spain, and they were extremely fortunate in their timing, since the sharpening of their interest immediately preceded the Spanish accession to world empire. Indeed, it was a Genoese, Francisco Pinelo, who, along with others, financed the first and second voyages of Columbus to the New World; in return, Pinelo was made a factor of the Casa de Contratación in Seville.[16]

Genoese support for the overseas adventure of their fellow countryman instituted a long and normally profitable relationship between Genoa and Seville that was strengthened by the peculiarities and failures of the Spanish economy. In return for loans, the Italians received concessions and trade privileges that were denied to others; after the first quarter of the sixteenth century, for example, the English found themselves less and less welcome in Spain, but the Genoese colony expanded and prospered. The rapid rise in Spanish population combined with debilitating governmental regulation of agriculture to cause Spain to teeter on the brink of famine for most of the century.[17] Similarly, the misguided mercantilist legislation that restricted industrial growth led to an inadequate supply of the manufactured goods that were essential for domestic consumption and for export to the colonies in the New World.[18] Together, the failures of Spanish agriculture and industry provided an ideal opportunity for a venerable trading republic like Genoa, and once loans had opened the door to the Spanish market, the Genoese capitalized on the rich commercial prospects that lay before them. Prosperity, of course, breeds prosperity and the dual earnings from commercial and financial enterprise multiplied Genoese capital and compounded profits. In 1595, the Venetian ambassador, Vendramin, estimated that the Genoese had received more than 24 million ducats in interest payments alone during the preceding sixty-four years.[19] Earnings, however, were not limited only to interest, and even this remarkable figure fails to reveal the riches – surpassing those from banking toward the end of the century – that Genoa drew from Spain as a carrier of foodstuffs to that hungry nation and as intermediary in the provision of the manufactured goods of France, England, and the Low Countries for domestic and overseas consumption. Genoa, in short, became one of the major conduits through which the wealth of the Spanish empire was dispersed across Europe.

Envy for the vast wealth that south German and Genoese financiers accumulated in their dealing with the Spanish government must be tempered by the events of the latter half of the sixteenth century. The Sevillian money market was immensely volatile, offering great rewards to the player who cashed his chips in time but bitter dreams of former wealth to those who played overlong. Simon Ruiz commented in 1592 that in his fifty years of experience no bank founded in Seville had avoided failure.[20] This instability is hardly surprising when the magnitude of public borrowing is compared to crown receipts; in every year of his reign, Charles V found it necessary to borrow money, and in sixteen separate years, the sums contracted for exceeded 1 million *ducados.* Since the normal crown revenues during this period lay in the range of to 1.5 million, it became clear that the Spanish empire was an increasingly insolvent giant. Under the ever weightier burden of debt, the crown resorted to more dangerous expedients of dubious legality and disastrous effect. *Juros,* interest-bearing obligations secured by the pledge of future revenues, had been a factor in Spanish finance since the fifteenth century, but their use was markedly extended under Charles V and his successor. Since the *juros* were an apparently sound investment and since the interest rate, often 7 percent, was satisfactory, substantial numbers of Spaniards and even foreign nationals freely purchased them.[21] One might add that, as the century progressed and the impact of industrial and agricultural regulation became more stultifying, the relative rate of return on the *juros* may have become more attractive in comparison with the possible returns on alternative invest ments. In any event, the proliferation of the *juros* appears to have absorbed and diverted immense quantities of domestic capital from investment in productive enterprise and transferred it to the Spanish crown, where it was largely squandered in hopeless military and political efforts at counterreformation. Not all *juros* were freely purchased. The Genoese and others who had claims in their private accounts on the bullion that arrived from the New World would surely have preferred to receive the precious metal that was rightfully theirs. Such desires, however, were ignored from the 1520s on, when the crown, under the plea of urgent need, began to confiscate private shipments of bullion and to compensate the owners with *juros,* issued either with set terms of redemption or as perpetual obligations and bearing interest rates well below those prevailing on the world market.[22] Under such circumstances, of course, the *juros* quickly depreciated in value, with the most precipitous decline occurring in those perpetual obligations that offered virtually no hope of capital recovery.

Spanish finances continued to deteriorate throughout the sixteenth century, but before returning to the calamitous later years and the impact of Spain's failures on world financial markets, it is well to observe that Spain's financial history was neither unique nor distinct from that of the other states of Europe. France, for example, did not encounter similar problems so early in the century and its overall experience was not so chilling, but the ingredients of its troubles were essentially the same. Until the 1540s, the French deficit – largely composed of advances from the tax collectors themselves – remained under control; thereafter, however, the joint pressure from increasing inflation and from the continuing and expanding expense of France's persistent but futile Italian campaigns forced the state into ever greater dependence on the money market. As we have already noted, Lyons had been an international city since the reign of Louis XI, and one that, through the financial needs and opportunities engendered by the international fairs, had grown into a center of world banking. So rich an asset could not long be ignored by a needy Renaissance monarchy and the frequency and scale of royal sorties into the Lyonaise money market consequently rose briskly after the early 1540s. As in Spain, credit was often given only reluctantly and under duress; when resistance was encountered, the monarchy employed force – directly against the French magistrates of Lyons, who were simply jailed until loans were forthcoming, and indirectly through tax threats against foreign merchant-bankers.[23] With the advent in 1555 of the *Grand Parti,* an arrangement for the consolidation of royal loans, crown finance appeared to be on the road to a more regular and reliable system of debt management. Fixed schedules of amortization were established and older debts were, in part, extinguished through exchange for the new obligations, but the crown continued to borrow and to assume heavy commitments to additional creditors, both domestic and foreign, without making adequate provision for repayment.[24]

The French equivalents of the Spanish *juros* were *rentes sur l'hôtel de ville,* which were interest-bearing obligations backed initially by the urban revenues of Paris. Until the death of Francis I in 1547, *rentes* were employed sparingly, the total issue coming only to some 725,000 livres, but they proliferated quickly thereafter; 6.8 million were sold in the next reign, and from 1559 to 1574, another 25.9 million livres of *rentes* were forced on an increasingly reluctant public.[25] As the pace of such borrowing accelerated, the scope of the base altered and *rentes* were issued against the revenues of a growing number of French cities. By the end of the century, the total public debt appears to have climbed to nearly 297 million livres, or roughly fifteen times the recorded crown receipts for the year 1600; a substantial portion of the debt was in the form of *rentes* yielding 8 percent interest.[26] Since crown revenues in 1600 were on the order of 20 million livres, a simple arithmetical calculation suggests that debt service alone, if it were faithfully performed, would have more than consumed the sum total of the annual crown revenues. The comparison is not strictly accurate, however, since the *rentes*, in theory at least, were alienations of urban taxes, not directly reflected in crown receipts; the immense magnitude of royal borrowing is highlighted, however, by measuring the requisite debt service costs against revenues.

Although the level of direct borrowing in France reached truly unwieldy proportions by the century's end, it did not constitute the only drain on French economic resources. Taxes, both ordinary and extraordinary, rose sharply, as indicated on Graph 3, and forced conversions of ecclesiastical lands became a matter of royal policy. In addition, the sale of public offices became firmly embedded in the state's fiscal structure. Instead of increasing the public debt by direct borrowing or by floating new issues of *rentes,* the sale of public offices was simply a device for capitalizing the future value of government salaries by allowing potential public officials to bid for the right to hold a position in government. Because the official was, in effect, purchasing a stream of income, payable over time, public office, under this sytem of venality, became quite similar to *rentes* and annuities; it often promised the added inducement of exemption from a variety of taxes. In this sense, investment in public office in sixteenth-century France stands in obvious parallel to present-day investment in tax-free municipal bonds, which sell at a price premium over those taxable issues sold by private companies to raise investment capital. Direct damage to the state's financial stability as a result of venality of office was initially limited, because the offices sold were already in existence and already received salaries. The prime danger arose from the likely deterioration in the quality of the bureaucracy that might be anticipated once wealth became the sole criterion for public office. Soon, however, the rapacity of the fisc conjoined with the ingenuity of the royal will to push venality of office to its logical extremes. If the sale of existing offices proved profitable, why not create new offices that could also be sold for handsome returns? Never slow to act once a revenue source was identified, the monarchy decreed by royal edict in 1554 that virtually all of the fiscal offices in France – the entire tax bureaucracy – must be doubled through the institution of an alternate for each preexisting functionary at the same salary as that of the incumbent.[27] The negative impact of the sale of these offices on the treasury, once the initial capital received was dissipated, was twofold. First, the added salary burden increased royal expenditures; second, the loss of revenue, consequent upon the tax exemption which the offices carried, lowered crown receipts. The broader economic impact of the legislation – particularly during later years, when the number of offices affected grew – was even more profound. Venality at once decreased the tax base and increased the costs of government at a time when expenditures were already rising exponentially. As a result, more and more devious financial expedients were required and utilized to buttress crown receipts. The role of local and national guild legislation as a guarantor of quality diminished, while the purely fiscal aspect expanded into a national system for siphoning money from industrial and commercial enterprise. Personal taxes and fees cut more deeply into personal incomes, and as they did, the advantages of exemption from the fiscal assault grew accordingly. Together, these factors amounted to a three-pronged attack on capital formation. Rising taxes were in themselves a direct drain on private capital. When they were applied to industrial enterprise, they precluded the retention and reinvestment of earnings, and simultaneously lowered profitability and the return on investment in manufacturing. This sequence, in turn, acted to dissuade potential entrepreneurs from further investment, because investment normally depends on optimistic estimates of future returns. Finally, as the rates of return in private investment declined under these cumulative pressures, the relative advantages of committing capital to the purchase of public office and tax-exempt status were highlighted. Such investment, when undertaken, simultaneously diverted capital from productive enterprise and enticed entrepreneurial talent from the productive sector of the economy to the public sector, where talent, if exercised at all, was more apt to have a pernicious than a positive effect on French economic development.

In the other states of Europe, financial problems became more severe during the later sixteenth century, but they were met with more prudence, luck, and skill. In the United Provinces, the struggle for independence placed heavy burdens on the small republic's financial resources. There each town was responsible for a portion of the war costs, and annuities, sold on a municipal basis, were taken up by the affluent burghers. Because many of the investors were also participants in government, self-interest inculcated deep concern for the provision of adequate funds to cover repayment of the obligations issued.[28] Taxes were increased to cover the debts, but world political and economic patterns were so favorable to the Dutch that the burdens, though heavy, never became so oppressive as to destroy the economic progress of the United Provinces. Cotemporal with the steep rise in war-induced debt were those events that aided the Dutch in the Mediterranean. The battle of Lepanto, which weakened the Turkish navy, coincided with the demographic expansion of Constantinople and the consequent reduction in the exportable surpluses of Anatolian grain. The efforts of the dukes of Tuscany to develop the port of Livorno and to find northern sources of grain favored the Dutch, who at the time were constantly extending their role in the Baltic carrying trade, and especially in the commerce of Danzig. Further, the prominent position that the Genoese occupied in Spanish finance diverted immense quantities of Spanish bullion to northern Italy, where it was employed, at least in part, for the purchase of Baltic grain carried by the Dutch and English. In a sense, one might say that, through this devious chain of circumstances, Spain at once forced its Dutch enemies to increase their debts and then provided them with the wealth to meet the obligations without more embarrassment than a fourteen-year suspension of interest payments during the war-torn years after 1572. The financial stability of Holland, in the face of military assault by the most formidable power in Europe, was a remarkable tribute to the republic's ability to mobilize the world's resources.

During the first half of the sixteenth century, under Henry VIII, a prince with grand ambition, England was borrowing heavily and stood in jeopardy of pursuing the same dreary path to insolvency that Spain had already embarked upon. In 1544, Henry borrowed 100,000 crowns from the south German Welser family's agent in Antwerp; in 1545, he owed the Fugger agents in that same city 152,180 Flemish pounds, an obligation contracted in a single loan; during one three-year period, he engaged himself for nearly a million pounds sterling.[29] These same years also witnessed some unfortunate efforts to dump huge quantities of lead, more than 26 million pounds, on the Antwerp market in order to raise cash; in both this and subsequent experiments with the massive sale of alum, English hopes were frustrated as prices quickly collapsed under the weight of excess supply.[30] Because Henry's early loans were often granted in commodities at inflated prices, interest rates were extremely high; one of the several achievements of Sir Thomas Gresham was to lower the royal interest rate from levels as high as 18 percent to something on the order of 12 percent. The second, and even more noteworthy accomplishment of the famous financier, was to keep the crown solvent. In 1566, Gresham claimed to have borrowed more than 1.84 million Flemish pounds in Antwerp during his fourteen years as royal agent and to have presided over the almost total repayment of that great sum.[31] The period of large-scale borrowing in Antwerp ended during the 1560s as English cloth was excluded from the city and as the political problems that were ultimately to ruin Antwerp intensified. The English crown turned to domestic sources, occasionally resorting to forced loans, but generally remaining cautious with regard to borrowing. Elizabeth's fabled parsimony coupled with her political circumspection to limit crown demands. Between 1575 and 1603, domestic borrowing totaled some 461,000 pounds,[32] a substantial sum, but, at only one and a half times annual crown receipts, not one that threatened England's financial stability.

Before returning to the failures of Spain, it is well to consider one more success story. Venice, during the early sixteenth century, teetered on the brink of insolvency induced by military demands; bonds that had sold at 102 at the beginning of the century, sold at 40 in 1509 and plummeted to 10 during the 1520s.[33] From 1530 on, however, the republic began to retire outstanding issues and to use state revenues to reduce debt; success bred success, and as debts decreased, more revenue was available for repayment instead of being dissipated in interest charges. By 1570, substantial progress was visible, but the War of Cyprus from 1570 to 1573 added 6 million ducats to the deficit and forced a setback in the program of debt reduction. Even so, the Venetians quickly resumed their efforts once peace returned, and by the beginning of the seventeenth century, the republic was not only completely free of debts but able to boast of a substantial cash reserve.

Comprehensive treatment of the complexities of public finance during the sixteenth century is clearly beyond the scope of this book, yet enough has been said to indicate the growing importance of access to money markets and the broad dependence of many governments upon their credit lines. Two further general observations are necessary, however, in order to demonstrate the crucial nature of public credit. On the one hand, as the century progressed and as the scale of public borrowing expanded, the credit markets became inextricably linked. On the other, money lending became a political act of critical significance. Each of these statements may be documented through consideration of the various Spanish bankruptcies that marked the latter half of our period. In 1557, for example, Philip of Spain, reviewing the catastrophic financial situation that comprised his inheritance, learned that virtually all the crown revenues were mortgaged for years to come and that all sources of credit had been exploited to the breaking point. Philip acted with dispatch, suspending all further payments to his creditors and confiscating two shipments of bullion that had been destined for the Fuggers at Antwerp. Repayment was beyond Spain's capacity, but the debts were honored in theory, if not in fact; by 1560, the Fugger's nominal lien against Spain totaled nearly 3 million ducats, a sum in excess of the firm's capital at the time.[34] Philip's default shook the financial world; credit dried up in Antwerp for all but a few favored borrowers. In France, the news of Philip's suspension of payment conjoined with a defeat of the French army to produce similar credit stringency in Lyons. The French crown, strapped for cash, arbitrarily lowered its interest payments in 1558, and, in its own turn, suspended all payments in the following year.[35] By mid-century, financial problems in one portion of Europe were quickly transmitted to the remainder. In a sense, this was fortunate, because it preserved the balance of power among nations. In an age of mercenary armies, money truly was the sinews of war, and backruptcy would have led directly to political defeat had the other side enjoyed continuing access to credit. As it was, the virtually simultaneous failures of Spain and France forestalled either from deriving an advantage from the other's weakness; instead, both sides were compelled to draw back and to resolve their grievances temporarily in the treaty of Cateau-Cambrésis in 1559. In passing, we may recall our earlier observation that the economic recovery of northern Italy dates from this period and the termination of the French adventure in that country.

The second great Spanish bankruptcy occurred in 1575, when Philip again suspended payments on his debts and again precipitated an international financial crisis. On this occasion, it seemed as if the world was devoid of cash. Within Spain two banks failed in 1576, and the Genoese refused further loans; even the Fuggers, who remained loyal to the crown, were able to offer only limited help.[36] Inevitably, debts were settled in depreciated *juros,* which had come to serve as a kind of capital levy against the creditors of the Spanish monarchy, and for several years, the credit of the crown was in world disrepute. Happily for Spain, however, bullion imports began to rise sharply during the late 1570s, trebling the level of the 1550s and doubling again in the 1580s.[37] The imports rescued Philip for a time and he was able to restore his credit, but before that occurred, a number of pan-European consequences flowed from the bankruptcy. The imperial troops in the Netherlands were mainly foreign mercenaries whose loyalty ceased with their pay; the failure of Spanish finances led directly to the first sack of Antwerp in 1576 and to the subsequent brutalization of the population that has come to be known as the "Spanish Fury" even though the troops were largely German. In France, Lyonaise and other bankers also suffered the ramifications of Spain's failure, and in 1575, Henry III discovered that his credit was also exhausted. The market that had absorbed an annual issue of 2.6 million livres of *rentes* during the reign of Charles IX accepted only 220,000 livres annually from 1575 to 1584.[38] The usual expedients were tried, offices were created and sold, domain lands were alienated, but funds were still insufficient. Financial pressures forced the king to treat with his young brother, Alençon, who was leading a powerful Huguenot faction, and to accept the Peace of Monsieur, which provided one of the temporary respites that occurred periodically during the confusion of the wars of religion.

Little appears to have been learned from the bankruptcies of 1557 and 1575. As soon as Spain's credit recovered, it went to the well again and the cycle of overextension, crisis, and default was repeated at twenty-year intervals until the middle of the seventeenth century. In 1596, the crown again suspended payments to its creditors and ultimately settled by converting debts into even larger issues of *juros.* During the sixteenth century, Spain's profitable international fairs and its financial hub were located at Medina del Campo, near Zamora in the Duero valley; the failure of 1596 completed the work of earlier failures in ruining the prosperity of the fairs and shifting the financial capital to Madrid.[39] This movement complemented the southward migration of the population and served further to withdraw the support and the benefits of economic interaction from Spain's most promising economic region – the north, the Duero valley, and Zamora

– while again confirming the dangers of a rapacious treasury and its capacity to stifle nascent industrial growth.[40] The political result of the failure inevitably was peace, in this case with France through the Treaty of Vervins in 1598. The international character of public finance at this time is further demonstrated by the simultaneous exhaustion of French finances. Debt consolidation was also unavoidable in France, and Henry IV's unilateral reduction, often halving, of interest payments was needed, despite the substantial hardship inflicted on the holders of royal *rentes*. In the French case, however, Sully, Henry's minister, was able to restore some order to the royal revenues and budget; combined with the religious toleration expressed in the Edict of Nantes, this permitted France to enjoy a period of recovery and economic resurgence during the first decades of the seventeenth century.

The last Spanish bankruptcy that concerns us occurred in 1607, but since the details of payment suspension and debt conversion merely repeat previous patterns, they need not be reiterated. Politically, the default led to a treaty with the Dutch in 1609 that had great economic significance for the remainder of the seventeenth century. Antwerp was already in decline during the last years of the sixteenth century, but the 1609 truce made that city's position hopeless by sealing the mouth of the Scheldt and severing access to the sea. For the Dutch, on the contrary, the treaty provided a respite from war and allowed the favorable confluence of economic circumstances that surrounded the republic to bestow their blessings. Dutch finances improved markedly, the Indies trade began to pay handsome dividends as Dutch penetration of the East deepened, and heavy investment in the armaments industry combined with virtual control of Sweden's copper output to make Amsterdam the world's armaments supplier just as the start of the Thirty Years' War in 1618 caused military demand to soar.[41]

Private capital needs

Private capital markets were not yet highly developed in the sixteenth century, so it is not possible to compare relative allocations of capital among governments, private industries, and commercial ventures. It seems obvious, however, that the desperate measures that constituted Spanish financial policy deeply damaged private capital accumulation. Forced loans and arbitrary and confiscatory taxes meant that investment decisions were largely controlled by the state; since the state chose to invest in empire and war and since this entailed substantial transfers of funds beyond Spain's borders, that nation remained a capital-starved and industrially backward country throughout the sixteenth and seventeenth centuries.[42]

In France, too, government demand for cash led to a war between public and private capital needs, with undoubtedly harmful, if unquantifiable, effects on economic development. If a particular industry was important to the state, however, capital was raised either by direct royal participation or by the grant of such extensive privileges as were necessary to attract it from other uses. Saltpeter, the basic ingredient in the manufacture of gunpowder, was so strategic a commodity that it quickly drew royal attention.[43] From the mid-fifteenth century, saltpeter production was subject to government regulation, and by the middle of the next century, royal warehouses existed in many towns and villages throughout the kingdom; by the reign of Henry IV, royal commissioners were charged with regulation of the most minute details of production, and, more to the point of our current discussion, with the provision of capital and capital equipment for the manufacture. State control produced fairly good results in the saltpeter industry, and a case can surely be made that such control was justified in an industry so vital to national interests. On the other hand, it is well not to overlook the price of success. If the conflict between public and private capital needs demanded that the state subsidize one industry, the price was paid by the others; taxes, whether generalized or specific, penalized the industries that were not favored, limiting both their profits and their access to private capital. Direct taxes on the output of iron manufacturers such as those imposed in 1542, for example,[44] appear to have been levied solely for revenue purposes, but they reduced the competitive position of iron manufacturing and, in effect, amounted to the indirect subsidization of one industry, saltpeter, by another. Such distortion of market relationships inevitably leads to less efficient capital allocation and to failure to attain the highest potential output of goods and services that the unhindered economy might otherwise have produced.

In England, the burden of fiscalism was lighter, but even there motives of national security engendered royal efforts to control the manufacture of saltpeter and gunpowder similar to those practiced across the Channel. In the early 1560s, George Evelyn was granted a royal monopoly for the manufacture of gunpower, and the patent remained in the family for decades.[45] Interestingly enough, it was possible for Evelyn to share his monopoly rights and to seek out private sources of capital among wealthy London merchants. In England, capital remained available for private investment, and although privilege directed it toward the gunpowder industry, capital was free to flow in the direction that maximized profit. Now saltpeter was difficult to collect, because the raw material was found in barns, outhouses, stables, and dovecotes widely dispersed throughout the kingdom. The grant of royal privilege, authorizing royal agents to search for and seize saltpeter-earth, outraged the individual's sense of privacy and of property, and provoked strong resistance when the collectors made their incursions into private estates. The crown's self-asserted rights were hotly contested and it was only through an argument based on the "preservation of the state" that saltpeter collection and the gunpowder monopoly were exempted for the 1624 statute that outlawed monopolies in England.[46] Even so, the crown's prerogatives in this sphere were severely limited by a decision of the twelve judges of England in the following year.[47] Overseas trading companies, like gunpowder, were expressly exempted from the provisions of the antimonopoly statute, because their activities demanded semigovernmental power – dealing with foreign princes, making treaties, and occasionally taking military action. One might also note that, since their commercial provenance lay beyond the borders of England, they could be granted such extraordinary powers without threatening the integrity of customary law within the kingdom.

The English experience is illuminating in several ways. As we have already observed, England's industrial growth during the sixteenth century proceeded faster and was more broadly based than that of any other major state in Europe. Such growth at once depended on and provided capital funds for further expansion, and the funds were available. The formation of overseas trading ventures was largely accomplished with private capital, and even domestic royal monopolies found willing private investors who had funds to contribute to a profitable enterprise. What sustained this fortunate situation in England? The fact that Britain was an island kingdom bestowed a political security that other states lacked, and by providing a natural line of defense, the sea limited the need for excessively expensive military commitments. This advantage diminished the exchequer's demands for defense funds and lightened the economically destructive treasury competition for the wealth required for commercial and industrial purposes. Tudor and especially Stuart monarchs, however, were not devoid of political aspirations, nor did they lack the imagination to invent means for squandering the nation's wealth overseas. Indeed, the history of the early Stuarts is in many ways the history of their endeavors to introduce economic, fiscal, and political policies that had already been inflicted on Continental economic systems with effects that ranged from harmful to devastating. Happily for England, their desires were frustrated and it is here that we return full circle to our earlier questions of law and the vocabulary of constraint.

The extended development of parliamentary control over English taxation and over the granting of subsidies is sufficiently well known that it need not be repeated here; we may note, however, that even the strongest of the Tudor monarchs had to contend with Parliament's reluctance to grant funds and that most were wise enough not overly to alarm that body. Turbulent debate in Elizabeth's last parliament, for example, made it emphatically clear, even though the requested funds were ultimately approved, that the national tolerance for heavy taxation was severely strained. The discussion of monopolies was even more acerbic, and under pressure, Elizabeth herself undertook to promise that some of the monopolies "would presently be repealed, some suspended, and none put into execution, but such as should first have a trial according to the laws for the good of the people."[48] Early in the reign of James I, the English courts ruled, in *Dàcy v. Allen*, that monopolies were prima facie violations of both common and statute law.[49] The language of both queen and magistrate and the confident assertion of a law beyond and above the crown would have had a hollow echo on the Continent at this time, even if it were still formulaically employed.

Since England, unlike France, had but one parliament, that body was a far more powerful spokesman of the national interest than either the various *parlements* or the regional estates of France. As spokesman, it benefited from a vocabulary drawn from customary law as well as statute that had remained intact in England, where the power of Roman law was weak and consequently not the effective tool for undermining custom that it became in the hands of Continental monarchs. As spokesman of the national interest, articulate in the vocabulary of precedent and custom, Parliament was effective in limiting crown revenue demands and thereby in preserving private wealth for capital accumulation, reinvestment, and economic growth.

7
Retrospect

The preceding chapters have touched upon three modes of perception of society – the nature and flux of systems of legal abstractions, the realities of political history, and the development of economic society. Emphasis has, of course, been primarily on the latter, as it must be in a book devoted to economic history, but my endeavor has been to interweave these themes without according dominance to any one in particular. To do so would be to falsify history. A crude economic determinism that made legal abstractions bend and political systems evolve solely in response to changes in the economic foundation of society would be a gross distortion and oversimplification of an extraordinarily complex period. So, too, would the converse view, which claimed that the dissolution of thirteenth-century value systems and the shattering of older, accepted legal and philosophical premises acted as the prime stimulus for the economic changes of the period and controlled their direction by redefining man and his relationship to the economic environment. Equally unsatisfactory would be a view that credited political leaders with the power to act in independence of the world around them or even the capacity to pose economic questions beyond the limits set by their own value systems.

The truth does reside, it seems to me, in the tension and interaction between and among the three elements that we have considered. The limitations of language force us to analyze the past in a linear fashion, beginning with one event or theme and proceeding to the next in sequential steps, and at the risk, therefore, of losing the wholeness of the field of multidirectional interaction that we seek to comprehend. If one starts with a political premise – for example, the statement that war became increasingly expensive during the sixteenth century – one can trace some of the consequences in a fairly convincing manner.

War required revenue; taxes and loans absorbed capital; national priorities diverted economic resources from other uses; and success or failure in battle directly altered trade patterns and the availability of raw materials. The need for taxes and raw materials also affected property rights, the integrity of the home, the behavior of the judicial system, and, consequently, confidence in the received body of legal abstractions. Recall here the problem of saltpeter collection and its effect on the individual, his liberty, and his domestic security.

This linear analysis is superficially viable, but one could enter the identical field from another angle and generate an equally convincing but alternate sequence by beginning with an economic premise. Rising population, for example, emphasized the scarcity of natural resources and forced states to take political action to preserve their economic independence. This led to increasingly expensive military involvements; mobilization of resources in support of war resulted in higher taxes, capital diversion, and a reduction in the liberties of the domestic population. Again, one might begin with a voluntarist premise – the prince is not bound by his own law and there is no sanction against his actions save the political power of another state. In order to increase their power, princes manipulated economic resources at home for the purpose of maintaining powerful armies and an invincible navy. The quest for further aggrandizement led to ever more expensive wars, additional mobilization, higher taxes, and assaults on individual rights and the legal structure.

Each of these three approaches produces a different perspective, though each considers essentially the same empirical phenomena and the same critical conflicts. Individually, no one of them is satisfactory, since the implied causality introduced by each linear sequence and its analysis precludes full awareness of the multiple interactions and mutual reinforcements present in historical reality. Taken together, they remind us that a sequential pattern is not necessarily a causal one, but such knowledge need not lead us to historical pyrrhonism or utter skepticism with regard to our capacity to understand the past.

It is useful, for example, to recognize that the preservation of custom and precedent in England was not merely an exogenous given of that nation's history; to be aware that political events reaching back to William the Conqueror and John contributed to their preservation; to know that the economic and demographic strength of London also aided in that noble enterprise; and to recall that the very existence of the vocabulary of custom and precedent, at every stage, exercised its influence on political and economic events. Yet awareness of such deep interaction does not detract from the value of an analysis that momentarily focuses, for example, on the power of custom and precedent for the purpose of illuminating England's fiscal structure in the sixteenth century and exploring its influence on economic growth.

By the same token, the observation that Holland's role as the most important commercial nation during the late sixteenth and most of the seventeenth centuries deeply influenced Hugo Grotius, the author of the first major explication of international law – one that was predicated upon a secular, nonreligious system of natural law – does not falsify history.[1] Nor is it irrelevant to note that England, where custom was strong, and Holland, where the East India Company could subsidize a treatise on natural and international law, were the two most successful nations in Europe in the quest for economic development. For Grotius, natural law once again sets limits to the power of princes to control trade and required free passage of goods and men across international borders; voluntarism was no longer the sole normative standard when princes confronted each other beyond their borders, and free trade was justified by the proscriptions of natural law. In the case of Grotius and Holland, it is perhaps legitimate to follow our tripartite analysis sequentially from the economic foundations, through the influence of political exigencies, to the ultimate perception of the abstractions of philosophy and law. Yet even in this apparently obvious instance, caution is demanded. Our proffered linear analysis may illuminate the origins of Grotius's commitment to doctrines of natural law and free trade, but it is only through awareness of the interactions among economic, political, and abstract intellectual forces that we may fully comprehend the man and the period. Despite the continuing growth of Holland's commercial strength in the seventeenth century and despite intensified military conflict and the increasingly obvious need for a system of law that could transcend national boundaries, Grotius's defense of free trade and his arguments for the transcendent role of natural law were not widely accepted until the Enlightenment of the eighteenth century. Holland grew more, rather than less, restrictive in its commercial policy, and Grotius, himself a victim of political and doctrinal cross currents, died in exile.

Notes

Chapter 1. The abstractions of law and property

1 Hauser, H., ed., *La Response de Jean Bodin àM. de Malestroit; 1568,* Paris, Armand Colin, 1932.
2 Bodin, Jean, *Les Six livres de la république,* Paris, 1576.
3 Bodin, Jean, *De la Démonomanie des sorciers,* Paris, 1580.
4 Petit-Dutaillis, C., "France: Louis XI," *Cambridge Medieval History,* VIII, Cambridge, Cambridge University Press, 1958, pp. 275–6.
5 Agricola, Georgius, *De re metallica,* trans. Herbert C. Hoover, New York, Dover Publications, Inc., 1950, pp. 217–18.
6 Machiavelli, Niccolo, *The Prince,* trans. G. Bull, Harmondsworth, Penguin Books, 1961, passim but especially pp. 90–92.
7 Marsilius of Padua, *The Defender of the Peace: Defensor Pacis,* trans. Alan Gewirth, New York, Harper & Row, Publishers, 1967.
8 Passerim D'Entrèves, A., *The Medieval Contribution to Political Thought,* New York, Humanities Press, Inc., 1959, p. 63.
9 Marsilius of Padua, *Defensor Pacis,* II, xii, para. 9.
10 Ibid., II, xii, para. 7.
11 Idem.
12 Ibid., II, xii, para. 8.
13 Ibid., I, xii, para. 3.
14 Ibid., I, xviii, passim.
15 Previté-Orton, C., *Marsilius of Padua* (from the *Proceedings of the British Academy,* Vol. XXI), London, Humphrey Milford Amen House E.C., 1935.
16 Passerim D'Entrèves, *The Medieval Contribution,* pp. 61, 85, 90.
17 William of Ockham, *Philosophical Writings,* trans. P. Boehner, Indianapolis, The Bobbs-Merrill Co., Inc., 1964, p. xxvii.
18 Ibid., p. 25.
19 Ibid., p. 39. *Summa totius logicae,* I, c. xv.

20 *Primo modo absolutum, secundo modo cum aliqua conditione, modificatione, vel specificatione, seu declaratione.* Quoted in Georges de LaGarde, *La Naissance de l'espirit laïque au déclin du moyen age, IV, Guillaume d'Ockham, défense de l'empire,* Louvain, Editions Nauwelaerts, 1962, p. 117, n. 17.

21 *Rursus ille modus regendi universitatem mortalium, qui aliquando fuit licitus et justus est expediens reputandus, quia omne licitum et justum est judicandum expediens.* Quoted in LaGarde, *La Naissance,* IV, p. 117, n. 15.

22 Bodin, Jean, *The Six Books of the Commonwealth,* trans. M. J. Tooley, Oxford, Basil Blackwell, no date, p. 188.

23 The literature is considerable but for an economist's view see J. A. Schumpeter, *History of Economic Analysis,* New York, Oxford University Press, 1954, pp. 73–142. Also worthy of note are Gabriel Le Bras, "Conceptions of Economy and Society," *The Cambridge Economic History,* III, Cambridge, Cambridge University Press, 1963, pp. 554–75; J. W. Baldwin, "The Medieval Merchant Before the Bar of Canon Law," *Papers of the Michigan Academy of Science, Arts, and Letters,* XLIV (1959) 287–99; W. J. Courtenay, "The King and the Leaden Coin: The Economic Background of 'Sine Qua Non' Causality," *Traditio,* XXVIII (1972) 185–210, and "Token Coinage and the Administration of Poor Relief During the Late Middle Ages," *Journal of Interdisciplinary History,* III (1972–73) 275–95; Raymond de Roover, "La Doctrine scholastique en matière de monopole et son application à la politique économique des communes Italiennes," *Studi in Onore di Amintore Fanfani,* I, Milan, Dott. A. Giuffré, 1962, pp. 151–79, and "Scholastic Economics: Survival and Lasting Influence from the Sixteenth Century to Adam Smith," *Quarterly Journal of Economics,* LXIX (1955) 161–90.

24 See p. 6 and note 19.

25 LaGarde, *La Naissance,* IV, p. 233.

26 O'Brien, George, *An Essay on Medieval Economic Teaching,* London, Longmans, Green and Co., 1920, p. 84.

27 Marsilius of Padua, *Defensor Pacis,* II, xii, para. 10.

28 Ibid., II, xvii, para. 16.

29 Idem., "And not only can the legislator lawfully, according to divine law, revoke the authority to distribute such temporal goods from the person or persons to whom it had entrusted it, but also it can sell or otherwise alienate these goods for a reasonable cause, since they belong to the legislator and are always rightfully in its power. . . ."

30 LaGarde, *La Naissance,* IV, pp. 211–12.

31 *Absque causa vel sine culpa.* Quoted in LaGarde, *La Naissance,* IV, p. 212.

32 *Unam sanctam.* Printed in R. H. Bainton, *The Medieval Church,* New York, D. Van Nostrand Company, 1962, pp. 158–9.

33 William of Ockham, *Philosophical Writings,* p. xiv.

34 LaGarde, *La Naissance,* IV, p. 37.

35 Hay, Denys, *Europe in the Fourteenth and Fifteenth Centuries,* New York, Holt, Rinehart and Winston, Inc., 1966, p. 312.

36 William of Ockham, *An princeps pro suo succursu, scilicet guerrae, possit recipere bona ecclesiarum etiam invito papa,* in J. G. Sikes, ed., *Guillemi de Ockham, Opera Politica,* 3 vols., Manchester, Manchester University Press, 1940, 1956, 1963. Vol. I, pp. 224–71, p. 231: *Sed allegationibus intendo monstrare patentibus quod praelati et clerici sibi subiecti ei in guerra sua iusta de bonis ecclesiae, et non solum de propriis, subventionis tenentur auxilium impertiri, et quod etiam verus summus pontifex de plenitudine potestatis eos prohibere minime posset, et si de facto prohiberet, prohibito sua ipso facto et iure nulla esset, nec alicuius esset omnino vigoris.*

37 McKisack, May, *The Fourteenth Century: 1307–1399,* Oxford, Clarendon Press, 1959, pp. 280–2.

38 Ibid., p. 290.

39 Marsilius of Padua, *Defensor Pacis,* II, xxiii, para. 13.

40 McKisack, *Fourteenth Century,* p. 283.

41 Bloch, Marc, *Feudal Society,* trans. L. A. Manyon, Chicago, Chicago University Press, 1961, p. 117.

42 Rashdall, H., "The Medieval Universities," *Cambridge Medieval History,* VI, Cambridge, Cambridge University Press, 1964, p. 579.

43 Bloch, Marc, *Feudal Society,* pp. 118–19.

44 Schipa, M., "Italy and Sicily under Frederick II," *Cambridge Medieval History,* VI, Cambridge, Cambridge University Press, 1964, pp. 148–9.

45 Livermore, H., *A History of Spain,* New York, Grove Press, Inc., 1960, pp. 138–9.

46 Ibid., p. 139.

47 *Ordonnances des rois de France de la troisième race recueillies par ordre chronologique,* Paris, Imprimerie Royale, 1724.

48 Doucet, R., *Les Institutions de la France au xvie siècle,* I, Paris, A. et J. Picard et Cie, 1948, p. 60.

49 *Ordonnances des rois de France.*

50 Sabine, G. H., *A History of Political Theory,* New York, Holt, Rinehart and Winston, Inc., 1961, pp. 169–70.

51 Bouwsma, W. J., "Lawyers and Early Modern Culture," *American Historical Review,* LXXVIII (1973) 326.

52 Franklin, J. H., *Jean Bodin and the Sixteenth Century Revolution in the Methodology of Law and History,* New York, Columbia University Press, 1963, pp. 19–27.

53 Ibid., p. 23.

54 For this paragraph I am heavily indebted to J. H. Franklin, *Jean Bodin,* pp. 36-79.
55 Quoted in J. H. Franklin, *Jean Bodin,* p. 69.
56 Butterfield, H., *The Origins of Modern Science, 1300-1800,* New York, Macmillan Publishing Co., Inc., 1958, pp. 34-35.

Chapter 2. Recovery: population and money supply

1 Lopez, R. S., H. A. Miskimin, and A. Udovitch, "England to Egypt, 1350-1500: Long-Term Trends and Long-Distance Trade," in M. A. Cook, ed., *Studies in the Economic History of the Middle East,* London, Oxford University Press, 1970, pp. 93-128.
2 Miskimin, H. A., "Monetary Movements and Market Structure - Forces for Contraction in Fourteenth and Fifteenth Century England," *The Journal of Economic History,* XXIV (1964) 470-90.
3 Vicens-Vives, J., *Historia social y económica de España y América,* II, Barcelona, Teide 1957, p. 91.
4 Lopez, R. S. and H. A. Miskimin, "The Economic Depression of the Renaissance," *The Economic History Review,* 2nd ser., XIV (1962) 408-26.
5 Ibid.
6 Cornwall, Julian, "English Population in the Early Sixteenth Century," *The Economic History Review,* 2nd ser., XXIII (1970) 32-44.
7 Mauro, F., *Le XVIe siècle Européen - aspects économiques,* Paris, Presses Universitaires de France, 1970, p. 160.
8 Braudel, F., *La Méditerranée et le monde Méditerranéen à l'époque de Philippe II,* I, Paris, Armand Colin, 1966, p. 370.
9 Helleiner, K., "The Population of Europe from the Black Death to the Eve of the Vital Revolution," in E. E. Rich and C. H. Wilson, *The Cambridge Economic History of Europe,* Cambridge, Cambridge University Press, 1967, pp. 32-33.
10 Gascon, R., "Immigration et croissance," *Annales: économies, sociétés, civilisations,* XXV (1970) 989.
11 Helleiner, K., "The Population of Europe," pp. 24-26.
12 Beloch, K. J., *Bevolkerungsgeschichte Italiens,* III, Berlin, Walter de Gruyter and Co., 1961, p. 354.
13 Lane, F. C., *Venice: A Maritime Republic,* Baltimore, Johns Hopkins University Press, 1973, p. 304.
14 Mauro, *Le XVIe siècle,* p. 161.
15 Lane, *Venice,* p. 19.
16 Vicens-Vives, J., *An Economic History of Spain,* trans. F. M. López-Morillas, Princeton, Princeton University Press, 1969, pp. 250, 253, 259.
17 Nef, J. U., "Mining and Metallurgy in Medieval Civilization," in M. M. Postan and

H. J. Habakkuk, eds., *The Cambridge Economic History of Europe*, II, Cambridge, Cambridge University Press, 1952, p. 457.

18 See, for example, Vannoccio Biringuccio, *De la Pirotechnia*, 1540, and Georgius Agricola, *De re metallica*, 1556.

19 Agricola, G., *De re metallica*, trans. Herbert C. Hoover, New York, Dover Publications, Inc., 1950.

20 Smith, C. S. and R. J. Forbes, "Mining and Assaying," in C. Singer, E. J. Holmyard, A. R. Hall, and T. I. Williams, eds., *A History of Technology*, III, Oxford, Clarendon Press, 1957, pp. 27-71.

21 Hamilton, E. J., *American Treasure and the Price Revolution in Spain*, Cambridge, Harvard University Press, 1934, p. 15.

22 Nef. J. U., "Silver Production in Central Europe, 1450-1618," *Journal of Political Economy*, XLIX (1941) 575-91.

23 Elliott, J. H., *Imperial Spain: 1469-1716*, New York, The New American Library, Inc., 1963, p. 61.

24 Parry, J. H., *The Establishment of the European Hegemony: 1415-1715*, New York, Harper & Row, Publishers, 1961, p. 46.

25 Throughout this paragraph I am indebted to J. H. Elliott, *Imperial Spain*, pp. 68-74.

26 Nef, J. U., "Mining and Metallurgy," pp. 451-8.

27 Idem., pp. 480-9.

28 Elliott, *Imperial Spain*, pp. 180-2.

29 Malestroit, J., *The Paradoxes of Malestroit*, trans G. A. Moore, in G. A. Moore, *Jean Bodin's Response (1568-78) to Malestroit's Paradoxes*, Chevy Chase, Country Dollar Press, 1946.

30 Hauser, H., *La Response de Jean Bodin à M. de Malestroit: 1568*, Paris, Armand Colin, 1932.

31 Schumpeter, J., *History of Economic Analysis*, New York, Oxford University Press, 1954, pp. 316-17.

32 Fisher, Irving, *The Purchasing Power of Money*, New York, Macmillan Publishing Co., Inc., 1926.

33 Supra, Table III.

34 Elliott, *Imperial Spain*, pp. 190-2 and J. Nadal Oller, "La Revolución de los Precios Españoles en el Siglo XVI," *Hispania*, XIX (1959) 503-29.

35 For a discussion of the monetary stock and an alternate view of the shortage see F. P. Braudel and F. C. Spooner, "Prices in Europe, 1450-1750," in E. E. Rich and C. H. Wilson, eds., *The Cambridge Economic History of Europe*, IV, Cambridge, Cambridge University Press, 1967, pp. 442-6.

36 Miskimin, H., "The Enforcement of Gresham's Law," to appear in the *Proceedings of the Quarta Settimana di Studio*, Prato, Istituto Internazionale di Storia Economica "Francesco Datini,"1972.

37 This paragraph is, in the main, extracted from H. Miskimin, "Population Growth and the Price Revolution in England," *The Journal of European Economic History*, IV (1975) 179–86.

38 E. H. Phelps Brown and Sheila Hopkins, "Seven Centuries of the Prices of Consumables Compared with Builders' Wage Rates," *Economica*, XXIII (1956).

39 Hamilton, E. J., "American Treasure and the Rise of Capitalism," *Economica*, XXVII (1929) 338-57.

40 Keynes, J. M., *A Treatise on Money*, II, London, Macmillan and Co., Ltd., 1930, pp. 159-63.

41 Nef, J. U., "Prices and Industrial Capitalism in France and England, 1540-1640," *Economic History Review*, VII (1937) 155-85.

42 Felix, David, "Profit Inflation and Industrial Growth: The Historic Record and Contemporary Analogies," *The Quarterly Journal of Economics*, LXX (1956) 441-63.

43 See, for example, Y. S. Brenner, "The Inflation of Prices in Early Sixteenth Century England," *Economic History Review*, 2nd ser., XIV (1961) 225-39, and "The Inflation of Prices in England, 1551-1600," *Economic History Review*, 2nd ser., XV (1962) 266-84.

Chapter 3. Agriculture: the rising demand for food

1 Braudel, F. P. and F. C. Spooner, "Prices in Europe from 1450 to 1750," in E. E. Rich and C. H. Wilson, eds., *The Cambridge Economic History of Europe*, IV, Cambridge, Cambridge University Press, 1967, pp. 470-5.

2 Miskimin, H. A., *Money, Prices, and Foreign Exchange in Fourteenth Century France*, New Haven, Yale University Press, 1963, pp. 102-4.

3 Bindoff, S. T., "The Greatness of Antwerp," in G. R. Elton, ed., *The New Cambridge Modern History*, II, Cambridge, Cambridge University Press, 1965, pp. 50-69.

4 Koenigsberger, H. G., "Property and the Price Revolution (Hainault, 1475-1573)," *Economics History Review*, 2nd ser., IX (1956) 1-15, Table 2.

5 De Vries, Jan, *The Dutch Rural Economy in the Golden Age: 1500-1700*, New Haven, Yale University Press, 1974, p. 149.

6 Ibid., p. 152.

7 Coornaert, E., *Les Francais et le commerce international à Anvers: fin du xve–xvie siècle*, II, Paris, Marcel Rivière et Cie, 1961, p. 100.

8 De Vries, J., *The Dutch Rural Economy*, p. 145.

9 Ibid., pp. 125-7.

10 Slicher van Bath, B. H., *The Agrarian History of Western Europe: A.D. 500-1850*, trans. Olive Ordish, London, Edward Arnold, Ltd., 1963, pp. 200-1.

11 Homan, B., "La Circolazione della monete d'oro in Ungheria del x al xiv secolo

e la crisi Europea dell'oro nel secolo xiv," *Rivista Italiana di numismatica,* 2nd ser., V (1922) 109–56.

12 Malowist, M., "L'Evolution industrielle en Pologne du xive au xviie siècle," *Studi in onore di Armando Sapori,* I, Milan, Istituto Editoriale Cisalpino, 1957, pp. 573–603.

13 Ibid., pp. 575–7.

14 Ibid., p. 587.

15 Hoszowski, Stanislow, "The Polish Baltic Trade in the 15th–18th Centuries," in *Poland at the XIth International Congress of Historical Sciences in Stockholm,* Warsaw, Polish Academy of Sciences, 1960, p. 130.

16 Ibid., p. 127.

17 Malowist, M., "L'Evolution industrielle en Pologne," p. 588.

18 Betts, R. R., "The Central Monarchies," in Denys Hay, *Europe in the Fourteenth and Fifteenth Centuries,* New York, Holt, Rinehart and Winston, Inc., 1966, p. 239.

19 Ibid., p. 238.

20 Hoszowski, S., "The Polish Baltic Trade," p. 128.

21 Idem.

22 Maczak, Antoni, "Export of Grain and the Problem of Distribution of National Income in the Years 1550–1650," *Acta Poloniae Historica,* XVIII (1968) 75–98.

23 Ibid., p. 82.

24 Doroshenko, V., J. Kahk, H. Ligi, H. Piirimäe, and E. Tarvel, *Trade and Agrarian Development in the Baltic Provinces,* preprint, Tallinn, Academy of Sciences of the Estonian S.S.R., 1974, pp. 5, 6.

25 Kirilly, Z. and I. N. Kiss, "Production de céréales et exploitations paysannes en Hongrie aux xvie et xviie siècles," *Annales: économies, sociétés, civilisations,* XXIII (1968) 1211–36.

26 Pach, Z. P., "En Hongrie au xvie siècle: l'activité commerciale des seigneurs et leur production marchande," *Annales: économies, sociétés, civilisations,* XXI (1966) 1212–31.

27 Ibid.

28 Weber, Max, *The Protestant Ethic and the Spirit of Capitalism,* trans. T. Parsons, New York, Charles Scribner's Sons, 1958.

29 Gade, J. A., *The Hanseatic Control of Norwegian Commerce During the Later Middle Ages,* Leiden, E. J. Brill, 1951, pp. 104–22.

30 Heckscher, E. F., *An Economic History of Sweden,* trans. G. Ohlin, Cambridge, Mass., Harvard University Press, 1954, p. 24.

31 Andersen, N. K., "The Reformation in Scandinavia and the Baltic," in G. R. Elton, ed., *The New Cambridge Modern History: The Reformation, 1520–1559,* Cambridge, Cambridge University Press, 1965, pp. 134–60.

32 Ibid., p. 148.

33 Ibid., p. 150.

34 Quoted in Benjamin Nelson, *The Idea of Usury: From Tribal Brotherhood to Universal Otherhood,* Chicago, University of Chicago Press, 1969, pp. 50–51.

35 Heckscher, *An Economic History of Sweden,* p. 117.

36 Abel, W., *Geschichte der deutschen Landwirtschaft vom frühen Mittelalter bis zum 19 Jahrhundert,* 2nd ed., Stuttgart, Verlag Eugen Ulmer, 1967, pp. 110–13.

37 Ibid., p. 155.

38 Holborn, H., *A History of Modern Germany: The Reformation,* New York, Alfred A. Knopf, Inc., 1959, pp. 57–59.

39 Ibid., pp. 59–60.

40 Abel, W., *Geschichte der deutschen Landwirtschaft,* pp. 184–7.

41 Ibid., p. 161.

42 Le Roy Ladurie, E., *The Peasants of Languedoc,* trans. John Day, Urbana, University of Illinois Press, 1974, pp. 135–6.

43 Ibid., pp. 137–8.

44 Ibid., p. 94.

45 In this section, I have drawn heavily on Marc Bloch, *French Rural History,* trans. J. Sondheimer, Berkeley, University of California Press, 1969, pp. 185–210.

46 Le Roy Ladurie, E., *The Peasant of Languedoc,* pp. 172–80.

47 Bloch, M., *French Rural History,* pp. 146–8.

48 Vicens Vives, Jaime, *An Economic History of Spain,* trans. F. M. López-Morillas, Princeton, Princeton University Press, 1969, p. 304.

49 Ibid., pp. 302–303.

50 Ringrose, D. L., "The Government and the Carters in Spain, 1476–1700," *Economic History Review,* 2nd ser., XXII (1969) 45–57.

51 For this paragraph, I am deeply indebted to J. Vicens Vives, *An Economic History of Spain,* pp. 346–7.

52 Vicens Vives, *An Economic History of Spain,* pp. 349–50.

53 Braudel, F. P., *La Méditerranée et le monde méditerranéen à l'époque de Philippe II,* 2nd ed., I, Paris, Armand Colin, 1966, pp. 530–35.

54 Vicens Vives, *An Economic History of Spain,* p. 340.

55 Braudel, *La Méditerranée,* I, p. 534.

56 Cipolla, C. M., "Une Crise ignorée: comment s'est perdue la propriété ecclésiastique dans l'Italie du nord entre le xie et le xvie siècle," *Annales: économies, sociétés, civilisations,* II (1947) 317–27.

57 Luzzatto, G., *An Economic History of Italy from the Fall of Rome to the Beginning of the Sixteenth Century,* trans. P. Jones, New York, Barnes & Noble Books, 1961, pp. 166–7.

58 Braudel, *La Méditerranée,* I, pp. 535–8.

59 Ibid., p. 537.

60 Barkan, Ömer, "The Problem of the Construction and Settlement of Istanbul

after the Conquest," paper delivered at Princeton University, Spring, 1974, unpublished.

61 Felix, David, "Profit Inflation and Industrial Growth: The Historic Record and Contemporary Analogies," *The Quarterly Journal of Economics,* LXX (1956) 441–63.

62 Fisher, F. J., "Commercial Trends and Policy in Sixteenth Century England," in E. M. Carus-Wilson, *Essays in Economic History,* I, New York, St. Martin's Press, Inc., 1966, pp. 152–72.

63 See the survey of the recent literature by A. R. Bridbury, "Sixteenth Century Farming," *Economic History Review,* 2nd ser., XXVII (1974) 538–56.

64 Nugent, E. M., *The Thought and Culture of the English Renaissance,* 2 vols., The Hague, Martinus Nijhoff, 1969, Vol. I, pp. 244–6; Vol. II, pp. 312–15.

65 See Chapter 1.

66 Marsilius of Padua, *The Defence of Peace: Lately Translated out of Laten in to Englysshe, with the Kynges moste gracyous Priuilege,* London, Robert Wyer for Wyllyam Marshall, 1535. This edition was printed with the following significant omissions: Discourse I, Chapter 3, *On the Origin of the Civil Community;* Disc. I, Chap. 14, *On the Qualities or Dispositions of the Perfect Ruler;* Disc. I, Chap. 18, *On the Correction of the Ruler;* Disc. II, Chap. 20, *To Whom Belongs or Has Belonged the Authority to Define or Determine Doubtful Sentences of Holy Scripture;* Disc. II, Chap. 22, *In What Sense the Roman Bishop and His Church Are The Head and Leaders of the Others;* and finally, Disc. III, Chap. 2, *In Which Are Explicitly Inferred Certain Conclusions.*

67 Mackie, J. D., *The Early Tudors: 1485–1558,* Oxford, Clarendon Press, 1952, pp. 370–2.

68 Youings, J., "The Church," in Joan Thirsk, ed., *The Agrarian History of England and Wales,* IV, Cambridge, Cambridge University Press, 1967, pp. 306–56.

69 Ibid., p. 340.

70 See, for example, J. H. Hexter, "Storm over the Gentry" in J. H. Hexter, *Reappraisals in History,* New York, Harper & Row, Publishers, Inc., 1961, pp. 117–62.

71 Thirsk, J., "Farming Techniques," in J. Thirsk, ed., *The Agrarian History of England and Wales,* IV, Cambridge, Cambridge University Press, 1967, p. 199.

72 Slicher van Bath, *The Agrarian History,* p. 85.

73 Phelps Brown, E. H. and Sheila V. Hopkins, "Seven Centuries of the Prices of Consumables, Compared with Builders' Wage Rates" in E. M. Carus-Wilson, ed., *Essays in Economic History,* II, New York, St. Martin's Press, Inc., 1966, pp. 179–96.

Chapter 4. Industry: technology and organization

1 See Chapter 2.

2 Felix, D., "Profit Inflation and Industrial Growth: The Historic Record and Contemporary Analogies," *Quarterly Journal of Economics,* LXX (1956) 441–63.

3 There is a substantial literature devoted to the English cloth industry; the following histories and monographs will serve as a guide: P. J. Bowden, *The Wool Trade in Tudor and Stuart England,* London, Macmillan and Co., Ltd., 1962; H. Heaton, *The Yorkshire Woollen and Worsted Industries,* Oxford, Clarendon Press, 1920; E. Lipson, *History of the Woollen and Worsted Industries,* London, A. and C. Black, Ltd., 1921, and by the same author, *A Short History of Wool and Its Manufacture,* Cambridge, Mass., Harvard University Press, 1953; T. C. Mendenhall, *The Shrewsbury Drapers and the Welsh Wool Trade,* London, Oxford University Press, 1953; and G. D. Ramsay, *The Wiltshire Woollen Industry,* Oxford, Oxford University Press, 1943.

4 Smith, Adam, *An Inquiry into the Nature and Causes of the Wealth of Nations,* New York, Random House, Inc., 1937, p. 4.

5 Böhm-Bawerk, E. V., *The Positive Theory of Capital,* trans. W. Smart, New York, G. E. Stechart, 1923, and *Capital and Interest,* 3 vols., South Holland, Ill., Libertarian Press, 1959.

6 Ramsay, *The Wiltshire Woollen Industry,* pp. 13–14.

7 This paragraph draws heavily on Mendenhall, *The Shrewsbury Drapers,* pp. 33–40.

8 Unwin, G., *Industrial Organization in the Sixteenth and Seventeenth Centuries,* New York, A. M. Kelley 1963 (first ed. 1904), pp. 137–41.

9 Unwin, *Industrial Organization,* p. 105.

10 For a fuller discussion of the political developments in the Low Countries see Pieter Geyl, *The Revolt of the Netherlands, 1555–1609,* Ernest Benn, Ltd., London, 1966.

11 Lipson, *History of the English Woollen and Worsted Industry,* pp. 21–26.

12 Bowden, P. J., "Wool Supply and the Woolen Industry," *Economic History Review,* 2nd ser., IX (1956) 44–58.

13 Bowden, *The Wool Trade,* figs. 1 and 2, pp. 28–29.

14 Schofield, R. S., "The Geographical Distribution of Wealth in England: 1334–1649," *Economic History Review,* 2nd ser., XVIII (1965) 483–510.

15 See Table II.

16 This discussion of the glass industry depends heavily on D. W. Crossley, "The Performance of the Glass Industry in Sixteenth Century England," *Economic History Review,* 2nd ser., XXV (1972) 421–33.

17 Ibid., p. 422.

18 Nef, J. U., *The Rise of the British Coal Industry,* 2 vols., London, George Routledge and Sons, Ltd., 1932, pp. 192–93, and Crossley, "The Performance of the Glass Industry," p. 431.

19 Bamford, P. W., *Forests and French Sea Power: 1660–1789,* Toronto, University of Toronto Press, 1956, p. 11.

20 Nef, *British Coal Industry,* pp. 192–93.

21 Ibid., p. 158.

22 Ibid., pp. 19-20.

23 Ibid., pp. 350-410.

24 See Chapter 2.

25 S. P. D., Eliz., Vol. XL. No. 87: Printed in R. H. Tawney and Eileen Power, eds., *Tudor Economic Documents,* 3 vols., London, Longmans Green and Co., 1924, Vol. I, pp. 249-50.

26 Nef, *British Coal Industry,* pp. 199-200.

27 Hall, A. R., "Early Modern Technology, to 1600," in M. Kranzberg and C. W. Pursell, eds., *Technology in Western Civilization,* 2 vols., London, Oxford University Press, 1967, Vol. I, pp. 79-103.

28 Crossley, D. W, "The Management of a Sixteenth Century Ironworks," *Economic History Review,* 2nd ser., XIX (1966) 273-88.

29 Ibid., p. 283.

30 Felix, "Profit Inflation," p. 446.

31 My discussion of the leather industry draws heavily on L. A. Clarkson, "The Organization of the English Leather Industry in the Late Sixteenth and Seventeenth Centuries," *Economic History Review,* 2nd ser., XIII (1960) 245-56.

32 Ibid., p. 246.

33 Malowist, M., "L'Evolution industrielle en Pologne du xive au xviie siècle," *Studi in Onore di Armando Sapori,* I, Istituto Editoriale Cisalpino, Milan, 1957, p. 588.

34 This paragraph depends heavily on Malowist, "L'Evolution industrielle."

35 Elliott, J. H., *Imperial Spain: 1469-1716,* New York, The New American Library Inc. 1963, p. 185.

36 Vicens Vives, J., *An Economic History of Spain,* trans. F. M. López-Morillas, Princeton, Princeton University Press, 1969, pp. 300-1.

37 Ibid., p. 352.

38 Ibid., pp. 354-5.

39 This discussion of crown revenues depends heavily on Elliott, *Imperial Spain,* pp. 196-204.

40 Vicens Vives, *An Economic History of Spain,* pp. 352-3.

41 For a discussion of the confiscations and a partial accounting of the receipts, see Henry Kamen, "Confiscations in the Economy of the Spanish Inquisition," *Economic History Review,* 2nd ser., XVIII (1965) 511-25.

42 Elliott, *Imperial Spain,* pp. 234-5.

43 See Chapter 2, Table I, *Urbanization in Selected Areas of Europe.*

44 Vicens Vives, *An Economic History,* p. 250.

45 Ibid., pp. 250-62.

46 Braudel, F., *La Méditerranée et le monde méditerranéen à l'époque de Philippe II,* 2 vols., Paris, Armand Colin, 1966, I, p. 370.

47 Elliott, *Imperial Spain*, p. 184.

48 Sella, D., "European Industries: 1500–1700," in C. Cipolla, ed., *The Fontana Economic History of Europe*, II, London, Fontana Books, 1974, pp. 362–3.

49 Barbour, V., "Dutch and English Merchant Shipping in the Seventeenth Century," *The Economic History Review*, II (1930) 261–90.

50 Gascon, R., "Immigration et croissance urbaine au xvie siècle; l'exemple de Lyon," *Annales: économies, sociétés, civilisations*, XXV (1970) 988–1001.

51 Bayard, F., "Les Bonvisi, marchands banquiers à Lyon, 1575–1629," *Annales: économies, sociétés, civilisations*, XXVI (1971) 1234–1269.

52 Davis, N. Z., "A Trade Union in Sixteenth Century France," *The Economic History Review*, 2nd ser., XIX (1966) 48–69.

53 Sella, "European Industries," p. 399.

54 Zeller, G., "Industry in France before Colbert," in R. Cameron, ed., *Essays in French Economic History*, Homewood, Ill., Richard D. Irwin, Inc., 1970, pp. 128–39.

55 Sée, H., *Histoire économique de la France*, Paris, Armand Colin, 1939, pp. 122–3.

56 Bayard, "Les Bonvisi," p. 1253.

57 Ibid., p. 1251.

58 Bodin, J., *The Six Books of the Republic*, trans. M. J. Tooley, Oxford, Basil Blackwell, no date.

59 Coornaert, E., *Les Corporations en France avant 1789*, Paris, Gallimard, 1941, pp. 130–33.

60 For a fuller discussion of these problems see J. U. Nef, *Industry and Government in France and England, 1540–1640*, Ithaca, Cornell University Press, 1957; and H. Hauser, *Les Débuts du capitalisme*, Paris, Librairie Félix Alcan, 1927.

61 Cipolla, C., *Before the Industrial Revolution: European Society and Economy, 1000–1700*, New York, W. W. Norton & Company, 1976, pp. 236–8.

62 Ibid.

63 This discussion of Venice depends heavily on F. C. Lane, *Venice: A Maritime Republic*, Baltimore, Johns Hopkins University Press, 1973, Chaps. 22–25.

64 Voet, L., *The Plantin-Moretus Museum*, Antwerp, Museum Plantin-Moretus, 1965, p. 11.

65 See Lane, *Venice*, pp. 361–84.

66 Cipolla, *Before the Industrial Revolution*, p. 238.

67 Schremmer, E., *Die Wirtschaft Bayerns: von hohen Mittelalter bis zum Beginn der Industrialisierung*, Munich, Verlag C. H. Beck, 1970, pp. 90–92.

68 Ibid., pp. 94–95.

69 Holborn, H., *A History of Modern Germany: The Reformation*, New York, Alfred Knopf, Inc., 1959, p. 69.

70 For the glass industry see Schremmer, *Die Wirtschaft Bayerns*, pp. 99–104.

71 Ibid., pp. 81–82.

Chapter 5. Trade patterns in the wider world

1 Wallerstein, I., *The Modern World-System: Capitalist Agriculture and the Origins of the European World-Economy in the Sixteenth Century,* New York, Academic Press, 1974.

2 Cipolla, C., *Guns, Sails, and Empires: Technological Innovation and the Early Phases of European Expansion, 1400–1700,* New York, Pantheon Books, Inc., 1965, passim.

3 See J. H. Parry, *The Establishment of the European Hegemony, 1415–1715,* New York, Harper & Row, Publishers, 1961, pp. 29–34.

4 Chaunu, P., *Conquête et exploitation des nouveaux mondes: xvie siècle,* Paris, Presses Universitaires de France, 1969, p. 316.

5 Curtin, P., *The Atlantic Slave Trade: A Census,* Madison, University of Wisconsin Press, 1969, p. 268.

6 On Antwerp see S. T. Bindoff, "The Greatness of Antwerp," *The New Cambridge Modern History,* II, Cambridge, Cambridge University Press, 1958, pp. 50–69.

7 Magalhães-Godinho, V., *L'Economie de l'empire portugais aux xve et xviie siècles,* Paris, S.E.V.P.E.N., 1969, p. 375.

8 Herbert, E. W., "The West African Copper Trade in the Fifteenth and Sixteenth Centuries," paper delivered at the XIV International Congress of Historical Sciences, San Francisco, 1975.

9 Magalhães-Godinho, *L'Economie de l'empire portugais,* pp. 375–6. The metrological conversions are my own.

10 Chaunu, *Conquête et exploitation,* p. 320. The metrological conversions are my own.

11 Lane, F. C., *Venice: A Maritime Republic,* Baltimore, Johns Hopkins University Press, 1973, pp. 292–3.

12 See Table VII.

13 Simkin, C. G. F., *The Traditional Trade of Asia,* London, Oxford University Press, 1968, pp, pp. 184–5.

14 Parry, *European Hegemony,* pp. 90–97.

15 Ibid., p. 95.

16 Chaunu, *Conquête et exploitation,* p. 316.

17 Simkin, *Traditional Trade,* p. 186.

18 Hazan, A., "En Inde aux xvie et xviie siècles: trésors americains, monnaie d'argent, et prix dans l'empire mogol," *Annales: économies, sociétés, civilisations,* 24 (1969), 835–59.

19 Mauro, F., *Le xvie siècle,* p. 155. The metrological conversions are mine.

20 Ibid., p. 155.

21 See Chapter 2.

22 Curtin, *Atlantic Slave Trade,* pp. 21–23.

23 Hamilton, E. J. *American Treasure and the Price Revolution in Spain, 1501–1650,* New York, Octagon Books, 1970, pp. 33–34.
24 Ibid., pp. 56–59.
25 Parry, J. H., *The Spanish Seaborne Empire,* New York, Alfred Knopf, Inc., 1966, p. 258.
26 Hamilton, *American Treasure,* p. 31, n. 3.
27 Parry, *Seaborne Empire,* p. 247.
28 For an excellent recent survey of the region see A. Attman, *Russian and Polish Markets in International Trade: 1500–1650,* Göteborg, Kungsbacka, 1973.
29 Ibid., p. 15.
30 Dollinger, P., *The German Hansa,* London, Macmillan & Co., Ltd., 1970, pp. 312–14.
31 Attman, *Russian and Polish Markets,* pp. 62–63.
32 Glamann, K., "European Trade: 1500–1700," in C. Cipolla, ed., *The Fontana Economic History of Europe,* II, Glasgow, Fontana Books, 1974, p. 446.
33 Attman, *Russian and Polish Markets,* p. 173.
34 Ibid., p. 120.
35 For a detailed history of political events in the Low Countries see Pieter Geyl, *The Revolt of the Netherlands,* London, Ernest Benn, Ltd., 1958.
36 Barbour, V., *Capitalism in Amsterdam in the Seventeenth Century,* Ann Arbor, University of Michigan Press, 1963, p. 17.
37 Baasch, E., *Holländische Wirtschaftsgeschichte,* Jena, Verlag von Gustav Fischer, 1927, p. 163.
38 Braudel, F., *La Méditerranée et le monde méditerranéen à l'époque de Philippe II,* 2nd ed., Vol. I, Paris, Armand Colin, 1966, pp. 535–38.
39 See Chapter 3.
40 Ramsay, G. D., *English Overseas Trade During the Centuries of Emergence,* London, Macmillan and Co., Ltd., 1957, pp. 50–51.
41 Braudel, *La Méditerranée,* pp. 543–44.
42 Baasch, *Holländische Wirtschaftsgeschichte,* p. 162.
43 Elliott, J. H., *Imperial Spain: 1469–1716,* New York, The New American Library Inc., 1963, pp. 287–9.
44 Parry, *European Hegemony,* p. 99.
45 Simkin, *Traditional Trade,* p. 193.
46 See Graph 2 for English cloth exports.
47 Figures for Narva and Archangel are derived from Attmann, *Russian and Polish Markets,* pp. 85–86.
48 For a recent study of the English East India Company see K. N. Chaudhuri, *The English East India Company,* London, Frank Cass and Company, Ltd., 1965.
49 Ramsay, *English Overseas Trade,* pp. 40–41.
50 Chaudhuri, *The English East India Company,* pp. 11–13.
51 Delumeau, J., *L'Aiun de Rome, xvᵉ–xixᵉ siècle,* Paris, S.E.V.P.E.N., 1962, pp. 214–15.

52 Ibid., pp. 237–9.

53 Ibid., pp. 214–15.

54 Ramsay, *English Overseas Trade,* pp. 75–76.

55 See H. Miskimin, *The Economy of Early Renaissance Europe, 1300–1460,* Cambridge, Cambridge University Press, 1975; and R. Lopez, H. Miskimin, and A. Udovitch, "England to Egypt, 1350–1500: Long-Term Trends and Long-Distance Trade," in M. A. Cook, ed., *Studies in the Economic History of the Middle East,* London, Oxford University Press, 1970, pp. 93–128.

56 Clough, S. B. and C. W. Cole, *Economic History of Europe,* Lexington, Mass., D. C. Heath & Company, 1941, p. 212.

57 Ibid., p. 206.

58 Ibid., p. 216.

59 Ibid., p. 226.

60 Hauser, H., *La Response de Jean Bodin àM. de Malestroit: 1568,* Paris, Armand Colin, 1932.

61 Bodin, J., *The Six Books of the Republic,* trans. M. J. Tooley, Oxford, Basil Blackwell, no date, p. 188.

62 See p. 132.

63 Jamieson, A., ed. trans., *Memoirs of the Duke of Sully,* II, London, G. and W. B. Whittaker, 1822, p. 282.

Chapter 6. Finances: private and public

1 Miskimin, H., *Money, Prices, and Foreign Exchange in Fourteenth Century France,* New Haven, Yale University Press, 1963, passim.

2 Parker, G., "The Emergence of Modern Finance in Europe: 1500–1730," in C. Cipolla, ed., *The Fontana Economic History of Europe,* II, London, Fontana Books, 1974, p. 530.

3 Hicks, J. R., "Mr. Keynes and the Classics: A Suggested Interpretation," *Econometrica* (1937) 147–59. See also A. Hansen, *Monetary Theory and Fiscal Policy,* New York, McGraw-Hill Book Company, 1949, pp. 43–82.

The reader is advised to consult the literature both for theoretical elegance and for the full explication of the necessary assumptions and caveats, but a simple representation is provided below:

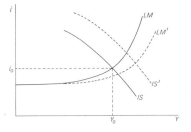

If the initial economic conditions are described by the curves *LM* and *IS*, the interest level is i_0 and income is Y_0. An increase in the money supply or a decrease in liquidity preference shifts the *LM* curve outward as indicated by the curve *LM'*, lowering interest rates and increasing income. Technological advance (i.e., a shift in the marginal efficiency of capital schedule) or an increase in the marginal propensity to consume would shift the *IS* curve outward as indicated by the curve *IS'*; this would result in a higher interest rate and an increase in income. If both curves shift outward together, income would increase but the effect on interest rates is indeterminate.

4 See pp. 27–28.
5 Miskimin, H., "The Enforcement of Gresham's Law," to appear in the *Proceedings of the Quarta Settimana di Studio,* Prato, Istituto Internazionale di Storia Economica "Francesco Datini," 1972.
6 See M. Wolfe, *The Fiscal System of Renaissance France,* New Haven, Yale University Press, 1972, pp. 205–13, for a discussion of this question.
7 See E. H. Hamilton, *American Treasure and the Price Revolution in Spain, 1500–1650,* New York, Octagon Books, 1970, pp. 211–21.
8 See Chapter 4.
9 See H. Miskimin, *The Economy of Early Renaissance Europe: 1300–1460,* Cambridge, Cambridge University Press, 1975, pp. 110–11, for a summary of the developments favoring Augsburg.
10 Ehrenberg, R., *Capital and Finance in the Age of the Renaissance,* trans, H. M. Lucas, New York, A. M. Kelley, 1963, pp. 66–67.
11 Ibid., p. 85.
12 Ibid., p. 77.
13 Ibid., pp. 81–82.
14 Ibid., p. 82.
15 Carande, R., *El Credito de Castilla en el precio de la politica imperial,* Madrid, Sucesores de Rivadeneyra, S.A., 1949, pp. 65–66.
16 Pike, R., *Enterprise and Adventure: The Genoese in Seville and the Opening of the New World,* Ithaca, Cornell University Press, 1966, p. 3.
17 See pp. 72–73.
18 See Chapter 4.
19 Lopez, R. S., "Il Predominio economico dei Genovesi nella monarchia Spagnola," in R. S. Lopez, *Su e giù per la storia di Genova,* Genoa, University of Genoa, 1975, p. 260.
20 Quoted in Pike, *Enterprise and Adventure,* p. 87.
21 Elliott, J. H., *Imperial Spain: 1469–1716,* New York, The New American Library, Inc., 1963, pp. 203–4.
22 Pike, *Enterprise and Adventure,* pp. 16–17.
23 Wolfe, *Fiscal System,* p. 108.

24 Ibid., pp. 109–13.

25 Ibid., p. 115.

26 Ibid., p. 233.

27 Ibid., p. 131.

28 Parker, G., "The Emergence of Modern Finance," pp. 572–4.

29 Outhwaite, R. B., "The Trials of Foreign Borrowing: The English Crown and the Antwerp Money Market in the Mid-Sixteenth Century," *The Economic History Review,* XIX (1966) 289–305; Ehrenberg, *Capital and Finance,* p. 268.

30 Richardson, W. C., "Some Financial Expedients of Henry VIII," *The Economic History Review,* VII (1955) 33–49.

31 Ehrenberg, *Capital and Finance,* p. 253.

32 Outhwaite, "Trials of Foreign Borrowing," p. 305.

33 I depend here on F. C. Lane, *Venice: A Maritime Republic,* Baltimore, Johns Hopkins University Press, 1973, pp. 324–7.

34 Ehrenberg, *Capital and Finance,* p. 116.

35 Wolfe, *Fiscal System,* pp 112–13.

36 Elliott, *Imperial Spain,* pp. 260–5.

37 See Table III.

38 Wolfe, *Fiscal System,* p. 154.

39 Elliott, *Imperial Spain,* pp. 283–4.

40 See Table III and Chapter 4 for a discussion of the importance of Zamora.

41 Barbour, V., *Capitalism in Amsterdam in the 17th Century,* Ann Arbor, University of Michigan Press, 1963, pp. 36–40.

42 Referring to note 3, one may observe that the collection and export of funds in Spain would act to move the *LM* curve inward, reducing investment, raising interest rates, and lowering gross national product.

43 See J. U. Nef, *Industry and Government in France and England: 1540–1640,* Ithaca, Cornell University Press, 1957, pp. 59–68.

44 Ibid., p. 73.

45 See Nef, *Industry and Government,* pp. 89–98.

46 Ibid., pp. 92–3.

47 For a discussion of the political context surrounding the monopoly issue see G. Davies, *The Early Stuarts: 1603–1660,* Oxford, Clarendon Press, 1959, pp. 24–25, pp. 331–6.

48 Black, J. R., *The Reign of Elizabeth, 1558–1603,* Oxford, Clarendon Press, 1959, p. 232.

49 Davies, *Early Stuarts,* p. 24.

Chapter 7. Retrospect

1 Grotius, H., *The Law of War and Peace,* trans. F. W. Kelsey, Indianapolis, The Bobbs-Merrill Co., Inc., 1925, passim.

Bibliography

Note

As indicated in the preface, a full bibliography, even one limited to economic history, would dwarf the present book. What follows is thus simply a list of works cited throughout the text and is designed merely to provide complete references to those works. Additional bibliographical material may be found in *The Cambridge Economic History of Europe* (E. E. Rich and C. H. Wilson, eds., New York, Cambridge University Press, 1967), where the works are arranged topically in support of individual chapters, and in F. Mauro (*Le xvie siècle Européen: aspects économiques,* Paris, Presses Universitaires de France, 1970), which offers material arranged by country of reference. On overseas expansion, the bibliography contained in P. Chaunu (*Conquête et exploitation des nouveaux mondes: xvie siècle,* Paris, Presses Universitaires de France, 1969) is valuable.

List of works cited

Abel, W., *Geschichte der deutschen Landwirtschaft vom frühen Mittelalter bis zum 19 Jahrhundert,* 2nd ed., Stuttgart, Verlag Eugen Ulmer, 1967.

Agricola, G., *De re metallica,* 1556.

De re metallica, trans. H. C. Hoover, New York, Dover Publications, Inc., 1950.

Andersen, N. K., "The Reformation in Scandinavia and the Baltic," in G. R. Elton, ed., *The New Cambridge Modern History,* II, Cambridge, Cambridge University Press, 1965, pp. 134-60.

Attman, A., *Russian and Polish Markets in International Trade: 1500-1650,* Göteborg, Kungsbacka, 1973.

Baasch, E., *Holländische Wirtschaftsgeschichte,* Jena, Verlag von Gustav Fischer, 1927.

Bainton, R. H., *The Medieval Church,* New York, D. Van Nostrand Company, 1962.

Baldwin, J. W., "The Medieval Merchant before the Bar of Canon Law," *Papers of the Michigan Academy of Science, Arts, and Letters,* XLIV (1959) 287-99.

Bamford, P. W., *Forests and French Sea Power, 1660-1789,* Toronto, University of Toronto Press, 1956.

Barbour, V., *Capitalism in Amsterdam in the Seventeenth Century,* Ann Arbor, University of Michigan Press, 1963.

"Dutch and English Merchant Shipping in the Seventeenth Century," *The Economic History Review,* II (1930) 261–90.

Barkan, O., "The Problem of the Construction and Settlement of Istanbul after the Conquest," paper delivered at Princeton University, Spring, 1974, unpublished.

Bayard, F., "Les Bonvisi, marchands banquiers à Lyon, 1575–1629," *Annales: économies, sociétés, civilisations,* XXVI (1971) 1234–69.

Beloch, K. J., *Bevolkerungsgeschichte Italiens,* III, Berlin, Walter de Gruyter and Co., 1961.

Bennett, M. K., *The World's Food,* New York, Harper & Row, Publishers, 1954.

Betts, R. R., "The Central Monarchies," in Denys Hay, *Europe in the Fourteenth and Fifteenth Centuries,* New York, Holt, Rinehart and Winston, Inc., 1966.

Bindoff, S. T., "The Greatness of Antwerp," in G. R. Elton, *The New Cambridge Modern History,* II, Cambridge, Cambridge University Press, 1965, pp. 50–69.

Biringuccio, V., *De la pirotechnia,* 1540.

Black, J. R., *The Reign of Elizabeth, 1558–1603,* Oxford, Clarendon Press, 1959.

Bloch, Marc, *Feudal Society,* trans. L. A. Manyon, Chicago, Chicago University Press, 1964.

French Rural History, trans. J. Sondheimer, Berkeley, University of California Press, 1969.

Bodin, Jean, *De la Démonomanie des sorciers,* Paris, 1580.

Les Six livres de la république, Paris, 1576.

The Six Books of the Commonwealth, trans. M. J. Tooley, Oxford, Basil Blackwell, no date.

Böhm-Bawerk, E. V., *Capital and Interest,* 3 vols., South Holland, Ill., Libertarian Press, 1959.

The Positive Theory of Capital, trans. W. Smart, New York, G. E. Stechary, 1923.

Bouwsma, W. J., "Lawyers and Early Modern Culture," *American Historical Review,* LXXVIII (1973) 303–27.

Bowden, P. J., *The Wool Trade in Tudor and Stuart England,* London, Macmillan and Co., Ltd., 1962.

Braudel, F. P., *La Méditerranée et le monde méditerranéen à l'époque de Philippe II,* 2 vols., Paris, Armand Colin, 1966.

and F. C. Spooner, "Prices in Europe, 1450–1750," *Cambridge Economic History of Europe,* IV, Cambridge, Cambridge University Press, 1967, pp. 378–486.

Brenner, Y. S., "The Inflation of Prices in Early Sixteenth Century England," *The Economic History Review,* 2nd ser., XIV (1961) 225–39.

"The Inflation of Prices in England, 1551–1600," *The Economic History Review,* 2nd ser., XV (1962) 266–84.

Bridbury, A. R., "Sixteenth Century Farming," *The Economic History Review,* 2nd ser., XXVII (1974) 538–56.

Buisseret, D., *Sully and the Growth of Centralized Government in France, 1589–1610,* London, Eyre and Spottiswoode, 1968.

Butterfield, H., *The Origins of Modern Science, 1300–1800,* New York, Macmillan Publishing Co., Inc., 1958.

Carande, R., *El Credito de Castilla en el precio de la politica imperial,* Madrid, Sucesores de Rivadeneyra, S.A., 1949.

Chaudhuri, K. N., *The English East India Company,* London, Frank Cass and Co., Ltd., 1965.

Chaunu, P., *Conquête et exploitation des nouveaux mondes: xvie siècle,* Paris, Presses Universitaires de France, 1969.

Cipolla, C., *Before the Industrial Revolution: European Society and Economy, 1000–1700,* New York, W. W. Norton & Company, Inc., 1976.

"Une Crise ignorée: comment s'est perdue la propriété ecclésiastique dans l'Italie du nord entre le xie et le xvie siècle," *Annales: économies, sociétés, civilisations,* II (1947) 317–27.

Guns, Sails and Empires: Technological Innovation and the Early Phases of European Expansion, 1400–1700, New York, Pantheon Books, Inc., 1965.

Clarkson, L. A., "The Organization of the English Leather Industry in the Late Sixteenth and Seventeenth Centuries," *The Economic History Review,* 2nd ser., XIII (1960) 245–56.

Clough, S. B. and C. W. Cole, *Economic History of Europe,* Lexington, Mass., D. C. Heath & Company, 1941.

Coornaert, E., *Un Centre industriel d'autrefois: la draperie-sayetterie d'Hondschoote,* Paris, Presses Universitaires de France, 1930.

Les Corporations en France avant 1789, Paris, Gallimard, 1941.

Les Francais et le commerce international à Anvers: fin du xve–xvie siècle, 2 vols., Paris, Marcel Rivière et Cie, 1961.

Cornwall, J., "English Population in the Early Sixteenth Century," *The Economic History Review,* 2nd ser., XXIII (1970) 32–44.

Courtenay, W. J., "The King and the Leaden Coin: The Economic Background of 'sine qua non' Causality," *Traditio,* XXVIII (1972) 185–210.

"Token Coinage and the Administration of Poor Relief During the Late Middle Ages," *Journal of Interdisciplinary History,* III (1972–3) 275–95.

Crossley, D. W., "The Management of a Sixteenth Century Ironworks", *The Economic History Review,* 2nd ser., XIX (1966), 273–88.

"The Performance of the Glass Industry in Sixteenth Century England," *The Economic History Review,* 2nd Ser., XXV (1972) 421–33.

Curtin, P., *The Atlantic Slave Trade: A Census,* Madison, University of Wisconsin Press, 1969.

Davies, G., *The Early Stuarts: 1603–1660,* Oxford, Clarendon Press, 1959.

Davis, N. Z., "A Trade Union in Sixteenth Century France," *The Economic History Review,* 2nd ser., XIX (1966) 48–69.

Delumeau, J., *L'Alun de Rome, xve–xixe siècle,* Paris, S.E.V.P.E.N., 1962.

DeVries, J., *The Dutch Rural Economy in the Golden Age, 1500–1700,* New Haven, Yale University Press, 1974.

Dietz, F. C., "English Government Finance, 1485-1558", *University of Illinois Studies in the Social Sciences,* IX (1920).

Dollinger, P., *The German Hansa,* London, Macmillan and Co., Ltd., 1970.

Doroschenko. V., J. Kahk, H. Ligi, H. Piirimäe, and E. Tarvel, *Trade and Agrarian Development in the Baltic Provinces,* preprint, Tallinn, Academy of Sciences of the Estonian S.S.R., 1974.

Doucet R., *Les Institutions de la France au xvie siècle,* 2 vols., Paris, A. et J. Picard et Cie, 1948.

Dowell, S., *A History of Taxation and Taxes in England from the Earliest Times to the Present Day,* 4 vols., London, Longmans, Green and Co., 1884.

Ehrenberg, R., *Capital and Finance in the Age of the Renaissance,* trans. H. M. Lucas, New York, A. M. Kelley, 1963.

Elliott, J. H., *Imperial Spain: 1469-1716,* New York, The New American Library, Inc., 1963.

Felix, D., "Profit Inflation and Industrial Growth: The Historical Record and Contemporary Analogies," *The Quarterly Journal of Economics,* LXX (1956) 441-63.

Fisher, F. J., "Commercial Trends and Policy in Sixteenth Century England," *The Economic History Review,* X (1940) 95-117.

Fisher, I., *The Purchasing Power of Money,* New York, Macmillan Publishing Co., Inc., 1926.

Franklin, J. H., *Jean Bodin and the Sixteenth Century Revolution in the Methodology of Law and History,* New York, Columbia University Press, 1963.

Gade, J.A., *The Hanseatic Control of Norwegian Commerce During the Later Middle Ages,* Leiden, E. J. Brill, 1951.

Gandilhon, R., *Politique économique de Louis XI,* Rennes, Imprimeries Réunies, 1940.

Gascon, R., "Immigration et croissance urbaine au xvie siècle: l'exemple de Lyon," *Annales: économies, sociétés, civilisations,* XXV (1970) 988-1001.

Geyl, P., *The Revolt of the Netherlands, 1555-1609,* London, Ernest Benn, Ltd., 1966.

Glamann, K., "European Trade: 1500-1700" in C. Cipolla, ed., *The Fontana Economic History of Europe,* II, London, Fontana Books, 1974.

Grotius, H., *The Law of War and Peace,* trans. F. W. Kelsey, Indianapolis, The Bobbs-Merrill Co., Inc., 1925.

Hall, A. R., "Early Modern Technology to 1600," in M. Kranzberg and C. W. Pursell, eds., *Technology in Western Civilization,* 2 vols., London, Oxford University Press, 1967, vol. 1, pp. 79-103.

Hamilton, E. J., *American Treasure and the Price Revolution in Spain,* Cambridge, Mass., Harvard University Press, 1934.

"American Treasure and the Rise of Capitalism," *Economica,* XXVII (1929) 338-57.

Hansen, A., *Monetary Theory and Fiscal Policy,* New York, McGraw-Hill Book Company, 1949.

Hauser, H., *Les Débuts du capitalisme,* Paris, Librairie Félix Alcan, 1927.

ed., *La Response de Jean Bodin à M. de Malestroit: 1568,* Paris, Armand Colin, 1932.

Hay, Denys, *Europe in the Fourteenth and Fifteenth Centuries,* New York, Holt, Rinehart and Winston, Inc., 1966.

Hazan, A. "En Inde aux xvie et xviie siècles: trésors americains, monnaie d'argent, et prix dans l'empire mogul," *Annales: économies, sociétés, civilisations,* XXIV (1969) 835-59.

Heaton, H., *The Yorkshire Woollen and Worsted Industries,* Oxford, Clarendon Press, 1920.

Heckscher, E. F., *An Economic History of Sweden,* trans. G. Ohlin, Cambridge, Mass., Harvard University Press, 1954.

Helleiner, K., "The Population of Europe from the Black Death to the Eve of the Vital Revolution," *Cambridge Economic History of Europe,* IV, Cambridge, Cambridge University Press, 1967.

Herbert, E. W., "The West African Copper Trade in the Fifteenth and Sixteenth Centuries," paper delivered at the XIV International Congress of Historical Sciences, San Francisco, 1975, unpublished.

Hexter, J. H., "Storm over the Gentry," in J. H. Hexter, *Reappraisals in History,* New York, Harper & Row, Publishers, 1961, pp. 117-62.

Hicks, J. R., "Mr. Keynes and the Classics: A Suggested Interpretation," *Econometrica,* V (1937) 147-59.

Holborn, H., *A History of Modern Germany: The Reformation,* New York, Alfred A. Knopf, Inc., 1959.

Homan, B., "La Circolazione della moneta d'oro in Ungheria del x al xiv secolo e la crisi Europea dell'oro nel secolo xiv," *Rivista Italiana di Numismatica,* 2nd ser., V (1922) 109-56.

Hoszowski, S., "The Polish Baltic Trade in the 15th-18th Centuries," in *Poland at the XIth International Conference of Historical Sciences in Stockholm,* Warsaw, Polish Academy of Sciences, 1960.

Jamieson, A., ed. trans., *Memoirs of the Duke of Sully,* II, London, G. and W. B. Whittaker, 1822.

Kamen, H., "Confiscations in the Economy of the Spanish Inquisition," *The Economic History Review,* 2nd ser., XVIII (1965) 511-25.

Keynes, J. M., *A Treatise on Money,* 2 vols., London, The Macmillan Co., Ltd., 1930.

Kirilly, Z. and I. N. Kiss, "Production de céréales et exploitations paysannes en Hongrie aux xvie et xviie siècles," *Annales: économies, sociétés, civilisations,* XXIII (1968) 1211-36.

Koenigsberger, H. G., "Property and the Price Revolution (Hainault, 1475-1573)," *The Economic History Review,* 2nd ser., IX (1956) 1-15.

LaGarde, Georges de, *La Naissance de l'esprit läique au déclin du Moyen Age, IV, Guillaume d'Ockham, Défense de l'empire,* Louvain, Editions Nauwelaerts, 1962.

Lane, F. C., *Venice: A Maritime Republic,* Baltimore, Johns Hopkins University Press, 1973.

Leber, C., *Collections des meilleurs dissertations, notices, et traités particuliers relatifs à l'histoire de France,* VII, Paris, G. A. Dentu, 1838.

LeBras, Gabriel, "Conceptions of Economy and Society," *Cambridge Economic History of Europe,* III, Cambridge, Cambridge University Press, 1963, pp. 554–75.

Le Roy Ladurie, E., *The Peasants of Languedoc,* trans. John Day, Urbana, University of Illinois Press, 1974.

Lipson, E., *History of the Woollen and Worsted Industries,* London, A. and C. Black, Ltd., 1921.

    A Short History of Wool and Its Manufacture, Cambridge, Mass., Harvard University Press, 1953.

Livermore, H., *A History of Spain,* New York, Grove Press, Inc., 1960.

Lopez, R. S., "Il Predominio economico dei Genovesi nella monarchia Spagnola," in R. S. Lopez, *Su e giù per la storia di Genova,* Genoa, University of Genoa, 1975.

Lopez, R. S. and H. A. Miskimin, "The Economic Depression of the Renaissance," *The Economic History Review,* 2nd ser., XIV (1962) 408–26.

Lopez, R. S., H. A. Miskimin, and A. L. Udovitch, "England to Egypt, 1350–1500: Long-Term Trends and Long-Distance Trade," in M. A. Cook, ed., *Studies in the Economic History of the Middle East,* London, Oxford University Press, 1970, pp. 93–128.

Luzzatto, G., *An Economic History of Italy from the Fall of Rome to the Beginning of the Sixteenth Century,* trans. P. Jones, New York, Barnes & Noble Books, 1961.

Machiavelli, Niccolo, *The Prince,* trans. G. Bull, Harmondsworth, Penguin Books, 1961.

Mackie, J. D., *The Early Tudors: 1485–1558,* Oxford, Clarendon Press, 1952.

McKissack, May, *The Fourteenth Century: 1307–1399,* Oxford, Clarendon Press, 1959.

Maczak, A., "Export of Grain and the Problems of Distribution of National Income in the Years 1550–1650," *Acta Poloniae Historica,* XVIII (1968) 75–98.

Magalhães-Godinho, V., *L'Economie de l'empire portugais aux xve et xvie siècles,* Paris, S.E.V.P.E.N., 1969.

Malestroit, J., *The Paradoxes of Malestroit,* trans. G. A. Moore, in G. A. Moore, *Jean Bodin's Response to Malestroit's Paradoxes,* Chevy Chase, Country Dollar Press, 1946.

Malowist, M., "L'Evolution industrielle en Pologne du xive au xviie siècle," *Studi in onore di Armando Sapori,* I, Milan, Istituto Editoriale Cisalpino, 1957.

Marsilius of Padua, *The Defence of Peace: Lately Translated out of Laten in to Englysshe with the Kynges moste gracyous Priuilege,* London, Robert Wyer for Wyllyam Marshall, 1535.

    The Defender of the Peace: Defensor Pacis, trans. A. Gewirth, New York, Harper and Row, Publishers, 1967.

Mauro, F., *Le xvie siècle Européen – aspects économiques,* Paris, Presses Universitaires de France, 1970.

Mendenhall, T. C., *The Shrewsbury Drapers and the Welsh Wool Trade,* London, Oxford University Press, 1953.

Miskimin, H. A., *The Economy of Early Renaissance Europe, 1300–1460,* Cambridge, Cambridge University Press, 1975.

"The Enforcement of Gresham's Law," to appear in *Proceedings of the Quarta Settimana di Studio,* Prato, Istituto Internazionale di Storia Economica, "Francesco Datini," 1972.

"Monetary Movements and Market Structure – Forces for Contraction in Fourteenth and Fifteenth Century England," *The Journal of Economic History,* XXIV (1964) 470–90.

Money, Prices and Foreign Exchange in Fourteenth Century France, New Haven, Yale University Press, 1963.

"Population Growth and the Price Revolution in England," *The Journal of European Economic History,* IV (1975) 179–86.

Nadal Oller, J., "La Revolución de los precios españoles en el siglio XVI," *Hispania,* XIX (1959) 503–29.

Nef, J. U., *Industry and Government in France and England, 1540–1650,* Ithaca, Cornell University Press, 1957.

"Mining and Metallurgy in Medieval Civilization," *Cambridge Economic History of Europe,* II, Cambridge, Cambridge University Press, 1952.

The Rise of the British Coal Industry, 2 vols., London, George Routledge and Sons, Ltd., 1932.

"Silver Production in Central Europe, 1450–1618," *Journal of Political Economy,* XLIX (1941) 575–91.

Nelson, B., *The Idea of Usury: From Tribal Brotherhood to Universal Otherhood,* Chicago, University of Chicago Press, 1969.

Nugent, E. M. *The Thought and Culture of the English Renaissance,* 2 vols., The Hague, Martinus Nijhoff, 1969.

O'Brien, G., *An Essay on Medieval Economic Teaching,* London, Longmans, Green and Company, 1920.

Ockham, Guillemi de, *Opera Politica,* J. G. Sikes, ed., 3 vols., Manchester, Manchester University Press, 1940, 1956, 1963.

Ordonnances des rois de France de la troisième race recueillies par ordre chronologique, Paris, Imprimerie Royale, 1724–.

Outhwaite, R. B., "The Trials of Foreign Borrowing: The English Crown and the Antwerp Money Market in the Mid-Sixteenth Century," *The Economic History Review,* 2nd ser., XIX (1966) 289–305.

Pach, Z. P., "En Hongrie au xvie siècle: l'activité commerciale des seigneurs et leur production marchande," *Annales: économies, sociétés, civilisations,* XXI (1966) 1212–31.

Parker, G., "The Emergence of Modern Finance in Europe: 1500–1730," in C. Cipolla, ed., *The Fontana Economic History of Europe,* II, London, Fontana Books, 1974.

Parry, J. H., *The Establishment of the European Hegemony: 1415–1715,* New York, Harper and Row, Publishers, 1961.

The Spanish Seaborne Empire, New York, Alfred Knopf, Inc., 1966.

Passerim D'Entrèves, A., *The Medieval Contribution to Political Thought*, New York, Humanities Press, Inc., 1959.

Petit-Dutaillis, C., "France: Louis XI," *Cambridge Medieval History*, VIII, Cambridge University Press, 1958, pp. 273–305.

Phelps Brown, E. H. and Sheila Hopkins, "Seven Centuries of the Prices of Consumables Compared with Builders' Wage Rates," *Economica*, XXIII (1956).

Pike, R., *Enterprise and Adventure: The Genoese in Seville and the Opening of the New World*, Ithaca, Cornell University Press, 1966.

Posthumus, N. W., *Geschiedenis van de Leidsche Laken Industrie*, 2 vols., Gravenhage, Martinus Nijhoff, 1908, 1939.

Previté-Orton, C., *Marsilius of Padua* (from *Proceedings of the British Academy*, Vol. XXI), London, Humphrey Milford Amen House E. C., 1935.

Ramsay, G. D., *English Overseas Trade During the Centuries of Emergence*, London, Macmillan and Co., Ltd., 1957.

The Wiltshire Woollen Industry, Oxford, Oxford University Press, 1943.

Rashdall, H., "The Medieval Universities," *Cambridge Medieval History*, VI, Cambridge, Cambridge University Press, 1964, pp. 559–601.

Richardson, W. C., "Some Financial Expedients of Henry VIII," *The Economic History Review*, 2nd ser., VII (1955) 33–49.

Ringrose, D. L., "The Government and the Carters in Spain, 1476–1700," *The Economic History Review*, 2nd ser., XXII (1969) 45–57.

de Roover, R., "La Doctrine scholastique en matière de monopole et son application à la politique économique des communes Italiennes," *Studi in onore di Amintore Fanfani*, I, Milan, Dott. A. Giuffré, 1962, pp. 151–79.

"Scholastic Economics: Survival and Lasting Influence from the Sixteenth Century to Adam Smith," *Quarterly Journal of Economics*, LXIX (1955) 161–90.

Sabine, G., *A History of Political Theory*, New York, Holt, Rinehart and Winston, Inc., 1961.

Schipa, M., "Italy and Sicily under Frederick II," *Cambridge Medieval History*, VI, Cambridge, Cambridge University Press, 1964, pp. 131–65.

Schofield, R. S., "The Geographical Distribution of Wealth in England: 1334–1649," *The Economic History Review*, 2nd ser., XVIII (1965) 483–510.

Schremmer, E., *Die Wirtschaft Bayerns: von hohen Mittelalter bis zum Beginn der Industrialisierung*, Munich, Verlag C. H. Beck, 1970.

Schumpeter, J. A., *History of Economic Analysis*, New York, Oxford University Press, 1954.

Sella, D., "European Industries: 1500–1700" in C. Cipolla, ed., *The Fontana Economic History of Europe*, II, London, Fontana Books, 1974.

"Les Mouvements longs: l'industrie lainière à Venise aux xvie et xviie siècles," *Annales: économies, sociétés, civilisations*, XII (1957) 29–45.

Simkin, C. G. F., *The Traditional Trade of Asia*, New York, Oxford University Press, 1968.

Slicher van Bath, B. H., *The Agrarian History of Western Europe: A.D. 500–1800*, trans. Olive Ordish, London, Edward Arnold, Ltd., 1963.

Smith, Adam, *An Inquiry into the Nature and Causes of the Wealth of Nations,* New York, Random House, Inc., 1937.

Smith, C. S. and R. J. Forbes, "Mining and Assaying," in C. Singer, E. J. Holmyard, A. R. Hall, and T. I. Williams, eds., *A History of Technology,* III, Oxford, Clarendon Press, 1957, pp. 27–71.

Steel, A., *The Receipt of the Exchequer, 1337–1485,* Cambridge, Cambridge University Press, 1954.

Tawney, R. H. and Eileen Power, *Tudor Economic Documents,* 3 vols., London, Longmans Green and Co., 1924.

Thirsk, J., "Farming Techniques," in J. Thirsk, ed., *The Agrarian History of Enland and Wales,* IV, Cambridge, Cambridge University Press, 1967.

Unwin, G., *Industrial Organization in the Sixteenth and Seventeenth Centuries,* New York, A. M. Kelley, 1963 (first ed. 1904).

Van der Wee, H., *The Growth of the Antwerp Market and the European Economy,* Louvain, Publications Universitaires, 1963.

Vicens-Vives, J., *An Economic History of Spain,* trans. F. M. López-Morillas, Princeton, Princeton University Press, 1969.

Historia social y económica de España y América, Barcelona, Teide, 1957.

Voet, L., *The Plantin-Moretus Museum,* Antwerp, Museum Plantin-Moretus, 1965.

Wallerstein, I., *The Modern World-System: Capitalist Agriculture and the Origins of the European World Economy in the Sixteenth Century,* New York, Academic Press, 1974.

Weber, M., *The Protestant Ethic and the Spirit of Capitalism,* trans. T. Parsons, New York, Charles Scribner's Sons, 1958.

William of Ockham, *Philosophical Writings,* trans. P. Boehner, Indianapolis, The Bobbs-Merrill Co., Inc., 1964.

Wolfe, M., *The Fiscal System of Renaissance France,* New Haven, Yale University Press, 1972.

Youings, J., "The Church," in J. Thirsk, ed., *The Agrarian History of England and Wales,* IV, Cambridge, Cambridge University Press, 1967.

Zeller, G., "Industry in France before Colbert," in R. Cameron, ed., *Essays in French Economic History,* Homewood, Ill., Richard D. Irwin, Inc., 1970.

Index